MAKING
DOLLS' HOUSE
INTERIORS

DECOR AND FURNISHINGS IN $^1/_{12}$ SCALE

MAKING
DOLLS' HOUSE
INTERIORS

DECOR AND FURNISHINGS IN 1/12 SCALE

— CAROL AND NIGEL LODDER —

TEXT AND DRAWINGS BY
VENUS AND MARTIN DODGE

PHOTOGRAPHY BY JONATHAN BOSLEY

David & Charles

A DAVID & CHARLES BOOK

Typeset by ABM Typographics Ltd, Hull
and printed in Singapore by C. S. Graphics Pte. Ltd.
for David & Charles
Brunel House   Newton Abbot   Devon

Contents

To our friends in the world of miniatures with thanks
for their help and encouragement over the years.
Carol and Nigel

Foreword

Martin and I first met Carol Lodder and her parents, Nigel and Greta, when Carol spotted her miniature pottery in pictures in one of our books and came to visit us. Since then we have spent many long summer evenings in the garden of their cottage sharing our interest in miniatures.

Carol already had an established reputation as a potter when, several years ago, Nigel began to make 'country-style' furniture to complement her pottery at exhibitions and fairs. The combination of beautifully painted porcelain and well-crafted wooden furniture proved so popular that the Lodders were encouraged to expand their range. Over the years they have devised some ingenious methods using commercial woods, mouldings and turnings, to make pieces which can be adapted from simple to sophisticated by adding detail and varying the painted finish.

Making Dolls' House Interiors was conceived during those summer evenings in the garden because we felt that the Lodders' designs and the simplicity of their methods would appeal to both beginners and experienced miniaturists alike. So, the book has been a collaboration between Carol and Nigel who designed and made all of the projects; Martin, who drew the patterns and illustrations; and myself, who planned and wrote it. We all hope you will enjoy the book and find it useful.

Venus A. Dodge (1994)

Introduction

Making Dolls' House Interiors is a book of ideas, plans and patterns for dolls-house rooms and furnishings in period styles from the sixteenth century to the present day. All of the projects in the book are in $1/12$ scale – one inch to the foot – which is the universally accepted scale for collectors' miniatures. The patterns have been designed to make full use of ready-cut commercial wood, woodstrip, mouldings and turnings, so no special skills or tools are required and many projects are simple enough for the absolute beginner. The furniture and accessory patterns are all drawn full-size and need only be taken from the page to use and full instructions are given for cutting, assembling and finishing every project.

Each chapter deals with a different room, ranging from Tudor through Georgian and Victorian to modern, and from country cottage to grand town house. Each room can be made as an individual room box – assembled from the plans in the book; or the methods can be adapted to the reader's own dolls' house.

Decorating schemes vary from simple wallpaper or paint to authentic period effects such as moulded ceilings and panelled or timbered walls, including windows and doors appropriate for the room. Instructions for making floors, fireplaces and a variety of fixtures, including a kitchen-range, copper, sink, washing machine and convector heater, can be found in the relevant chapters. A small garden with a veranda has been included, and some ideas for customising furniture kits.

In Chapter 1 you will find advice on buying or building a dolls' house if you do not already have one. There are also full details of the materials and simple tools needed to make the projects, including the wood, woodstrip and mouldings we recommend for furniture, and the paints and craft materials we use for decorating and making fixtures and accessories. Chapter 1 also covers the basic methods of construc-

tion which are used for pieces throughout the book, and tips for getting the best results from the patterns and methods described in the following chapters.

Chapters 2–9 give plans, patterns and making-up instructions for individual rooms, including making the room box, structural adaptations such as windows, doors, chimney breasts and partition walls, decorating schemes and lighting. Methods for painting realistic stones, flags and tiles for fireplaces and flooring, and patterns for the fixtures, furniture and accessories shown in the photographs, can be found in the appropriate chapters. Full instructions are given for a variety of painted finishes for furniture, from natural wood to elaborate decorative effects, and suggestions are offered for adapting the methods to other rooms or period styles. In Chapter 10 you will find patterns for the garden and veranda and ideas for making plants for the dolls' house. At the end of the book are lists of stockists of the materials you will need for the projects, books you may find useful and dolls-house magazines.

If you are a newcomer to miniatures, we recommend that you subscribe to one or more of the specialist magazines, in which you will find up-to-date information about dolls' houses old and new, craftsmen and suppliers, and miniatures fairs. Making and furnishing dolls' houses is a very popular and fast-growing hobby and the beginner is often surprised at the wealth of do-it-yourself materials and ready-made miniatures which are available. There are many shops and fairs, and the magazines carry advertisements for them, so finding something in your own area should not be difficult. There are also many dolls-house clubs which offer a warm welcome to new members.

A word of warning about copyright: all the plans and patterns in this book are intended for private use; it is illegal to use them for commercial purposes without the written consent (license) of the authors.

CHAPTER ONE

Getting Started

CHOOSING A DOLLS' HOUSE

If you are planning to buy or build a dolls' house, take a little time to consider the options. There may be a family dolls' house tucked away in the attic which you could refurbish, or you might buy an old house from an antique shop or auction. You could commission a craftsman to build the dolls' house of your dreams or buy a ready-made whitewood dolls' house which you could adapt or 'customise'. You might buy a dolls-house kit, or design and build a house yourself.

The first consideration is how much time and money you want to spend. Antique dolls' houses are expensive, even in relatively poor condition, and they were often built to no specific scale which can make furnishing difficult. Occasionally, old houses turn up in country sales, car boot sales – or attics! If you are lucky enough to find a house which is suitable for the period style you want and the right size for $^1/_{12}$ scale furniture, then it will probably only need cleaning and treating with Rentokil or a similar fluid to prevent woodbeetle before you are ready to decorate and furnish.

Craftsman-made dolls' houses range from modestly priced to 'the sky's the limit', depending on how large and elaborate a house you want. If you want to commission a house you will need a fairly clear idea of your requirements, perhaps with some sketches or photographs of life-sized houses, before approaching a craftsman whose work you like. The specialist magazines can be an excellent reference source, or look around at the larger miniatures fairs. If the craftsman you want to commission is very popular you may have to wait some time. You will need to come to an understanding about how much work you want him to do and how payment will be arranged. Many of the craftsmen who sell ready-made whitewood houses are prepared to adapt a stock design to a customer's requirements for a modest extra cost – this can be a very viable alternative to commissioning a 'one-off'.

The range of ready-made whitewood houses is very wide, and most of them can be supplied quickly, either from the craftsmen who make them or through most dolls-house shops. If you buy catalogues you can compare styles and prices and will usually find something suitable which requires the minimum of 'customising'. Give some thought not just to the period style you want, but also to the size of the rooms, as many ready-made houses have small rooms and this can be frustrating if you want to furnish a grand house. Check also whether the staircase can be removed for decorating and whether skirting (baseboard), cornice, architraves, doors and windows are supplied, or whether you need to add the cost of these to the price of the house. Many ready-made houses have add-on extensions such as attics, basements or conservatories which can be bought later, and some are made in such a way that you can slot extra floors in if you want to extend the house. Consider also if you would prefer a shop with living accommodation above.

Many of the craftsmen who sell ready-made houses also sell kits, which usually cost approximately half as much as an assembled house. Kits generally come supplied with full assembly instructions and, as the time-consuming measuring and cutting are already done, they are relatively quick and simple to put together. The original design can often be adapted by moving a partition wall or staircase; and, as nothing is fixed, you can decorate as you assemble. This can be particularly convenient if you want to apply elaborate decorative effects like the Tudor plaster and beams or the Georgian panelling described in this book.

With a little imagination, commercial houses can be 'customised' almost beyond recognition by adding a porch, balcony, veranda, or basement area with steps up to the front door, or by changing the doors and windows. Two small houses could be adapted to make one large house, or a large house could be converted to a pair of semi-detached cottages. Houses can be transformed by different decorating schemes; a standard Victorian house, given different windows and doors and decorated appropriately, could become a Tudor, Gothic or 1920s house.

The dolls' house shown on page 10 is typical of moderately priced commercial whitewood houses. It is well made in good quality marine plywood and the proportions are good with fairly large rooms. The staircase, with its nicely turned balusters, is removable for decorating and holes are ready-drilled in the carcase to accommodate the wires for lighting. Doors and windows can be chosen from a range, and we have added a partition wall with a door in one of the downstairs rooms to make a scullery and built-in larder. We glazed the hall windows with stained-glass panes and decorated the house to emphasise its Victorian style, with embossed brick 'cladding' and slate roofing.

If you decide to build your own dolls' house there are a number of books to help you, some of which are listed at the back of this book. If you have not built a dolls' house before, you might consider making one

The Victorian dolls' house is a ready-made whitewood house, decorated and furnished from patterns in the book

or two room boxes from the plans in the book to try out your skills and to see if one period style suits you better than another. Room boxes are also an excellent option for anyone who does not want the restriction imposed by a dolls' house where each room is usually in the same period. If you choose to make four room boxes from the same plan, and decorate them in the same period, they could be assembled together to make a simple dolls' house.

The dolls-house hall showing a stained-glass window,
and the panelled dado

THE WORKSPACE

As the projects in the book are planned room by room, little space is needed to make them and most of the projects can be made on the kitchen table; however, there are a few considerations which will make your work easier.

The first is good lighting. As miniatures are small, and some parts very small, you need to see clearly what you are doing and if it is not possible to work in daylight, a good spotlight which will throw light from above on to the work surface is the next best thing. Daylight simulation light bulbs are available from most craft shops and many people find them very helpful, or you may prefer an ordinary 100 watt bulb. If you are planning to buy a spotlight, consider the type with a built-in magnifying lens which are available from craft suppliers.

Comfort is also important, as assembling small pieces of furniture needs a considerable amount of concentration and you may well be spending some time making things for your dolls' house. Choose a chair which gives good support to your back at a height where you can rest your elbows on the work surface and reach without straining. If you are fortunate enough to have a special work place, it will prob-ably have a perfectly flat work surface, but if not a piece of kitchen worktop, perhaps three feet long, will provide an excellent alternative. Offcuts of melamine worktop are often available from DIY shops relatively cheaply and provide the ideal solid, tough, wipe-clean surface for cutting and gluing.

Storage is the next priority, so you can find what you need, when you need it. Wood, woodstrip and mouldings are easily warped or broken so they should be stored flat – in a drawer or shallow box, or in strong cardboard postal tubes. Tiny hinges, handles and screws, and small mouldings and spindles are easily lost, so sets of small plastic or metal drawers where they can be 'filed' according to size and type are very useful. As hoarding is virtually a requirement for making miniatures, you will need somewhere to keep all the scraps of fabric and trimmings, pictures and cut-outs and all the 'might come in useful' odds and ends which accumulate. One of the simplest and cheapest storage systems is a collection of plastic tubs of the type used for ice-cream. These are large enough to hold most things and are usually given away at places where ice-cream is sold – try your local super-market or garden centre.

TOOLS

WOODWORK (Fig 1)

As the furniture patterns in this book have been designed to make use of commercial woods, woodstrip and mouldings in ready-prepared thicknesses, and both cutting and construction are very simple, you will need only basic hand tools to make all of the projects. If you intend to make a room box you will need an all-purpose saw, a fretsaw to cut the window and door openings and a small plane or sandpaper to clean the plywood edges.

For furniture making you will need a small razor saw, a Stanley knife and a good craft knife with a selection of different shaped blades. A selection of abrasive papers will be useful, from medium-grade sandpaper for rough shaping to fine-grade (eg 400 grit) silicon carbide paper. You will also need a mitre box for cutting accurate mitres and a metal ruler to use as a straight edge for cutting. For accurate right angles, we recommend using a small engineers' set-square and a jig designed for miniatures.

A cutting mat is useful as it provides a non-slip, self-healing cutting surface. A number of small clamps are also handy to hold pieces firmly together as glue dries. Holes for knobs, handles and hinges are made with a fine bradawl and drilled with a small bit in a pin-vice or drill, and a pair of tweezers is useful for holding these tiny items as they are fitted. If you have difficulty applying small amounts of glue neatly, try using a plastic syringe with a curved nozzle, which will put a dot of glue exactly where you want it.

PAINTING

Most of the furniture pieces in the book have a painted finish, either coloured or to represent natural wood, and for the best results good quality artists' paint-brushes are essential. We recommend that you buy a selection of soft brushes in the best quality you can afford, including flat and round ½in wide, fine-detail and fine-liners. They will last for years if well cared for, so are a good investment.

Cheap brushes will also be needed for applying metallic paints and similar finishes, which make the brush very difficult to clean so these should be regarded as disposable.

CRAFTS

Simple tools required for the various craft projects in the book include an old rolling-pin for rolling out air-drying clay for floors and bricks, and a stylus or similar pointed tool for impressing patterns. Other tools are mentioned where appropriate and can be found in most homes or easily improvised. These include well sharpened HB pencils for drawing patterns, masking tape, rubber bands and cotton buds which will be useful for a number of purposes.

Small, sharp scissors are needed for many projects including soft furnishings and plant making, and dressmakers' pins, small needles, a bodkin, a pair of pliers and a small bradawl will all be useful.

MATERIALS

ROOM BOXES

If you are planning to make a room box from one of the patterns in the book you will need good quality plywood; birch-faced marine ply is best in ⅜in thickness. Some DIY shops sell good plywood, but if you have difficulty finding the right quality, it might be easier to buy from a marine chandler (see British Telecom's *Yellow Pages*). Do buy the best quality you can find. The difference in cost for the small quantities required is minimal and good plywood will produce much better results with less effort in cutting and sanding. When choosing your plywood, look for a piece which is not warped, by sighting at eye-level along the edges. The patterns show the amount of wood needed for each room, and you will find that offcuts are usually quite large enough rather than buying a whole sheet of plywood.

Patterns are given throughout the book for a variety of structural adaptations to the room box, including attic ceilings, chimney breasts and partition walls — most of which can be adapted to existing dolls-house rooms. Plywood can be used for these adaptations if you wish, but a simple alternative is Foamcore, which is a layer of polystyrene foam sandwiched between two layers of cardboard. Foamcore is available from art and craft shops and is very easy to use as it can be cut with a craft knife and is lightweight. Balsa wood, which is bought in ¼in or ½in thick blocks from craft suppliers, is also lightweight and easily cut with a small razor saw. It is a useful alternative for chimney breasts.

Patterns for doors and windows which can be used for the room boxes or adapted to the rooms in a dolls' house, are given in several chapters. Doors are made in the same wood and framed with similar mouldings

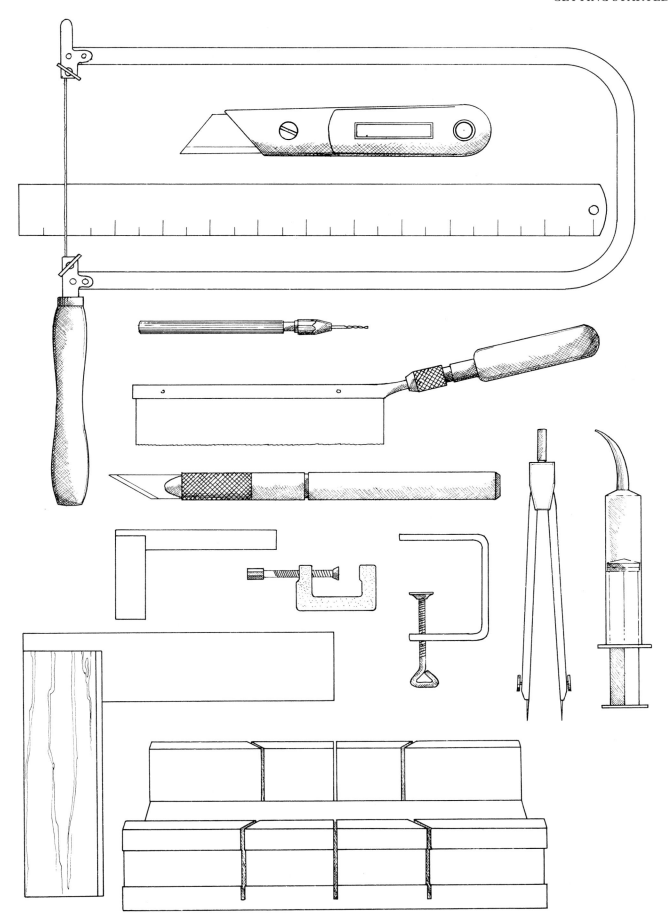

Fig 1 The simple hand tools needed to make the furniture

to those used for furniture and described below. Windows can be glazed with glass (ideally 1½–2mm (¹/₁₆in) thick), which can be bought cut to the required size from most glass merchants; however, this is not recommended for a child's dolls' house. Perspex is safer, (though it is more difficult to clean and inclined to scratch) and can be bought from most craft shops. You might also consider using the commercial doors and windows which are available from specialist suppliers. These range from simple four-panelled and more elaborate six-panelled doors to fixed or working sash windows, most of which can be supplied ready-made or as kits. Door furniture, such as handles, hinges, knockers and letter boxes (mail-slots) are made in a large range of styles and prices to suit all types of door and are available from most dolls-house shops.

You may also want to take advantage of the wide variety of staircases, panelling, beams and ceiling mouldings which are available from the same suppliers. Wood mouldings for architraves, skirting (base-board), cornice, picture-rail and dado can be found in most dolls-house shops and from mail-order suppliers. Doors, windows and architectural mouldings should be chosen to complement the style and period of the room or dolls' house. (See Acknowledgements for details of the items we have used.)

LIGHTING

The lighting methods in the rooms, shown in the photographs, are described in the relevant chapters. If you are planning to light a dolls' house, several of these methods can be adapted or you might consider a lighting kit, using either a wire or a copper tape system. Your local dolls-house shop or a specialist supplier will be able to advise you if you are not sure about the most suitable system and there are several booklets as well as a video to guide you through the installation. Lights are available to suit all styles and periods, ranging from 'candles' and chandeliers for Tudor and Georgian (Colonial) rooms, through 'gas' and 'oil' lamps to modern electric lights. You might also consider fitting a 'flickering fire' unit in a fireplace or fairy lights on a Christmas tree.

FLOORS

Several rooms in the book have paved or tiled floors (and brick fixtures) made in air-drying clay and painted with acrylic paints. There are a number of these hobby clays available from art and craft shops which are all very similar and easy to use. We recommend Das, which is made in both light grey and terracotta colours, because paint colours will blend well

A collection of decorating materials and accessories suitable for period rooms – from Georgian through Regency, Victorian and Edwardian, to the present day

on the porous surface to create realistic effects. We have also used a number of the commercial floorings which are available from specialist dolls-house suppliers, including simple tile-effect papers, embossed 'cladding' bricks and very realistic wooden planking with a self-adhesive backing. If you cannot find these in your local shop, they are available by post (see Acknowledgements).

WALLPAPER

Dolls-house wallpapers are available from almost all dolls-house shops and from many of the specialist mail-order suppliers who usually provide samples to help you choose. They are sold in sheets, so you need to measure the area of the room before buying as it can be difficult to match a paper later. Papers printed for dolls' houses have small patterns – in an enormous variety suitable for most periods – but life-size papers with small patterns can also be used. These are usually a cheaper alternative – often free – if you are permitted to tear off a large piece from the sample roll at the local DIY store.

For plain-coloured walls, try watercolour papers from an art shop, or large sheets of writing paper. You might also consider printing your own wallpaper using the method described in Chapter 6 for printing fabric. In the DIY store you will also find embossed wallpapers which make excellent dados and 'moulded plaster' ceilings, if you choose a pattern small enough for the proportions of the room. For the best results on painted walls, the walls (and ceiling) should be papered with lining paper first. Wallpaper (and lining paper) is best applied with ordinary household wallpaper paste.

PAINT

If you prefer painted walls, household emulsion paint with a matt finish – bought in small sample pots from the DIY store – is most effective and economical.

For the paintwork in each room – and for the furniture – we have used water-based acrylic paints. There are two types of acrylic paint: artists' acrylics which are available from art shops, and 'hobby' acrylics which are available from craft suppliers, art shops and often, haberdashery (notions) departments. Artists' acrylics are translucent and are available in the same range of colours as oil paints. We use these mixed to a very watery wash to 'stain' the wood to represent pine or mahogany or any other wood finish. The 'hobby' acrylics are opaque and are often sold in sets of colours, eg 'Country Colours' or 'Victorian Colours'. These are the shades we use for painting woodwork and for painted furniture.

Several of the fixtures such as the kitchen range and brick-copper bowl are painted to represent metal and you can use either acrylic paint in matt black and grey, or a metallic enamel paint such as Humbrol enamel, available from craft and DIY shops. If you prefer acrylic colours, a good burnished finish can be achieved by rubbing 'Treasure Gold' or a similar metallic wax on to the dry, painted piece with your finger. These metallic wax finishes are sold in art shops for picture-frame restoration.

PLASTER

For the plastered walls and the 'beaten earth' floor in the Tudor room, we have used Tetrion – a ready-mixed household filler available from DIY stores. This also makes a good grout for flagged floors and bricks and is useful for filling any small structural gaps before decorating.

FURNITURE

All of the furniture patterns in the book are designed to make use of commercial wood, woodstrip, mouldings and turnings which are supplied by firms such as Borcraft and are also widely available in America from craft and hobby shops, dolls-house shops and mail-order suppliers. If you have any difficulty finding them in Britain or Australia we recommend that you contact Borcraft (see Stockists) who have an excellent mail-order catalogue.

If you intend to make several pieces of furniture, it is well worth buying a good selection of materials before you begin, so that you will have everything you need 'in stock' and will not have to wait for a shopping trip or mail order. As the standard thicknesses of commercial woods and woodstrips can vary a little from batch to batch, it is also useful to have enough in stock to complete a project.

Furniture can be made in 'real' woods, planed to the required thickness, or in one of the hardwoods sold for crafts, such as obeche, bass and jelutong, which can be stained or painted to resemble real wood. Our own preference is for jelutong and you will find instructions for a paint-washed finish to represent pine or mahogany, as well as several decorative painted finishes in the book.

These craft woods are very simple to work with as they are easy to cut with basic tools, to sand and assemble, and jelutong is probably the ideal choice for the beginner. The wood is supplied in a variety of thicknesses – for most of the projects you will need wood $\frac{1}{8}$in, $\frac{1}{16}$in, and $\frac{3}{32}$in thick – which is sold in lengths of approximately 3ft by 2–4in wide (which might be cut in half to post). We recommend buying several pieces of each thickness.

Woodstrip, which is available in jelutong and other woods, is supplied in the same thicknesses, in a variety of widths. Having a good stock in all the standard widths will enable you to make any furniture piece in the book with the minimum of cutting. We recommend that you buy a selection in $\frac{1}{4}$in, $\frac{1}{8}$in, $\frac{3}{8}$in, $\frac{1}{16}$in, $\frac{3}{16}$in and $\frac{3}{32}$in widths.

MOULDINGS AND TURNINGS

Wood mouldings, which are used to add a decorative finish to furniture, are supplied in a variety of designs. The most useful widths are ⅛in, 3/16in and ¼in, but it is best to have a selection of these too so that they can be varied from piece to piece. We also use commercial skirting-board (base-board) to make plinths for some furniture pieces. This is available from the same suppliers in several widths.

Ready-made turned items including table legs, baluster spindles and bedposts are very useful if you do not have a lathe and we have used them for a number of projects. They are available in whitewood and mahogany from most dolls-house shops. Whitewood turnings will accept the painted finishes described in the book and can be used on any furniture piece made in jelutong.

The furniture is assembled with butt joints, so you will need a good whitewood glue – we recommend Evostick Resin W. For finishing your furniture, we recommend a pure beeswax furniture polish for the best results.

Tiny knobs, handles and hinges are essential to complement miniature furniture and can be bought from most dolls-house suppliers in styles suitable for everything from wooden knobs for simple rustic pieces to elaborate brass drop-handles for period furniture. We use small brass knobs, painted with white gloss enamel paint to represent china, on a number of cupboard doors and drawers. Hinges are often supplied with tiny pins, but it is better to fix both hinges and handles or knobs with a non-drip or gel superglue. Drawer plates and escutcheons can be found in period styles from the same suppliers and these too are fixed with superglue.

SOFT FURNISHINGS

Lightweight fabrics with small patterns in colours appropriate to the room are the key to successful soft furnishings. Shops which sell fabrics for patchwork are often the best source of supply and usually carry an enormous range of cottons in plain colours and tiny prints.

There are also suppliers who specialise in fabrics and trimmings for dolls' houses and who stock the American range of dolls-house wallpapers with matching fabric. Natural fabrics like cotton or silk are usually more effective than man-made fibres, especially for curtains, as they hang better.

If you want to create the impression of age in a room, old fabric might be more realistic than new, and charity shops or jumble sales can be good sources. Heavier fabrics like furnishing velvet or thick cottons make good fitted carpets or rugs and pieces of woven or tapestry fabric also make effective rugs, with threads drawn from each end to make fringes.

Braids, ribbons, lace and trimmings are available in dolls-house scale from the specialist suppliers to make pelmets, cushions, antimacassars and doilies for period or modern homes.

Making hems and attaching trimmings in this scale can be very fiddly so one of the fabric glues which dries clear is often a better option than sewing, and Fraycheck or a similar product can be used to seal edges to prevent fraying. Both fabric glue and Fraycheck can be found in most craft shops or haberdashery (notions) departments. Iron-on interfacing, such as Vilene, can be used on the back of any fabric to give it 'body' or weight and will also prevent cut edges from fraying. It is especially useful for backing rugs and for stiffening fabrics to make pelmets for curtains.

Padding for upholstered furniture can be either terylene wadding (batting) of the type used for quilting, or foam, which might be taken from packaging or bought from the craft shop or market.

The upholstered furniture in the book is made on a base of Foamcore or balsa wood or cardboard – which should be good quality art card, not packaging or cartons.

NOTES ON SAFETY

Providing that you work in good light and that you are not over-tired or unwell, only the simplest precautions should be necessary to ensure safety, as the hand tools described above do not pose the same potential hazards as power tools.

Blades in cutting tools should always be clean and sharp because a blunt tool needs more pressure and increases the risk that the blade might slip. Always cut away from your fingers and body, rather than towards. Keep the work area clear so that you avoid damaging yourself or your tools accidentally, and keep things where you can reach them easily without straining.

If you use air-drying clay to make bricks or floors, it may need sanding to make a smoother or more even surface, and the dust from this clay can be harmful so it is best to wear a mask – these are available from most craft suppliers.

If you are lighting your dolls' house or room box, always use the appropriate transformer (or batteries). *Never* plug the lights directly into the main power supply.

BASIC METHODS

ROOM BOXES (Fig 2)

Dimensions for each room box shown in the photographs are given on the plans. Draw the pieces on to the plywood, including the outline for windows (and doors if you wish to make opening doors), using a well-sharpened pencil. Check that your lines are accurate and that the angles are precise.

Cut the plywood pieces with a rip-style saw (designed to cut both with and across the grain of the wood) fractionally proud of the drawn line and plane the edges to the line with a small block plane. Cut the window holes (and doorways) with a 12in fretsaw with a No 3 or 4 blade by first drilling a small hole in each corner and inserting the fretsaw blade through the hole. With a little practice very straight lines can be cut with the fretsaw, so aim to cut along the drawn line and sand the cut edge if necessary.

Assemble the room box pieces with simple butt joints, with whitewood glue along the edges and 1in veneer pins tapped in at approximately 3in intervals. When the glue is dry, sand the box thoroughly inside and out with medium-, then fine-grade abrasive paper to make a good smooth surface for decorating. The outside of the room box can be stained or painted as you prefer, with woodstain or two or three coats of emulsion paint. The front edges can be faced with woodstrip (stained or painted) and glued in place with contact adhesive.

Full instructions for making the windows and doors and architectural adaptations can be found in the individual chapters and most of these can be adapted to dolls-house rooms.

DECORATING

Before you begin decorating, fill any gaps between the walls and between the cornice and ceiling with Tetrion or a similar filler. Apply with a craft knife and smooth in with a finger, making sure that any excess is cleaned away with a damp cloth or cotton buds. Check that the chimney breast fits flush against the wall and that there are no gaps between flooring and wall, and fill if necessary.

If you are fitting door and window-frames, skirting and picture-rails, these should be stained or painted first and it is usually easier to glue them in place after the room is painted and/or papered. Turn the room box upside-down to paint the ceiling (and cornice) and let the paint dry before papering the walls.

Wallpapering can be simplified by making a paper template for each wall, cutting out door and window holes and using the template as a pattern to cut the wallpaper. Apply a light coat of wallpaper paste to the walls, then paste the wallpaper. Begin with the back wall and lap the paper about 1/2in on to the side walls to soften the sharp angles in the corners, then paper the side walls, fitting the paper up to the back corners. Check that ceiling and floor edges are straight, and take care to match any pattern. Smooth the paper carefully over the walls to remove any air bubbles with a pad of cotton wool or a soft cloth and let it dry thoroughly before gluing skirting-boards and door and window-frames in place, as dolls-house wallpapers are thin and can tear easily when wet. Flooring is usually fitted before door frames and skirting-boards to give the neatest finish.

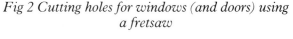

Fig 2 Cutting holes for windows (and doors) using a fretsaw

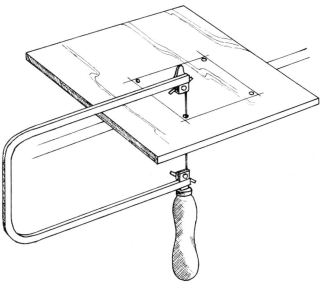

FLOORING (Fig 3)

To make flagstones or tiles in air-drying clay, roll out the clay with an old rolling-pin or something similar, on a sheet of plastic or piece of cloth so that you can lift it easily. To ensure an even thickness, guide rails of scrap woodstrip of the required thickness can be laid either side of the clay so that the rolling pin rests on the guide rails as the clay is rolled.

If you wish to impress the texture of slate or stone into the surface of the clay, use a piece of the appropriate life-size material as a mould, such as a roofing slate or paving stone. Lift the rolled clay carefully and press the upper surface gently on to the mould material to impress the pattern or texture, then peel it off and leave to dry leather-hard.

Cut the individual tiles or flags when the clay is leather-hard with a craft knife and metal ruler for a clean straight edge, or with scissors for a rougher rounded edge, and leave them to dry thoroughly. Remember that air-drying clay shrinks slightly as it dries, so allow for this when measuring the area of floor to be paved. Paint the individual flags or tiles with acrylic paints in the appropriate colours, mixing shades of paint to vary the colours. (Full details are given in the relevant chapters.) Seal the dry colour with a matt or gloss acrylic spray if required. Clay flooring can be glued directly on to the floor with UHU or a similar tacky craft glue, or on to a paper template cut to fit the floor area and then glued in place. The second method is useful if you want to lay a pattern or if the floor is awkward to reach.

Clay bricks and stones, which are used for chimney breasts and several of the fixtures described in the book, are made in the same way and glued on to a backing of Foamcore with UHU or similar glue. Apply ready-mixed Tetrion (or a similar filler) with a craft knife as grouting between flags and bricks and clean off excess grout immediately with a damp cloth or cotton bud.

FIXTURES

Patterns and instructions for a variety of fixtures are given in the relevant chapters. When making fixtures it is important to use the appropriate glue for the material and to read the assembly instructions care-

*Constructing a wardrobe from the full-size patterns in
the book, using simple hand tools*

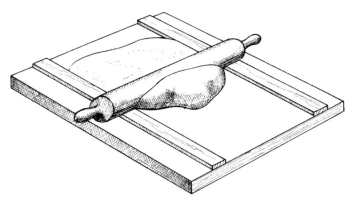

*Fig 3 Rolling out air-drying clay to an even thickness
using guide rails*

fully before you begin. The patterns are written with step-by-step instructions and it is often necessary to allow joined pieces to dry thoroughly before proceeding with the next step. This does require patience but it can be critical in achieving good results. (You may like to work on two or three projects at the same time so that you can move from one to another.)

We have used white-metal kits (see Acknowledgements) for fixtures in several rooms. These kits are an inexpensive way to make realistic miniatures, and when well painted are very impressive. The kits come with full assembly instructions and are put together with an epoxy-resin adhesive (or superglue) and painted with metal primer and enamel or acrylic paints as described in the individual projects.

FURNITURE

If you intend to use the painted pine or mahogany finish described on pages 34 and 73, the wood should be painted before cutting to prevent warping – details

are given with the individual projects – and sufficient wood should be prepared before you begin. If you intend to use woodstain, the cut pieces should be stained before assembly because woodstain will not 'take' over wood glue. Colour-painted finishes and 'ageing' can be applied to the furniture after assembly.

Cutting and assembly instructions are given with the patterns in the relevant chapters for each piece of furniture shown in the photographs, and we recommend that you read them right through before beginning a project. The following notes apply to projects throughout the book, so rather than repeating them, we suggest that you use them to supplement the individual cutting or assembly instructions as necessary.

Patterns (Fig 4)

The furniture patterns are all drawn full size. To use them, take the measurements from the page with

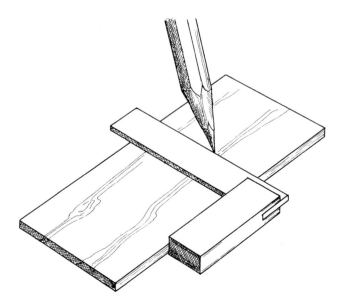

*Fig 4 Marking out an accurate right angle with an
engineer's set-square*

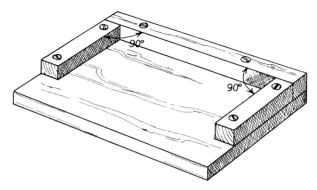

*Fig 5 A simple jig used to support furniture pieces at
right angles as the glue dries*

dividers and draw on to the wood with a well-sharpened pencil, ensuring that the grain of the wood runs in the correct direction on each piece. Where a measurement is not obvious on the pattern it is given in the assembly instructions for the individual piece. Check that all measurements are accurate and angles are precise by using an engineer's square.

Cutting

Straight edges on wooden furniture should be cut with a razor saw. When cutting across the grain of the wood, score the cutting line first with a craft knife and metal ruler to make a clean groove to guide the saw.

Curves can be cut with a fretsaw or roughly cut with a Stanley knife and refined with a craft knife and sandpaper. Sand all wooden pieces carefully with fine-grade abrasive paper wrapped around a small block of wood to avoid rounding edges before assembly. Try (dry-fit) the pieces together to check that they fit well before gluing and assembling.

Assembly (Fig 5)

Apply glue sparingly and evenly to both surfaces and clean off any excess glue immediately with a damp cloth or cotton bud. As all the furniture is assembled with simple butt joints, some pieces will require supporting while the glue dries and often, pressure will need to be applied to the joint as it dries. Various methods can be used as appropriate, including elastic bands, small cramps or a jig, or simply placing the item under a weight or applying pressure with your hands.

Finishing

Assembled furniture pieces should be given a final sanding with very fine-grade abrasive paper wrapped around a small block of wood to avoid rounding edges. Wood-painted or stained pieces should be polished with a good quality wax furniture polish and

well buffed with a soft cloth after any final details such as knot-holes or graining have been painted in and allowed to dry. Several other painted finishes are described in the relevant chapters, including simple colour-painted, decoratively painted and 'aged' effects. These should be applied to the bare wood, as described, and when thoroughly dry, may also be wax polished.

Hinges (Fig 6)

Hinges, knobs and handles are usually fixed with a non-drip gel superglue after the piece is painted. We have used two different types of hinge for the furniture pieces in the book – the butt hinge and the offset hinge and you can use whichever you prefer. The butt hinge is fixed on to the surface of the piece and can be a decorative feature; the offset hinge is fixed to the inside of the piece so that only the barrel is visible.

To fix a butt hinge, mark the hinge position on the front of the door. Hold the hinge with tweezers and apply gel superglue sparingly to the back of one flange. Position the glued flange on the door and hold in place as the glue dries with a fine bradawl pushed through one of the pin holes in the flange. When the glue is dry, use the bradawl to make pin holes in the wood, and push the pins into the pin holes with tweezers. Use a drop of superglue in the holes to secure the pins if necessary. Fit the door into the frame, and fix the other flange of the hinge to the frame in the same way.

Offset hinges have right-angled flanges designed to fit specific thicknesses of wood. For the furniture projects in the book you will need 1/8in offset hinges. To fix the hinge, mark the hinge position on the edge of the door and cut a rebate in the door edge, deep enough to accommodate one flange and the gap between the flanges. Apply gel superglue sparingly to the front face of one flange, position the glued flange on the door and hold in place as the glue dries with a fine bradawl pushed through one of the pin holes in the flange.

When the glue is dry, use the bradawl to make pin holes in the wood and push the pins into the pin holes with tweezers. Glue the door knob in place before fitting the door into the frame. Cut a sliver of thin card to fit between the flanges of the hinge as a spacer and close the hinge over the card. This will ensure that the flanges remain parallel as the hinge is fitted. Apply superglue to the front face of the second flange and carefully fit the door into the frame against the front edges of the shelf and bottom shelf – which will support the door as the glue dries. When the glue is dry, open the door and remove the card spacer.

Fig 6 The butt hinge and offset hinge showing how they are fixed in place

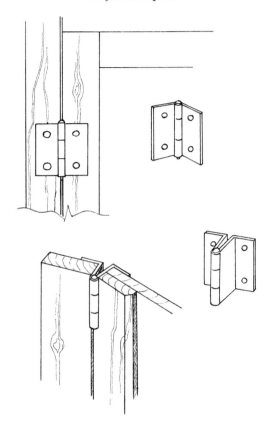

— CHAPTER TWO —
The Country Kitchen

The room in this chapter is designed as a kitchen or kitchen-parlour in a Victorian cottage, though the simple decorating scheme with its cream-painted walls and slate floor might be found in the kitchen of a much grander house of the period, and the traditional furniture would be equally appropriate in a cottage up to the present day.

The Victorian cottage kitchen, where the range burned all day, was the warmest place in the house and family life was usually centred there. During the daytime it was the cottage wife's workplace, and in the evening the family would gather there for tea. As most cottages had a scullery where the messier jobs were done, the kitchen was used as a place to cook and eat but it was also the living room, as the best parlour was reserved for Sundays and special occasions.

THE ROOM BOX
(Fig 7, photograph pages 26–7)

The pattern in Fig 7 will make a room box 14in wide, 10in deep and 8in high – a good size for a room in a cottage or small house. Our kitchen has a large chimney breast to accommodate the kitchen-range, a small (non-opening) window and a (non-opening) door in a planked partition wall. The floor is laid with

flags modelled in air-drying clay painted to represent slate and the ceiling is beamed. The measurements shown on the pattern and given below in brackets are for the room shown in the photograph but the methods can easily be adapted to fit any dolls-house room.

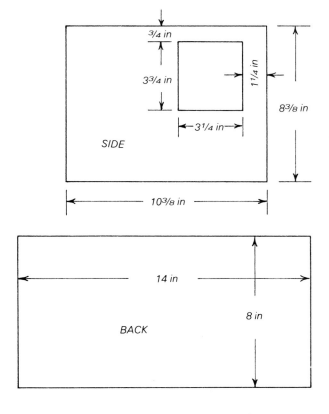

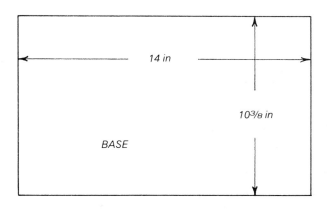

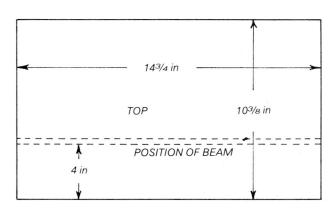

Fig 7 Plan for the Cottage Kitchen room box

To make the room box, you will need good quality ³/₈in plywood, an all-purpose (universal) saw and a fretsaw to cut the window opening. The room box is assembled with wood glue and 1in veneer pins. You will also need a small plane and sandpaper. The front edge of our room box is finished with a frame of woodstrip after the room is decorated.

Draw the pattern (Fig 7) on to the wood with a sharp pencil, and cut one base, one back, one top and two sides. For the best results, saw fractionally outside the drawn lines and use the plane to smooth the edges back to the line. Sand each piece.

Draw the window opening and cut out with a fretsaw on the drawn line. Clean the edges of the window opening with sandpaper.

Glue and pin the back on to the base ensuring that the pieces form a right angle.

Glue and pin one side on to the back and base, then the other side.

Glue and pin the top on to the back and sides as shown in Fig 8a and sand thoroughly.

If you wish, the outside of the room box can be stained or painted.

To frame the front edges, cut woodstrip with mitred corners, stain if required, and glue in place with contact adhesive (eg Evostick or similar) after the interior of the room is decorated.

CHIMNEY BREAST (Fig 8b)

The chimney breast is made in balsa wood block and faced with ¹/₈in thick plywood (or Foamcore). Use wood glue or UHU (or similar) to assemble the pieces. This chimney breast is designed to accommodate the range described below – if you intend to use a different range, adapt the pattern as necessary.

Cut two pieces of (1¹/₈ × 1⁵/₈in) balsa block to fit from floor to ceiling (8in).

Cut the chimney breast front (6¹/₄ × 8in) in plywood. Mark the chimney opening (4³/₄in high × 3³/₄in wide) and cut out with a fretsaw.

Cut two chimney breast sides (1⁵/₈ × 8in) in plywood. Glue each side to the corresponding face of the balsa blocks.

Glue the front on to the balsa block and side assemblies as shown in Fig 8b.

Glue the chimney breast to the centre of the back wall.

WINDOW (Fig 9)

The window in the room box projects beyond the outside wall to accommodate a realistic window-sill. The window-frame is made of woodstrip, ⁵/₈ × ³/₃₂in and ¹/₈in square, with glazing bars in ¹/₁₆in square strip. The window-sill is ³/₄in deep, made in ³/₃₂in woodstrip. The glazing may be glass or perspex, but should be no thicker than ¹/₁₆in or 2mm – our window is 3 × 3¹/₂in. It is easier to paint the window-frame and sill before

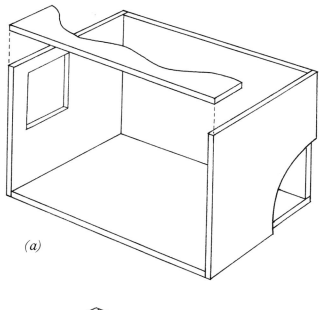

(a)

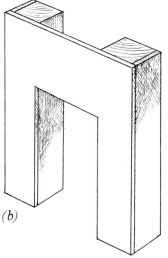

(b)

Fig 8 Patterns for (a) assembly and (b) chimney breast for the Cottage Kitchen

assembly – we have used cream acrylic paint.

Cut the window-sill (A) (3⁵/₈in wide), a little wider than the window opening. Cut notches at each end so that the sill fits into the window opening and projects ¹/₈in into the room (Fig 9b).

Face the top and sides of the window opening with ³/₃₂in woodstrip (B) to fit flush with the inside wall and project on the outside wall (Fig 9b).

Make a frame of ¹/₈in square woodstrip (C) glued into the opening to fit flush with the outside edge (Fig 9c).

Fit the glass against the frame and glue a second frame of ¹/₈in square woodstrip into the opening, butted against the glass (Fig 9d).

Cut the vertical divider (D) in ¹/₈in square strip and glue on to the glass (with UHU or similar).

Cut the glazing bars (E) in ¹/₁₆in square strip and glue in place to frame each 'pane' separately. (Cut the vertical glazing bars in batches of four to ensure that

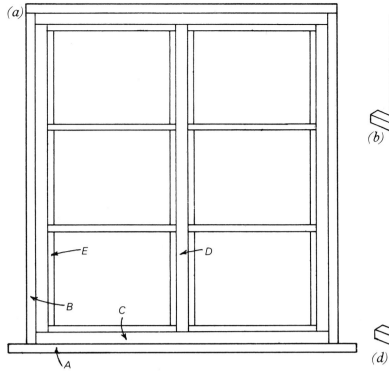

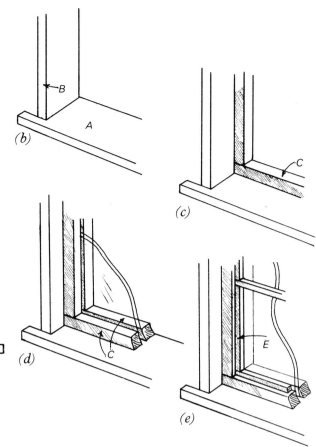

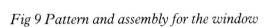

Fig 9 Pattern and assembly for the window

they are exactly the same length on each pane.) Fit the bottom horizontal bar first, followed by the lower four vertical bars, then two horizontal, four vertical etc to complete the window (Fig 9e).

We used the loop from a hook and loop fastening glued in place to represent a window catch.

DECORATING

We papered the walls and ceiling of the room with lining paper – including the window reveals, and applied two coats of magnolia matt emulsion paint. The ceiling is beamed with two pieces of ½in square woodstrip, slightly 'distressed' with a small hammer and stained or painted to represent old oak. Commercial beams could be used.

The inside of the chimney opening in the cottage kitchen is papered with a tile-pattern paper covered with transparent Fablon (or a similar self-adhesive plastic) for a glazed effect.

LIGHTING

We fitted a concealed light in the Cottage Kitchen room box, hidden behind the ceiling beam. This is a 12 volt bulb, wired through a hole in the ceiling to a transformer. Concealed lights can be used in any room or dolls' house where you do not wish to use obvious light fittings. The oil lamp in the kitchen-parlour is wired through a hole in the wall to the transformer (see Acknowledgements).

SLATE-FLAGGED FLOOR *(Fig 10b)*

The flagged floor is made in air-drying clay and painted with acrylic paints to represent slate. If you prefer to paint 'stone' flags see Chapter 9. You will need an old rolling-pin (or similar) to roll out the clay, a craft knife and metal ruler to cut the flags, and Tetrion (or similar) for grouting.

Roll out the clay to an even ⅛in thickness, over a piece of cloth or plastic sheet (so that it can be lifted easily).

If you wish to make a realistic texture in the flags, use a roofing slate as a mould. Lift the rolled out damp clay and press the top surface on to the roofing slate to impress the texture into the clay. Peel the clay off the slate carefully and leave it flat to dry leather-hard.

Make a template for the floor area in thick cartridge paper. Cut the clay into individual flagstones with a craft knife and metal ruler – allowing a little for shrinkage – to fill the template floor. Leave the flagstones to dry thoroughly.

Paint the flagstones individually, mixing green and purple acrylic paints to make a slate-blue colour and varying the shades from stone to stone by adding a little black or white to the colour. Allow the paint to dry, then paint or spray the flags with a matt acrylic sealer and allow to dry.

Working on the template, glue the flags to the paper with UHU or similar tacky craft glue, starting with the front row and working to the back – leaving a

*The Cottage Kitchen as the sun shines through the
window, lighting the bustle of baking day*

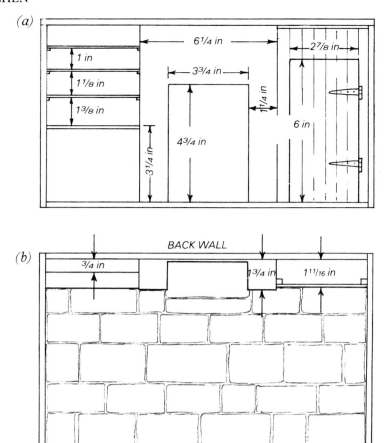

Fig 10 Patterns for (a) wall and
(b) floor for the Cottage Kitchen

small gap between each stone for grouting.

Glue the back of the paper template and press it in place on the kitchen floor. Finish the front edge with a piece of fine woodstrip if required.

Using the Tetrion in small amounts at a time, apply the grouting between the flags with a craft knife, toothpick or similar small tool. Wipe off excess grout immediately with a slightly damp sponge or cloth. Fill any gaps between the walls and floor and allow to dry. Colour the grouting with a wash of burnt umber paint applied with a fine brush.

PLANKED PARTITION WALL AND DOOR (Fig 10a)

The partition wall fits into the alcove beside the chimney breast – the (non-opening) door and wall are made in one piece, though you could hinge the door to open if you prefer. You will need approximately 6ft of 1/2in wide, 1/32in thick woodstrip – we have used tongue and groove floorboarding. Woodstrip should be chamfered along one edge so that the planks will resemble tongue and groove when butted together.

Cut sufficient planks to fit across the alcove from floor to ceiling (eight pieces). Glue and butt the planks together and allow to dry.

Mark the outline of the door and cut out with a craft knife or fretsaw.

Cut two woodstrip battens 1/2in wider than the door (33/8in) and glue the battens to the back of the door – one 1/2in from the top and one 1/2in from the bottom – so that they protrude 1/4in at each side.

With the planking face down, glue the protruding batten ends to the back of the planking to 'hang' the door. (Note that if you prefer to hinge the door into the doorway to open, the battens should fit, not protrude beyond the door.)

Cut a support of 1/16 × 3/4in woodstrip and glue to the front of the planking across the top edge. Sand the assembly.

Cut mock hinges in thin cardboard and hinge barrels from a wooden toothpick and glue on to the door. Add drops of gesso (a liquid plaster available from art shops), to resemble screw heads – as shown in Fig 10a.

Paint the partition wall and door – we have used cream acrylic paint; and fit the door knob – we have used a painted white-metal lockbox with a brass knob.

To support the partition wall, cut two strips of 1/8in square wood, and glue to the side wall and chimney breast side, recessed approximately 1/4in from the front of the chimney breast. Glue the back edges of the partition and fit in place against the supports.

FIXTURES

KITCHEN-RANGE (Fig 11, photograph pages 26–7)

The open kitchen-range was in use throughout the nineteenth century, and in some country areas where gas and electricity were unavailable, ranges like this were still in use until the 1950s.

Our range is made in 1/16in and 1/8in wood (we have used jelutong) with 1/16in square woodstrip for the grate bars and 1/8in wood-moulding for trimming. The oven door is made from thin, stiff cardboard and the fire bricks are modelled in air-drying clay. The handles on the oven door, ashpan and damper are small commercial brass drawer knobs.

The range is painted with matt black acrylic paint and can be finished with black-lead polish. The oven-door frame and latch, and the maker's label and

Fig 11 Pattern for the kitchen-range

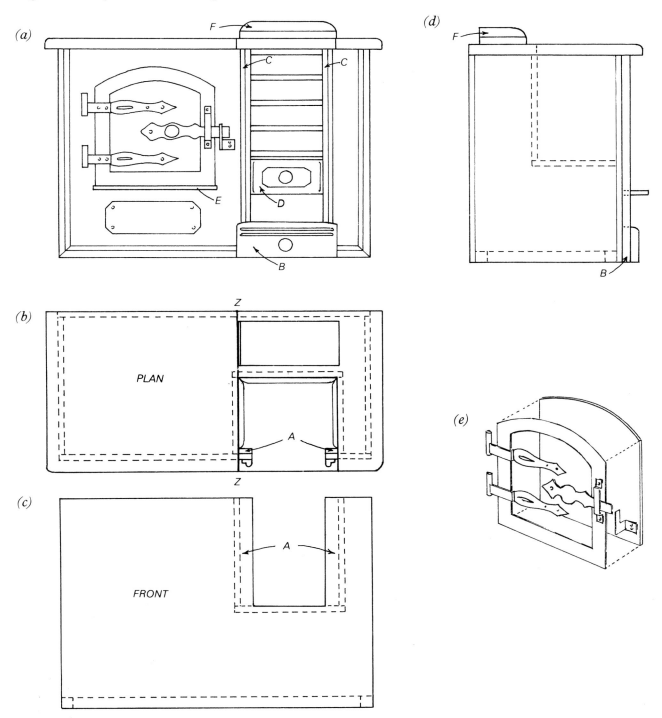

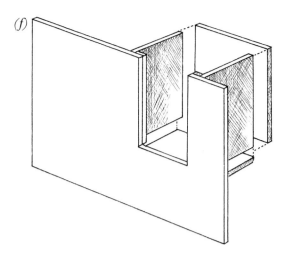
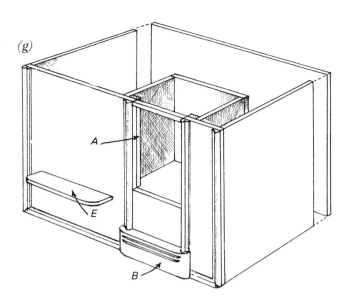

Fig 11 Assembly of the kitchen-range

damper front-panel are coloured with a gilt metallic wax (eg 'Treasure Gold') sold in art shops for finishing picture frames. This is simply rubbed into the cardboard with a finger.

Cut the range front in 1/16in wood from the pattern (Fig 11c).

To make the fire box, cut two sides, one back and one base in 1/16in wood from the pattern Fig 11c.

Cut two fire box support strips (A) and glue on to the back of the range front as shown above. Glue the fire box sides in place against the supports as shown in Fig 11f.

Glue the fire box base to the sides and to the range front. Glue the fire box back in place.

Cut two range sides in 1/16in wood and glue to the back of the range front as shown by the dotted lines on the pattern and in Fig 11g.

Cut the range back in 1/16in wood and glue on to the sides.

Model the fire bricks in air-drying clay as shown on the pattern and leave to dry. Sand each piece to chamfer the top and side edges, paint matt grey, and then glue into the fire box.

Cut the range top in 1/8in wood. (Note, that our top is cut in two pieces, joined at (Z–Z) with slightly chamfered edges to make the join more apparent; but the top may be cut in one piece if you prefer.) Glue the top on to the range so that the back edges are flush.

Cut the ashpan front (B) in 3/16in wood and score grooves as shown on the pattern, and glue into place.

Cut two pieces of moulding (C) to fit either side of the fire box opening and glue in place.

Cut the damper front (D) in 1/16in wood and glue in place.

Cut four grate bars in 1/16in square strip and glue between the fire box supports.

Cut moulding pieces with mitred corners and glue in place to frame the range front as shown on the pattern.

Cut the flue (F) in 3/16in wood, round the front and side edges as shown, and glue to the range top.

Cut pieces of 1/8in square strip and glue to the in-

side lower edge of the range to support and strengthen the assembly.

Score indented circles on the range top to represent boiling rings (or glue on metal washers after painting). Paint the range with two coats of matt black paint.

Cut the oven door and door frame, hinges, latch, makers' label and damper panel in thin cardboard. Cut two hinge barrels from a wooden toothpick and add drops of gesso (liquid plaster) to indicate rivet heads on the hinges. Paint the oven door matt black. Colour all other pieces with metallic wax.

Assemble the oven door, frame, hinges and latch as shown in Fig 11e and glue on to the range front. Glue the makers' label and damper panel in place.

Cut the oven rest (E) in 1/16in wood, paint matt black and glue below the oven door.

Apply black-lead polish if required, then drill small holes and glue brass knobs in place.

To make the fire in the fire box, we have used tiny pieces of wood, coal and paper, assembled with craft glue and sprinkled with ash and red and gold glitter while the glue is wet.

WHITE-METAL KITCHEN-RANGE
(photograph page 39)

This kitchen-range is one of several types which can be made from white-metal kits (see Acknowledgements). We assembled the range with epoxy-resin adhesive using the instructions supplied with the kit, then painted it with metal primer and two coats of matt-black Humbrol enamel spray paint – allowing each coat of paint to dry thoroughly before applying the next. The painted range was polished with black-lead grate polish, applied with an old toothbrush and buffed to a shine.

If you intend to use a kit or a commercial kitchen-range, check that the opening in the chimney breast will accommodate the range, and adapt the pattern as necessary.

FURNITURE

BUILT-IN CUPBOARD
(Fig 12, photograph pages 26–7)

Built-in cupboards were popular in cottages where space was at a premium and the alcoves by the chim- ney breast in kitchens and parlours were often used this way. Our cupboard is designed to fit into the alcove by the chimney breast in the room box, but is assembled before fitting, so check the pattern measurements and adapt as necessary to fit other rooms. The

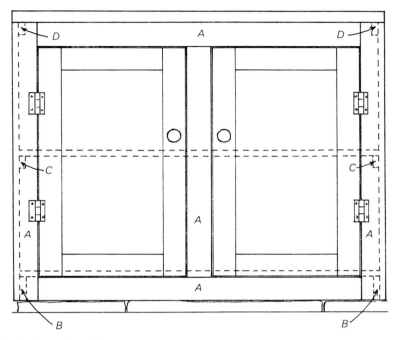

Fig 12 Pattern for the built-in cupboard

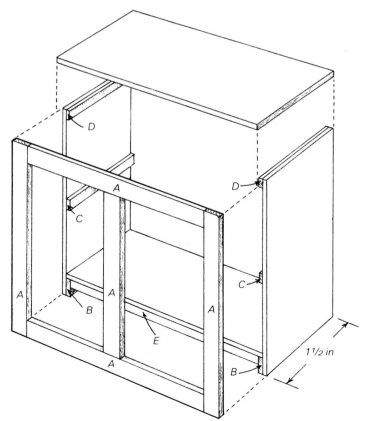

Fig 13 Assembly of the built-in cupboard

Country furniture showing a kitchen dresser, food-safe and rush-seated chair painted with a realistic pine finish

cupboard is made in $\frac{1}{16}$in and $\frac{1}{8}$in wood, and $\frac{1}{4} \times \frac{1}{8}$in and $\frac{1}{8}$in square woodstrip. You will also need four $\frac{1}{4}$in butt hinges and two small door knobs. Our cupboard front is painted cream, and the top is painted to represent pine (see page 34). If you prefer woodstain, stain the pieces before assembly.

Cut five front frame pieces (A) from the pattern in $\frac{1}{4} \times \frac{1}{8}$in woodstrip. Assemble the front frame as shown in Fig 13.

Cut two sides ($1\frac{1}{2} \times 3$in) in $\frac{1}{16}$in wood. Glue the sides behind the front frame.

Cut the lower shelf supports (B) in $\frac{1}{8} \times \frac{1}{16}$in strip, and glue to the inside bottom edge of the sides.

Cut shelf supports (C) in $\frac{1}{8} \times \frac{1}{16}$in strip and glue to the sides as shown on the pattern and in Fig 13.

Cut two top supports (D) in $\frac{1}{8} \times \frac{1}{16}$in strip and glue them to the top edge of the sides.

Cut two shelves in $\frac{1}{16}$in wood to fit, and glue in place on the supports (B) and (C).

Cut the base front (E) in $\frac{1}{8}$in square strip and glue it beneath the front edge of the bottom shelf.

Cut two door panels in $\frac{1}{16}$in wood to fit into the door openings. Cut door frames in $\frac{1}{4} \times \frac{1}{16}$in strip and glue the frames on to the door panels as shown. Glue and pin the hinges to the doors and front frame.

Paint the cupboard front (and inside if required), allow to dry and drill holes to receive the door knobs. Fit the cupboard into the alcove with a little glue to secure.

Cut the cupboard top in $\frac{1}{8}$in wood to fit snugly into the alcove with an $\frac{1}{8}$in overhang at the front edge. Sand the front edge so it is slightly rounded, paint as required and glue the top in place on to the cupboard.

Fig 14 Pattern for the kitchen dresser

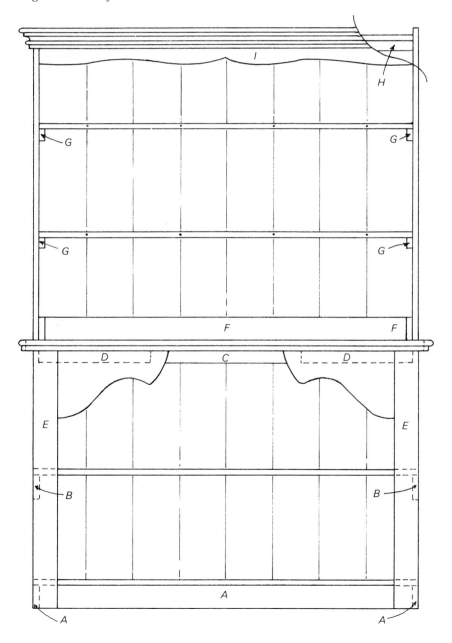
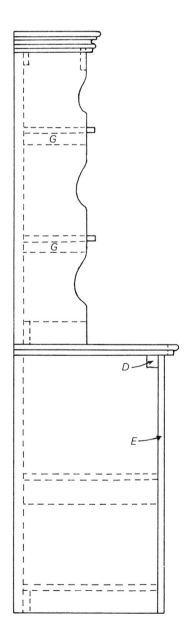

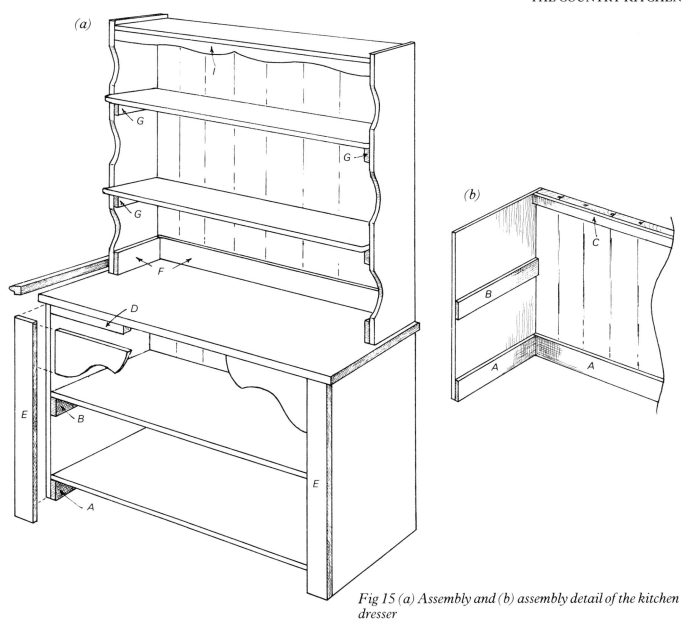

Fig 15 (a) Assembly and (b) assembly detail of the kitchen dresser

ALCOVE SHELVES

The shelves are cut in $\frac{1}{8}$in wood to fit into the alcove on battens of $\frac{1}{8} \times \frac{1}{16}$in woodstrip. Our shelves and battens are $\frac{3}{4}$in deep, painted to represent pine, and edged with narrow cotton lace.

Cut two battens for each shelf, and cardboard spacer templates as shown in Fig 10a. Glue the battens to the walls, using the card templates to ensure that they are level.

Cut the shelves, paint or stain them as required and glue lace trim to the front edge. Glue the shelves on to the battens.

DRESSER (Fig 14, photograph page 31)

The kitchen dresser is made in two parts, a base and top, which are glued together after assembly. Both parts are made in $\frac{1}{8}$in and $\frac{1}{16}$in wood with planked backs made from $\frac{1}{2} \times \frac{3}{32}$in woodstrip – we have used tongue and groove floorboarding. Woodstrip should be chamfered along one edge so that the boards resemble tongue and groove when butted together, and you will need approximately 5ft to make the top and base. The dresser is trimmed with $\frac{3}{16}$in and $\frac{1}{8}$in moulding and we have used eight commercial cup hooks on the shelves. Our dresser is painted with an acrylic wash to represent pine (see page 34 for instructions). If you use this finish the wood should be painted before cutting to prevent warping. If you prefer woodstain, stain the pieces before assembly.

THE BASE

Cut $\frac{1}{2}$in woodstrip planks for the back, glue and butt together as shown on the pattern to give a total width of $3\frac{7}{8}$in.

Cut two sides in $\frac{1}{16}$in wood and glue to the outside edges of the back.

Cut the pot-board supports (A) in $\frac{1}{16} \times \frac{1}{4}$in woodstrip and glue to the bottom edge of the back and sides.

Cut the shelf supports (B) in ¹/₁₆ × ¹/₄in strip and glue to the sides as shown on the pattern.

Cut the pot board and shelf in ¹/₁₆in wood and glue on to the supports and to the back.

Cut the top in ¹/₈in wood and glue on to the sides and back.

Cut a top support (C) 3⁷/₈in long in ¹/₁₆ × ¹/₈in strip and glue across the back, butted under the top, as shown in Fig 15b.

Cut two bracket supports (D) in ¹/₈in square strip and glue to the underside of the top – flush with the front edge of the sides, as shown on the pattern.

Cut two side-front pieces (E) in ¹/₄ × ¹/₁₆in strip and glue on to the sides – flush at the outside edges and overhanging the inside edges.

Cut two decorative brackets in ¹/₁₆in wood with a fretsaw or craft knife, sandpaper to refine the shaping, and glue to the side fronts and bracket supports.

Cut ¹/₈in moulding with mitred corners and glue to the front and side edges of the top.

THE TOP

Cut woodstrip planks for the back, glue and butt together as shown on the pattern to give a total width of 3⁷/₈in.

Cut two sides in ¹/₁₆in wood and shape the curved edges with a craft knife and sandpaper. Glue the sides to the outside edges of the back. (Note, that the sides are higher than the back.)

Cut supports (F) in ¹/₄ × ¹/₁₆in strip and glue to the bottom edge of the back and sides as shown in Fig 15a.

Cut shelf supports (G) in ¹/₈ × ¹/₁₆in strip and spacer templates in cardboard. Glue the shelf supports to the sides using the card templates to ensure that they are level.

Cut a top support (H) 3⁷/₈ long, in ¹/₈ × ¹/₁₆in strip and glue across the back, at the top edge.

Cut two shelves in ¹/₁₆in wood, round the front corners, and glue on to the shelf supports to protrude beyond the sides.

Cut the top in ¹/₁₆in wood (³/₄in wide) to fit between the sides. Glue the top on to the back, between the sides.

Cut the frieze (I) in ¹/₁₆in wood, shaping the curved edge with a craft knife and sandpaper. Glue the frieze to the front underside edge of the top, between the sides.

Cut ³/₁₆in moulding with mitred corners, and glue to the front and side edges of the top.

Glue the dresser top on to the base and allow to dry. Apply wax polish and buff to a soft sheen. Drill tiny holes in the front edge of the shelves to receive the cup hooks and glue in place with superglue.

PAINTED PINE FINISH

The dresser in the Cottage Kitchen (and other furniture throughout the book) has been painted rather than stained, to represent pine. This is a particularly useful finish if you are making furniture in jelutong

(or similar wood) as the wood can be coloured and grained, complete with knot-holes perfectly in scale. The colour is usually applied to the wood (and woodstrip and mouldings) before the piece of furniture is cut and assembled, so that the watery wash of paint will not affect glued joints or cause the piece to warp. The detail of graining and knot-holes is painted after the furniture piece is assembled.

You will need translucent colours of artists' acrylic paint in burnt umber for colouring the wood and artists' acrylic or watercolours in burnt sienna, yellow ochre and sepia for the detail. Brushes should be good quality artists' ¹/₂in round soft brush, and fine-liner and fine-detail brushes. The paints are mixed with water and an old plate makes a good palette. Protect

The Kitchen Parlour on a winter evening with the curtains drawn and the kettle on the range

the work surface with paper towels.

Mix burnt umber acrylic paint with water to make a very watery wash – virtually dirty water – in sufficient quantity to coat the whole piece of wood. To vary the shade, add minute amounts of burnt sienna and yellow ochre to the wash.

Load the ½in round soft paint-brush with paint, hold the piece of wood with your finger tips, and apply paint to the edges of the wood all around. As soon as the edges are painted, hold the wood by the edges and paint both surfaces, all over, as quickly as possible to minimise warping. Support the painted wood and leave to dry naturally – turning as necessary.

When the wood is thoroughly dry, cut and assemble the furniture piece. Touch in paint wash on any unpainted edges exposed by cutting. Sand the assembled piece lightly with small pieces of fine-grade abrasive paper to smooth the surface and to emphasise areas of light and shade on the painted finish – particularly areas where wear naturally occurs, such as mouldings and edges. Leave the back and base of the piece unsanded to represent unfinished wood.

Mix a little burnt umber paint so that it is fluid but not runny, and with the tip of the fine-detail brush, paint round and/or oval knot-holes on the piece. (It helps to use a life-size piece of wood as a guide and experiment on scrap wood.) Knot-holes vary in size and shape and the effect is more convincing in miniature if you have fewer than in life-size.

When the painted knots are dry, dilute the burnt umber paint to a watery wash and add a little burnt sienna. Using the tip of the fine-liner brush and a very light touch apply paint to highlight the grain of the wood and emphasise the grain around the knot-holes.

With the tip of the brush add a little burnt sienna paint to define the outline and shape of some of the knot-holes and tiny touches of sepia to vary the colour – but don't overdo it!

When the paint is thoroughly dry, apply a coat of beeswax polish and buff to a soft sheen.

PINE SETTLE *(photograph pages 34–5)*

The settle is made from the pattern Fig 34 and instructions in Chapter 3, in wood painted to represent pine before cutting (see above).

SMALL CUPBOARD
(Fig 16, photograph pages 34–5)

The small cupboard is made from the pattern Fig 61 and instructions in Chapter 5 for the pot cupboard, (omitting the decorative spindles), in wood painted to represent pine before cutting.

The panel is made from 1/2in tongue and groove boards, glued and butted together and cut diagonally. Note, that because the finished thickness of this door is 5/32in, the shelf supports (B and C) and the shelves should be set back 1/32in from the front edge of the sides to accommodate the extra thickness of the door.

TABLE *(Fig 17, photograph pages 26–7)*

The kitchen table is made in 1/8in wood with legs of 5mm (1/8in) square dowelling. The legs on our table are simply shaped with a craft knife and sandpaper to represent turning, but if you prefer, a set of commercial turned legs might be used instead. We have painted the frieze and legs brown and sanded the top to represent scrubbed deal. If you prefer woodstain, stain the pieces before assembly.

To make the legs, cut four blanks 2 1/2in long, and use the craft knife and sandpaper to pare and shape the legs to resemble turning, as shown on the pattern. Note, that the top 1/2in of the leg is left square and the remainder is rounded.

Cut two short and two long friezes in 1/8 × 3/8in woodstrip.

Using a scrap of 1/16in wood as a spacer, glue legs to each end of the short friezes as shown in Fig 18a and leave to dry.

Stand the assembly upside-down to glue the long friezes in place, and support as the glue dries. Paint the assembled legs and frieze as required.

Cut the table top in 1/8in wood and sand thoroughly. Place the top upside-down on the work surface and glue the leg assembly in place. Apply pressure until the glue is dry.

LADDERBACK CHAIRS
(Fig 19, photograph page 31)

The ladderback chairs are made in 1/8in wood, 1/8in square woodstrip, and 1/8, 1/4 and 1/2in × 1/16in woodstrip. Our chairs are painted with a thin wash of

Fig 16 Pattern for the small cupboard

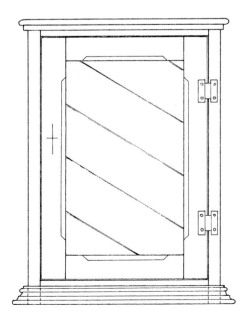
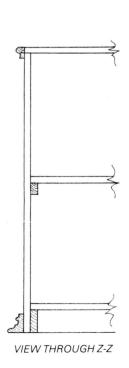

VIEW THROUGH Z-Z

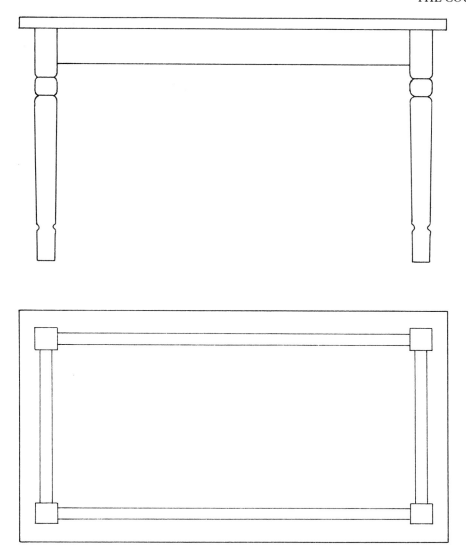

Fig 17 Pattern for the kitchen table

Fig 18 (a) Method for assembling the legs using a spacer
and (b) assembly for the kitchen table

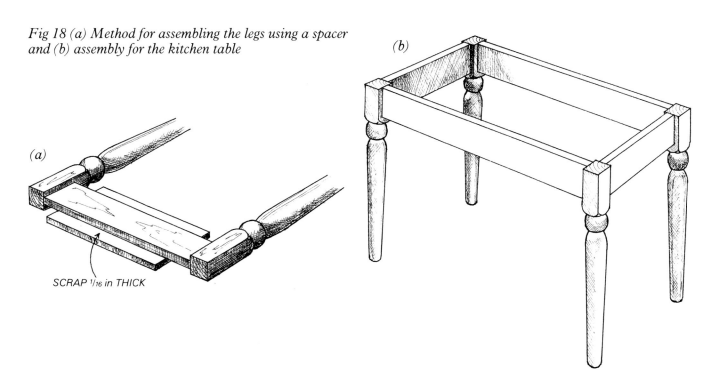

SCRAP 1/16 in THICK

acrylic paint, one to represent pine and the other in soft green (see pages 26–7). If you use a similar acrylic wash or woodstain, paint or stain the pieces before assembly so that any glue seepage will not affect the colour. If you prefer a painted finish the chair can be painted after assembly.

Cut two front and two back legs in ⅛in square woodstrip. Shape the top end of the back legs by cutting a shallow groove around the piece, ⅛in from the end with a craft knife, and sand the end to form a knob.

Cut the seat in ⅛in wood and cut ⅛in square notches in each back corner to accommodate the legs.

Cut two plain back rails in ¼in strip and one top rail in ½in strip. Shape the curved edge on the top rail with a craft knife and refine the shaping with fine sandpaper.

Cut one front, one back and two side stretchers in ⅛in strip.

To assemble the chair, lay one back leg on the work surface and glue the seat in place, ensuring that it is at a right angle to the leg.

Glue the three back rails and the back stretcher to the leg, using scraps of ¼in wood as spacers. Check that the assembly is square and allow the glue to dry thoroughly. Glue the second back leg into place.

Glue the front stretcher between the front legs and allow to dry.

Turn the chair on to one side and glue the front legs to the underside of the seat. Glue the side stretcher between the front and back legs, allow to dry, then turn the chair and glue the other side stretcher in place.

Sand the completed chair gently to define the shaping, paint if required and apply wax polish.

RUSH-SEATED CHAIR (photograph page 31)

The rush-seated chair is made from the pattern Fig 65 and the instructions in Chapter 5, in wood painted to represent pine.

FOOD-SAFE (Fig 20, photograph page 31)

The food-safe is a ventilated cupboard which could be floor-standing or hung on the wall in the kitchen or scullery and was used to keep food, especially meat, safe from rodents and insects. Our food-safe is made in wood, painted to represent pine, with side and door panels of fine-gauge aluminium gauze. Metal gauze of this type is available from some pottery suppliers, but if you cannot find anything suitable an excellent alternative is nylon net (available from fabric shops), painted with a metallic silver paint, eg 'Hammerite'. (Lay a piece of net on plastic sheet and

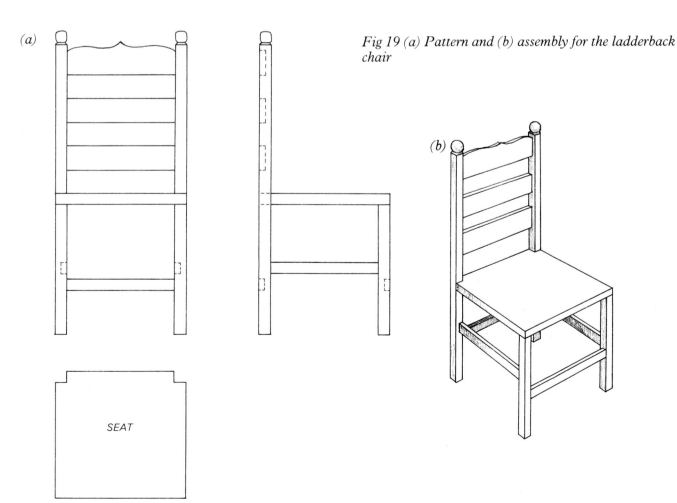

Fig 19 (a) Pattern and (b) assembly for the ladderback chair

SEAT

paint one side with metal paint using an old paint-brush, lift it off the plastic and paint the other side. Lift, and allow the painted net to dry thoroughly before use.)

You will need, ¹⁄₁₆in wood and ¼in, ⅛in, and ¹⁄₁₆in square woodstrip, and ⅛ × ¼in, ⅛ × ¹⁄₁₆in, and ¹⁄₁₆ × ¼in woodstrip. You will also need ⅛in, ³⁄₁₆in and ³⁄₃₂in mouldings. The door opens with two ¼in butt hinges and has a small wooden knob.

Note, that the sides are a pair – one right, one left –

Making bread the old-fashioned way, in a wooden dough trough

not both the same. For each side, cut four frame pieces in woodstrip from the pattern, and glue and assemble the frame as shown in Fig 21a.

Lay the side frame flat and glue ¹⁄₁₆in square strip to frame the inside edge of the opening as shown in Fig 21b.

Cut a gauze panel to fit, and lay in place on the

Fig 20 Pattern for the food-safe

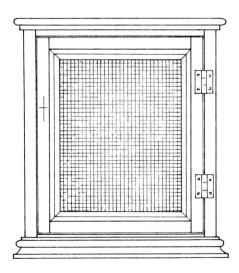
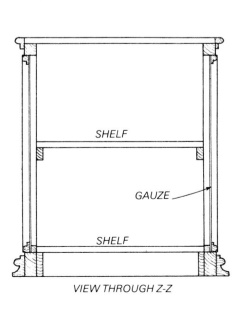
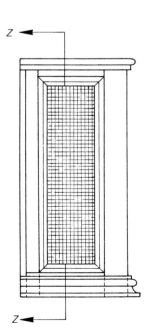

SHELF

GAUZE

SHELF

VIEW THROUGH Z-Z

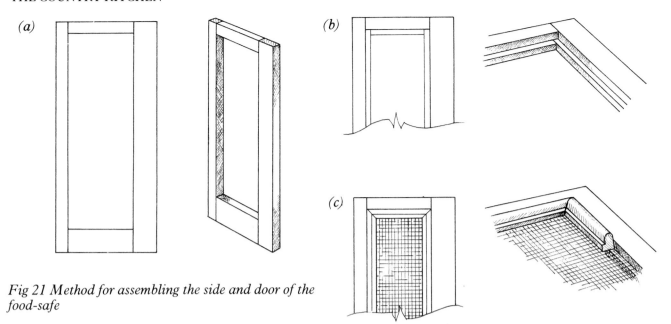

(a) *(b)* *(c)*

Fig 21 Method for assembling the side and door of the food-safe

inside-edge frame.

Cut a second frame of ³/₃₂in moulding with mitred corners, and glue to the outside edge of the opening as shown in Fig 21c, sandwiching the gauze panel and slightly overhanging the edge of the opening.

Cut the back from the pattern in ¹/₁₆in wood. Glue the sides on to the back and allow to dry thoroughly.

Cut the front-frame top (A) in ¹/₈in square strip. Cut the front-frame bottom (B) in ¹/₄in square strip. Glue both pieces in place between the sides.

Cut the centre shelf supports (C) in ¹/₈ × ¹/₁₆in strip. Cut the bottom shelf supports (D) in ¹/₁₆ × ¹/₄in strip. Glue the supports in place. Note, that the centre shelf supports are set back ¹/₈in from the front of the frame to allow the door to close.

Cut two shelves to fit in ¹/₁₆in wood. Note, that both shelves are set back ¹/₈in from the front edge. Glue the shelves on to the supports.

Cut the top in ¹/₁₆in wood and glue on to the carcase.

To make the door, cut four door-frame pieces in ¹/₈in square strip and assemble to fit snugly into the opening.

Cut the inside-edge frame in ¹/₁₆in square strip, the door panel in gauze, and the outside-edge frame in ³/₃₂in moulding, and assemble the door in the same way as the sides.

Drill a small hole to receive the doorknob and glue and pin the hinges to the door and door frame with superglue.

Cut ¹/₈in moulding with mitred corners and glue to the front and side top edges. Cut ³/₁₆in moulding with mitred corners and glue to the front and side bottom edges.

Paint the outside of the food-safe as required. For details of the painted pine finish, see page 34.

DOUGH TROUGH *(Fig 23, photograph page 39)*

When people made their own bread they usually made enough to last a week at a time and the dough was mixed in a large wooden trough. Our dough trough is made in ¹/₈in wood with legs of ³/₁₆in square woodstrip. We have used jelutong and painted the trough to represent bleached and aged wood.

Cut the base (B) but do not chamfer the edges at this stage.

Cut two ends (A) and glue on to the base as shown, and allow to dry.

Cut two sides (C). Chamfer the bottom edges so that the sides butt against the base, and chamfer the top edges to follow the angle of the ends. Glue the sides on to the base and to the ends.

Chamfer the edges of the base to follow the angle of the sides.

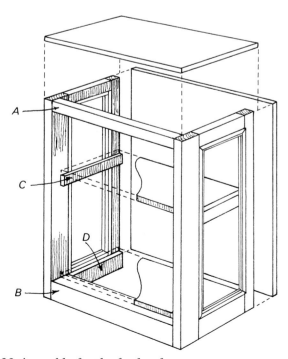

Fig 22 Assembly for the food-safe

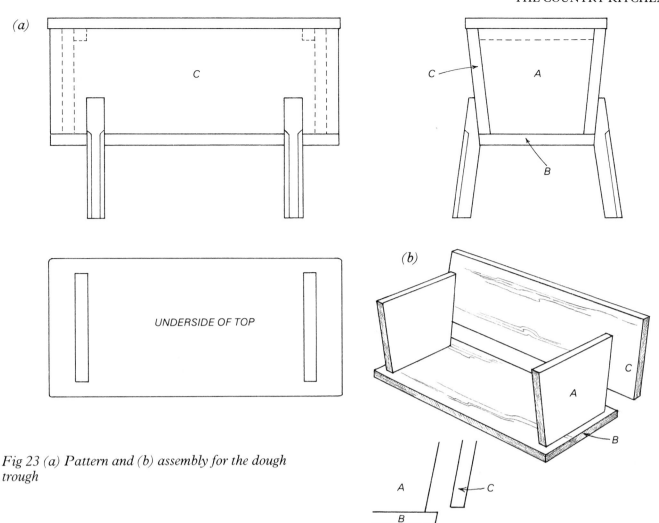

Fig 23 (a) Pattern and (b) assembly for the dough trough

Cut four leg blanks in ³/₁₆in woodstrip. Measure ½in from the top and pare the inside edge of each leg as shown on the pattern. Pare and shape the outside edges of each leg as shown. Glue the legs on to the sides and allow to dry.

Cut the lid in ⅛in wood. Cut two battens and glue on to the underside of the lid. Sand the edges rounded on both lid and battens.

Paint the outside of the dough trough to represent bleached wood (see page 53) adding touches of grey-green at the bottom of each leg.

UPHOLSTERED CHAIR *(photograph pages 34–5)*

The chair is made from the pattern Fig 52 and the instructions in Chapter 4.

ACCESSORIES

RAG RUG *(photograph pages 26–7)*

This type of rug was usually made at home on long winter evenings by the fire, using scraps from dressmaking or old clothes and household linens, saved in the 'rag-bag'. Traditionally, the rugs were made on a backing of old hessian sacks, but our rag rug is made with strips of cotton fabric on a backing of plastic embroidery canvas (available from needle-work suppliers). You will need six or eight toning patterns of a cotton fabric which does not fray badly –

such small amounts are needed that these could be scraps. The fabric strips are threaded with a bodkin – a needle with a very large, flat eye.

Cut a piece of plastic canvas to the required size of the rug – our rug is 4 × 2in – with a clean finished edge all around.

Cut the cotton fabrics into ¼in strips, 7 or 8in long and squarely on the grain of the fabric.

To work the border, thread the fabric strip into the bodkin and whip (oversew) the edge, one hole deep, working around the rug. Leave short ends on the underside and add in matching new strips as necessary. Ensure that the plastic-canvas edge is completely covered.

Work the centre of the rug in half-cross stitch (one hole diagonally at a time) in rows across the piece. Choose colours to form a pattern, leaving the short ends on the underside and adding new strips as required.

When the area is filled, trim the ends on the underside and press lightly with an iron if required.

SIMPLE GATHERED CURTAINS
(photograph pages 26–7)

The Cottage Kitchen curtains are made in printed cotton and hung from a pole of fine dowelling, suspended from small eyes screwed into the wall.

Cut two curtains to fit the window with allowance for hems and casing, and matching any pattern. Fold narrow hems down both sides and a wider hem at the bottom, press, and secure the hems with fabric glue. Fold in the top edge of each curtain and stitch a casing to take the dowelling pole.

Thread the pole through the casings and draw the curtains up equally. Pin the curtains on to the ironing board, set the folds by hovering a steam iron just above the fabric, and leave to dry.

Screw small eyes into the wall and push the ends of the curtain pole through the eyes.

TABLE-CLOTH (photograph pages 34–5)

The table-cloth in the kitchen parlour is made in printed cotton, trimmed with narrow picot braid.

Measure from the centre of the table to just above the floor, and draw a circle with this radius onto the fabric. Seal the drawn line with Fraycheck or similar and leave to dry. Cut out the table-cloth and glue on the braid to slightly overlap the edge. Dampen the cloth in steam from the kettle and put it on the table, smoothing the folds with your fingers until they hang well. Our lace cloth is an old lace doily, centred on the cotton cloth.

MANTELSHELF WITH DRYING RAIL
(Fig 24a, photograph pages 26–7)

The brackets and shelf are made in ⅛in wood to fit across the chimney breast with a drying rail of ¹⁄₁₆in diameter brass rod (available from model shops).

Cut two brackets and drill holes to receive the rail. Cut the shelf, 9 × ¾in. Stain or paint the brackets and shelf as required.

Glue one bracket to the underside of the shelf, ½in from the end and flush with the back edge.

Fit the rail and glue the other bracket into place. Glue the assembly to the wall.

MANTEL CLOTH (photograph pages 34–5)

The cloth was used as a decorative finish for mantelshelves in kitchens and parlours, but also helped to prevent smoke blowing into the room from a draught down the chimney. Our mantel cloth is a strip of velveteen an inch wide, cut to fit around the sides and front of the shelf with the edges sealed with Fraycheck. The lower edge is trimmed with picot braid, glued on to overlap the edge, and the top is folded in, pressed, and glued to the edge of the mantelshelf.

GUN BRACKETS (Fig 24b, photograph pages 26–7)

The brackets which support a commercial shotgun above the mantelshelf are made in ¹⁄₁₆in wood, painted or stained as required.

Cut two supports and two brackets. Glue the brackets on to the supports as shown, noting that one is slightly higher than the other so that the gun lies horizontally across them. Stain or paint as required and glue the supports to the wall.

SALT BOX (photograph page 39)

The salt box is made from the pattern Fig 131 and the instructions in Chapter 9.

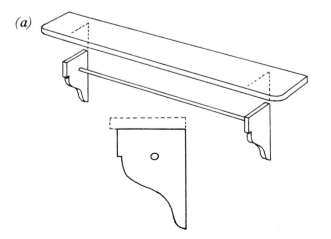

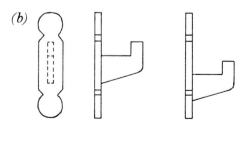

Fig 24 Pattern for (a) the mantelshelf with drying rail and (b) the gun brackets

— CHAPTER THREE —
The Scullery

The scullery, in all but the poorest houses, was an important room until well into the twentieth century when piped hot water and labour-saving machines made it obsolete, though the spirit of the scullery lingers on in the modern 'utility room'. It was in the scullery, not the kitchen, that most houses had their main water supply, and this was where the laundry (and the Christmas pudding) was boiled in a brick copper and where the washing-up was done.

In a country cottage, the scullery was often as large as the kitchen and was used for storing logs and tools and housing the chickens, as well as being a workshop for the cottager who repaired his family's boots and made hurdles or furniture. As all water had to be pumped (in some remote areas well into the twentieth century), water would have been heated in the copper and ladled into a bowl or bucket in the sink for washing-up. After the laundry was done, hot soapy water from the copper could be used to bath the family in a tin bath, kept on the scullery wall.

In the more sophisticated town house, the scullery was usually a small room behind the kitchen and its function was purely domestic. Most town houses built after 1860 had piped water and after 1900 most had hot water and bathrooms, so the scullery was used mainly for food preparation, laundry and washing-up. In the limited space of a town house, a larder was often built into a corner of the scullery – preferably against a north-facing wall – as it was convenient to store food where it would be prepared.

THE ROOM BOX
(photograph pages 46–7)

The room box shown in the photograph is made from the pattern Fig 7 and the instructions in Chapter 2, in the same way as the kitchen but omitting the window. The Scullery has a corner chimney breast behind the built-in brick copper, the walls and ceiling are papered with lining paper and emulsion-painted and the ceiling is beamed. The (non-opening) door is simply planked and the floor is laid with quarry tiles made in air-drying clay.

CORNER CHIMNEY BREAST (Fig 25)

The corner chimney breast is simple to make in 5mm (⅛in) Foamcore (available from art and craft shops), and is cut to fit the height of the room, before or after the floor is laid, as you prefer.

Cut three chimney breast supports in Foamcore, as shown on the pattern. Glue one support into the corner of the room, on the floor, one to the ceiling and one about half-way up the wall.

Cut the chimney breast in Foamcore, lengthening the pattern as appropriate for the height of the room. (The room box is 8in high.)

On the back of the chimney breast, mark the 'bending' line in pencil.

Cut a V-shaped groove with a craft knife and metal

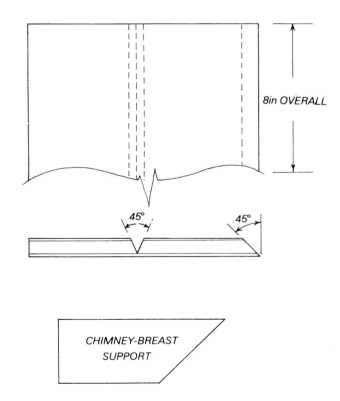

Fig 25 Pattern for the chimney breast and support

ruler through the back layer of card and the foam – but not the front layer of card, as shown in Fig 25. Trim the back-wall edge to an angle of 45° as shown.

Bend the chimney breast along the grooved line and glue in place to the walls and supports with UHU or a similar tacky craft glue. Allow to dry thoroughly.

DECORATING

We papered the ceiling and walls of the room, including the chimney breast, with lining paper and applied two coats of magnolia emulsion paint to represent whitewash. In an old-fashioned room of this type magnolia is a more realistic colour than a modern, bright white.

In the cottage scullery, areas of the walls – in corners, behind the sink and by the copper and an area of the ceiling above the copper – were painted with a very watery wash of burnt umber acrylic paint to indicate patches of dampness or discolouration by smoke. These painted areas should be applied with a very light touch, with a paint-brush or a small piece of natural sponge. We have added some definition to the chimney breast above the copper by stamping a brick pattern lightly on to the painted surface with a brick-shaped piece of potato, using very dilute burnt umber paint. At the bottom of the walls and under the sink, we have painted 'cracks' in the plaster with a fine-liner brush and burnt umber or dark grey paint.

The ceilings in both sculleries are beamed with two pieces of ½in square woodstrip (or commercial beams). In the cottage the beams were slightly 'distressed' with a hammer and stained to represent oak. The town scullery beams were painted to represent 'whitewash'. Hammer small black-painted pins into the beams before they are glued in place if you want to hang game-birds or bacon joints and bunches of herbs.

Note, that if you intend to fit a built-in larder (see page 45) the larder should be built and fitted before the scullery is decorated.

LIGHTING

We have fitted a concealed light in the room box, hidden behind the beam. In the town scullery the oil lamp and the light in the larder are part of the dolls-house copper-tape wiring system.

PLANKED AND BRACED DOOR (Fig 26)

Our door is built into the door frame and simply glued on to the wall, but the pattern and method may be adapted to make an opening door for a room box or dolls-house room. You will need approximately 3ft of ½ × ³/₃₂in woodstrip for the planks and 1ft of ½ × ⅛in woodstrip for the braces – we have used tongue and groove floorboarding. Woodstrip should

be chamfered along one edge to represent tongue and groove when the planks are butted together. The door frame is made in ³/₃₂ × ⅜in and ³/₃₂ × ⁵/₃₂in woodstrip.

Cut the planks and glue and butt them together as

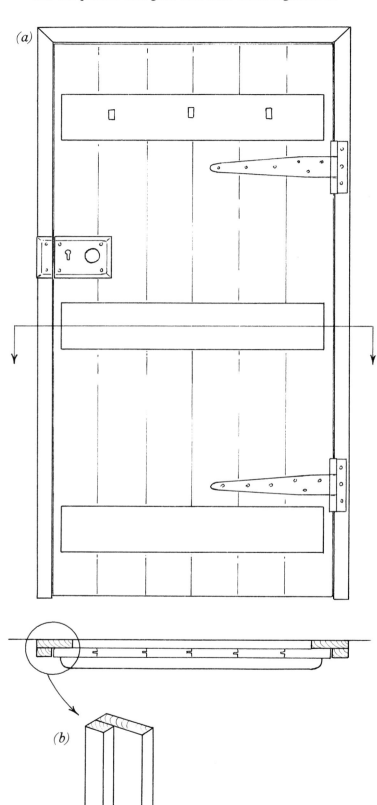

Fig 26 Pattern and assembly for the planked and braced door

shown on the pattern. Cut three braces and glue them across the planks as shown.

Sand the door thoroughly and stain or paint as required. We have painted our door with an acrylic-paint wash to represent pine (see page 34).

For the door frame, prepare two pieces (6½in long) and one piece (3½in long) of narrow woodstrip glued to wide woodstrip as shown in Fig 26b. Paint or stain as required.

Cut the woodstrip with mitred corners to frame the door leaving a slight gap all around. Glue the door into the door frame.

Cut mock hinges in thin cardboard with hinge barrels from wooden toothpicks and drops of gesso or liquid plaster to represent screw heads. Paint the hinges matt black and glue on to the door. We have used a commercial white-metal lockbox painted black, with a small brass knob. Add small black-painted pins or coathooks as required.

Cut a doorstep (if required) from a block of ½in scrap wood, sand a hollow in the tread to resemble wear and paint the doorstep with matt grey paint to represent stone. Glue the doorstep to the floor and wall. Glue the back of the door frame and position the door on the wall above the doorstep.

QUARRY-TILED FLOOR

The quarry-tiled floor is made from air-drying clay (eg terracotta-coloured Das) and can be painted with red, ochre and brown acrylic paints mixed to vary the terracotta colour. You will need an old rolling-pin (or similar) to roll out the clay and a craft knife and metal ruler to cut the tiles. (If you have a suitable small, square plastic container with sharp edges this could be used like a pastry-cutter to stamp out the tiles.)

Roll out the clay to an even ⅛in thickness on a plastic sheet and leave until the clay is leather-hard.

Cut individual tiles, all the same size, with the craft knife and ruler or cutter – our tiles are 1in square. Leave the tiles to dry thoroughly.

Paint the individual tiles, mixing the paints to vary the shades of colour and allow to dry. Paint or spray the tiles with acrylic matt sealer if required, and allow to dry.

Make a template for the floor area in thick cartridge paper if required.

Working on the template (or the floor of the room), glue the tiles to the paper with UHU or similar tacky craft glue, starting with the front row and working to the back, butting the tiles closely together. Trim the tiles as necessary on one side, the back edge (and around the chimney breast) to fit the template. Our tiles are not grouted.

Glue the back of the paper template and press the tiles in place on the floor. Finish the front edge with a piece of fine woodstrip, stained or painted if required.

Note, that if your tiles are a little thick or uneven, you may prefer to make and fit the brick copper first, then cut a paper template and tiles to fit around the copper.

BRICK FLOOR *(photograph pages 58–9)*

A brick floor can be made in air-drying clay in the same way as the tiled floor described above, but as a simple alternative, brick-patterned 'cladding' (see Acknowledgements), or simply brick-patterned paper cut to fit the floor area and pasted in place is very effective.

FIXTURES

BUILT-IN LARDER
(Fig 27, photograph pages 58–9)

The built-in larder shown in the town kitchen can be incorporated into the room box above, or into a dolls-house room. It is built as a three-sided unit and fitted into the required space with a partition wall (and opening door if required) fitted in front. The measurements given on the pattern and in brackets below can be adjusted to make a larger or smaller larder – perhaps to fit into an alcove in the dolls-house kitchen or scullery. Our larder walls are made in 5mm (⅛in) Foamcore, and the shelves in ⅛in wood. We have fitted a small window in the back wall, covered with a mesh panel made from a small piece of nylon net (available from fabric shops) which has been stiffened with Fraycheck and painted on both sides with metallic silver paint, eg Humbrol enamel or Hammerite. The window opening is framed with ⅛ × ¹⁄₁₆in and ⅛ × ¼in woodstrip.

Cut the back (6 × 8in) in Foamcore and cut out the window opening as shown in Fig 27. Face the window opening with ⅛ × ¼in woodstrip, glued in place to fit flush with the front edge.

Cut two sides (2¼ × 8in) in Foamcore and glue the sides to each side of the back.

Cut a 1in wide top support (A) in ⅛in wood to fit across the assembled back and sides and glue in place with the back edges flush.

Paper or paint the inside of the larder as required. We have used magnolia emulsion paint and glued a strip of paper tiles covered with a transparent self-adhesive plastic to the wall above the large shelf.

Cut a painted net panel (2 × 2½in). Cut the

The Cottage Scullery on washing day with a brick copper, mangle and wooden laundry accessories

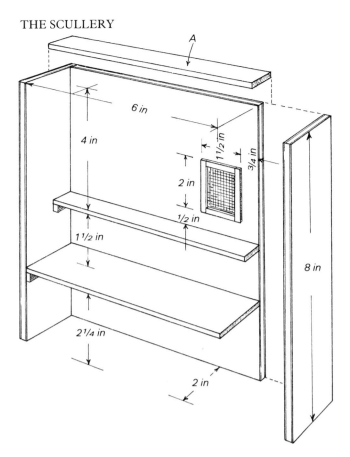

Fig 27 Plan and assembly for the built-in larder

window-frame in ⅛ × ¹/₁₆in wood to fit around the window opening and assemble the window-frame on the net panel. When the glue is dry trim away excess net and glue the window over the window opening. Glue a piece of tracing paper over the back of the window opening if required, to obscure the view through the window.

Cut large and small shelves in ⅛in wood to fit the width of the larder. We have painted the large shelf to represent marble (see page 53) and the small shelf to represent pine (see page 34).

Cut shelf supports in ⅛ × ¼in strip and glue to the side walls. Glue the shelves on to the shelf supports and to the walls. (In a wider larder the shelves may need the additional support of brackets.)

Cut a small wall shelf with brackets (see page 57), paint as required and glue to the wall beside the window.

Fit the assembled larder in place, gluing the back (and side/s) to the wall of the room. Fit flooring if it is something different from the floor of the room – for example, the kitchen or scullery might have a wooden floor and the larder a brick floor.

Our partition wall was cut in 5mm (⅛in) Foamcore (or plywood) to fit across the full width of the room, with a doorway (cut to fit a ready-made door) in front of the larder. The partition wall was glued on to woodstrip battens, glued to the walls, ceiling and floor in front of the larder before the room was deco-

rated. The door and door frame were painted to represent pine and fitted into the doorway after the room was decorated.

Note that if you wish the larder door to open into the larder, the partition wall should be fitted far enough in front of the larder to allow clearance for the door. If the door is to open outwards, the partition wall can be butted against the side walls of the larder.

BRICK COPPER *Fig 29, photograph pages 46–7)*

The copper is made in 5mm (⅛in) thick Foamcore, covered with bricks modelled in air-drying clay. The bowl is made in clay, using an eggcup as a mould, and the lid is made from scraps of ³/₃₂in woodstrip.

To make the bowl, coat the inside of an eggcup with a thin film of oil or vaseline to prevent the clay from sticking to it, and press two pieces of narrow tape inside to help lift the bowl out of the mould.

Knead and roll the clay to an even thickness and press it into the eggcup to shape the bowl against the sides and slightly splayed at the top edge as shown in Fig 28. Smooth and trim the clay and leave to dry. Use the tapes to lift the bowl out of the mould, smooth the edges thoroughly and paint to represent metal.

Cut the copper side in Foamcore from the pattern Fig 29. On the back of the piece, cut V-shaped grooves at a 45° angle as shown, with a craft knife and metal ruler – this allows the side to bend.

To make the fire box, cut two sides 1 × 1½in in Foamcore and glue to the back of the opening as shown in Fig 30. Cut the back to fit and glue on to complete the box. Paint the inside of the fire box matt black.

Cut the copper top from the pattern Fig 29 in Foamcore, checking that the hole for the bowl is the correct size for your eggcup mould.

Bend the side piece, running glue along the grooves, and glue the top on to the side with UHU or similar tacky craft glue as shown in Fig 31.

To make the bricks, roll out the clay to ¹/₁₆in thickness. Lay the assembled copper on its back and cut a piece of clay slightly larger than required to cover the copper sides, to allow for shrinkage. Trim around the fire box opening, and leave the clay on the copper to dry leather-hard. Mark the bricks into the clay with a pointed tool and leave the clay on the copper to dry thoroughly. Glue the clay to the Foamcore with UHU or a similar glue.

Stand the clay-covered copper upright, and fit the bowl into the hole in the top, using Tetrion or a similar filler to secure it in place and fill any gaps. Smooth Tetrion all over the top of the copper to meet the brick sides, and slightly round off the edges. Clean off surplus Tetrion, especially from the bowl, and leave to dry thoroughly.

Paint the bricks with acrylic paints in shades of brown, red and ochre, mixing the paints to vary the colours from brick to brick. When the paint is dry, grout the bricks with a little Tetrion or a similar filler,

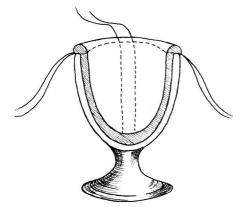

Fig 28 Method for making the bowl for the brick copper

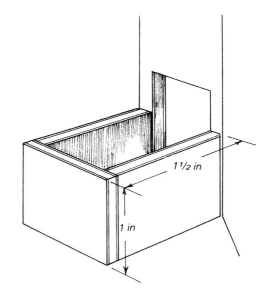

Fig 30 Assembly of the fire box for the brick copper

Fig 29 Pattern for the brick copper

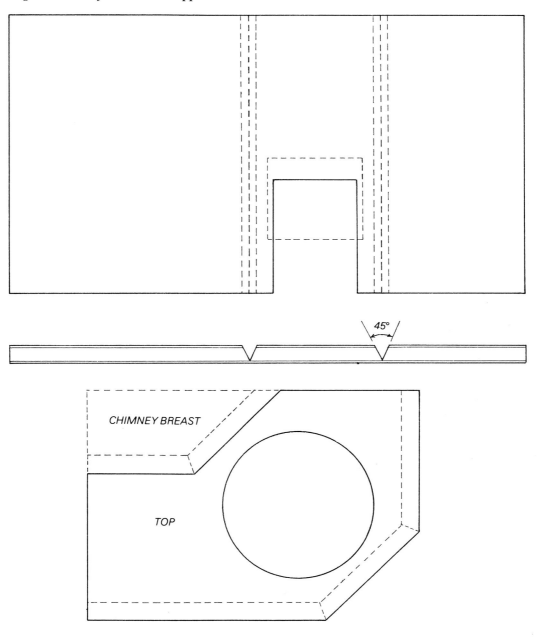

CHIMNEY BREAST

TOP

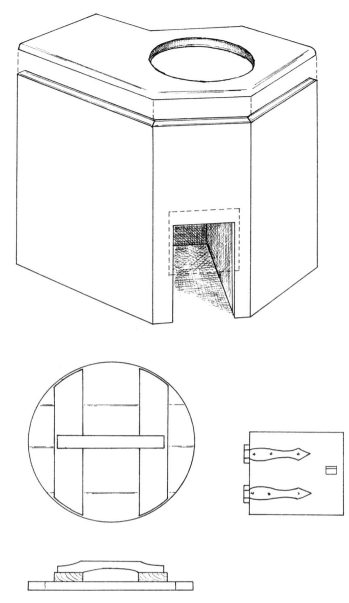

Fig 31 Assembly of the brick copper and pattern for the lid and fire box door

and apply matt sealer if required and leave to dry. The copper shown in the photograph on pages 46–7 has been painted with a coat of thin off-white acrylic paint over the painted (or unpainted) brick to resemble whitewash.

Cut the fire box door from the pattern Fig 31 in thin stiff card, mock hinges and handle in card, and hinge barrels from wooden toothpicks with drops of gesso to represent rivet heads. Assemble the door, paint to represent metal, and glue to the front of the copper as shown.

To make the circular wooden lid, cut four 2in long pieces of scrap woodstrip, glue and butt together. Draw the pattern, Fig 31, on to the wood and cut out with a fretsaw or craft knife. Cut two battens, trimming the ends to curve, and glue on to the lid as shown. Sand the edges to round off slightly.

Cut the handle from a scrap of 1/8in square woodstrip, shape as shown on the pattern with a craft

knife, and glue the handle across the battens. Paint the lid to represent bleached wood (see page 60).

BELFAST SINK ON BRICK PIERS
(Fig 32, photograph pages 46–7)

The Belfast sink, made in white glazed pottery, came into use early in the twentieth century and rapidly became popular, as it was easier to clean and more hygienic than porous fire-clay and stone or wooden sinks. Our sink is modelled in air-drying clay and painted to represent glazed pottery. The brick piers are modelled in clay over 10mm (1/4in) balsa or Foamcore blocks and the draining board is made in 1/16in wood with 1/8in moulding and brackets of 1/32 × 1/4in woodstrip.

To make the sink, roll out the clay to an even thickness of 3/32in and cut pieces for the bottom and sides. Punch out the plug-hole in the bottom and leave the pieces to dry leather-hard.

Assemble the bottom and sides as shown on the pattern, using slip (clay mixed with water) to join the pieces and to round off the top edge and the corners, inside and outside. Smooth with water and a soft paint-brush and leave to dry thoroughly.

Sand gently with fine-grade abrasive paper if necessary, to refine and smooth the shaping, and paint the sink with white acrylic or enamel paint – a coat of gloss over one or two coats of matt enamel will make a very effective porcelain finish. A metal eyelet can be glued into the plug-hole if required.

To make the piers cut two 10mm (1/4in) blocks, 1 1/8in wide × 1 3/4in tall, in balsa or Foamcore.

Roll out clay to 1/16in thickness and wrap clay around each block. Trim the clay and leave to dry leather-hard on the blocks. Mark the bricks with a pointed tool and leave the clay to dry thoroughly on the blocks. Paint the bricks as described on page 48, seal if required and glue the piers to the underside of the sink with UHU or a similar glue.

Cut the draining board in 1/16in wood and score grooves as shown on the pattern. Cut 1/8in moulding with mitred corners and glue in place to frame the board.

Cut three pieces for each bracket as shown on the pattern (Fig 32) and assemble, noting that the brackets do not form exact right angles. Glue the brackets to the underside of the draining board as shown, and to the sink, so that the draining board overhangs the sink slightly. The draining board is not stained or painted.

PUMP

The pump is made from a white-metal kit (see Acknowledgements), painted with metal primer and black enamel paint. It is mounted on a block of 1/2in square wood with metal straps cut from wine bottle caps and painted black.

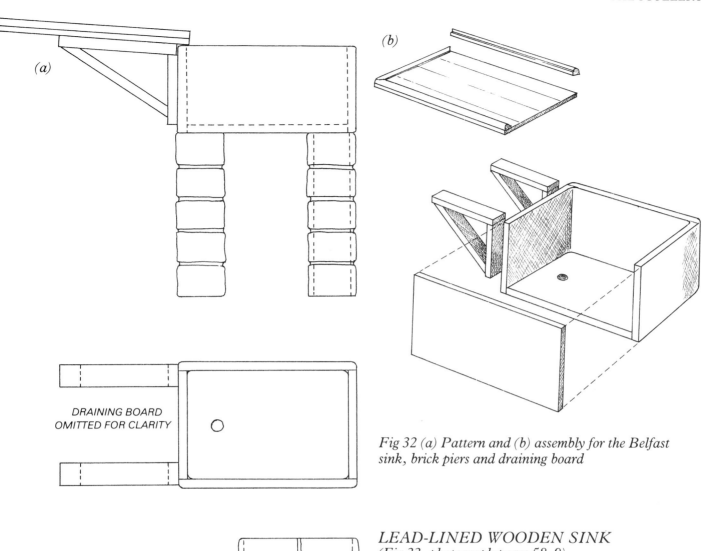

(a)

DRAINING BOARD
OMITTED FOR CLARITY

(b)

Fig 32 (a) Pattern and (b) assembly for the Belfast sink, brick piers and draining board

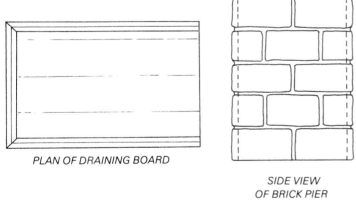

PLAN OF DRAINING BOARD

SIDE VIEW
OF BRICK PIER

TAPS

We have used a pair of commercial brass taps and white-metal pipes glued to the wall above the sink on small blocks of wood. Taps, pipes and waste pipes are available from most dolls-house shops in brass and white-metal. The plumbing in a Victorian house should be fairly obvious and, if you wish, additional pipes could be glued to the wall to appear to bring hot water into the room from a tank above.

LEAD-LINED WOODEN SINK
(Fig 33, photograph pages 58–9)

The hardwood sink lined with lead was used throughout the late eighteenth and nineteeth centuries as an alternative to shallow stone or fire-clay sinks, but as it was more expensive it was usually found in middle or upper class town houses. Our sink is made in ⅛in wood, stained or painted to represent teak. The 'lead' lining is made from soft metal taken from the caps of wine bottles. Slit the cap with a craft knife and remove it carefully from the bottle to preserve as large a piece of metal as possible. Open out the metal and press it flat, smoothing the surface with a piece of dowelling or similar to remove the creases. You will need two or three caps to provide sufficient metal to line the sink.

Cut the sink base (2 × 1⅛in), two sides 2¼ × ¾in, and two ends (1⅛ × ¾in), in wood.

Glue the ends butted to each end of the base. Glue the sides to the base and ends and allow to dry. Paint the sink to represent bleached wood (see page 60) and paint dovetail joints if required down each corner.

Cut pieces of smoothed metal to line the sink ends and glue into the sink with UHU or similar glue, with the bottom edges lapped on to the base and the top edges rolled over the ends. Cut metal to line the sides and base of the sink and glue in place with the top edges rolled over the sides. Use a piece of dowelling or

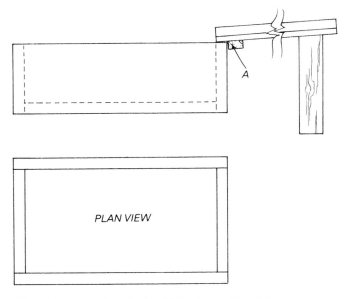

PLAN VIEW

Fig 33 Pattern for the lead-lined wooden sink

similar tool to rub the lead firmly and smoothly on to the wood, ensuring that there are no gaps in the corners of the sink. Trim the top edge neatly, flush with the outside edge of the sink. Drill a plug-hole if required through the base of the sink.

Make the brick piers as for the Belfast sink and glue the sink on to the piers.

Cut the draining board and assemble as above. Cut a support (A) in 1/8 × 1/16in strip and glue to the underside of the draining board as shown. Cut the bracket in 1/4 × 1/8in strip and glue to the underside of the draining board and to the wall. Paint the draining board to represent bleached wood, then glue the sink and draining board in place. We have added a small printed-cotton curtain, which is hemmed and gathered and then glued to the front edge of the draining board.

Cut a splashback, 2 × 1/2in, in 1/8in thick wood. Paint and then glue the splashback to the wall behind the sink.

(a)

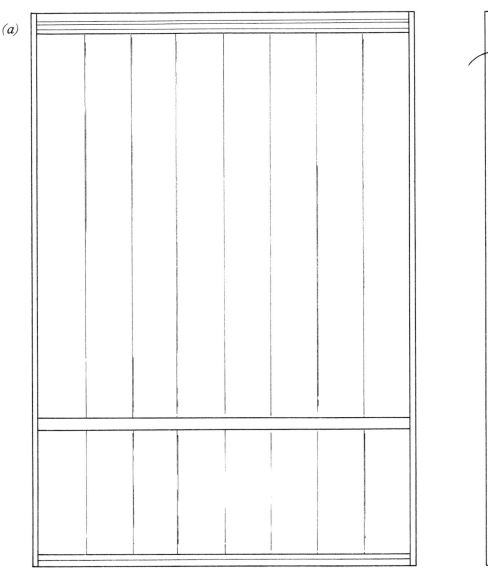

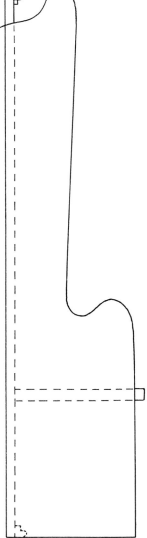

FURNITURE

THE SETTLE *(Fig 34, photograph page 54)*

The settle is a typical piece of country furniture which was found in grander houses in the sixteenth century, but progressed down the social scale to farmhouses and cottages by the nineteenth century. Our settle is made in ⅛in and 1/16in jelutong and finished with ⅛in and 3/16in mouldings. The back is planked, but it could be cut in one piece (and scored to represent planking) if you prefer. You will need approximately 4½ft of ½in woodstrip to make a planked back – we have used tongue and groove floorboarding. Woodstrip should be chamfered along one edge to represent tongue and groove when butted together. The settle can be stained or painted to represent pine as shown in the kitchen-parlour in Chapter 2, or colour-painted and 'aged' as shown in the scullery. If you choose woodstain or a paint wash, colour the pieces before assembly (see page 34), but the painted finish can be applied after the settle has been assembled if you wish.

Cut, glue and butt woodstrip planks together (or cut and score wood) to make the back as shown on the pattern (Fig 34a).

Cut a piece of 3/16in moulding and glue across the top of the back. Cut a piece of ⅛in moulding and glue across the bottom of the back as shown on the pattern.

Cut two sides in 1/16in wood, shaping the curved edges with a fretsaw or craft knife, and sand all the front edges so they are slightly rounded.

Cut the seat in ⅛in wood and sand the front edge and corners rounded.

Glue the seat to the back as shown. Glue the sides to the back and seat and leave to dry thoroughly.

Sand the assembly and paint as required. Our settle was painted dark blue-green over brown and 'aged' to show wear (see below).

PAINTED AND 'AGED' FINISH

The settle in the Scullery (and other pieces of furniture throughout the book) has been painted to represent old furniture re-painted several times over the years and aged with wear. You will need acrylic colours, and the technique is particularly effective if you use different colours for the undercoat(s) and top coat – applying as many layers of paint as you wish. You will also need fine-grade abrasive paper, eg 320-grit.

Sand the piece of furniture thoroughly and remove all traces of dust before you begin painting. Apply the first undercoat and allow to dry. Sand with fine-grade abrasive paper, and apply a second undercoat in the same or different colour, as you wish. When the paint is dry, sand again, and apply a very light coat of wax furniture polish.

Paint the top coat in the required colour over the wax polish and allow to dry.

Decide where on your piece of furniture wear would naturally occur, for example, on the front edge of the seat, the ends of the arms and the bottom of the sides and back. Consider where the piece has been, for example, our settle has been standing on the damp floor in the scullery so the bottom of the sides and back would have become damp, causing the paint to peel. Using fine-grade abrasive paper and a light touch, gently sand these areas to remove the top coat of paint. Sand some areas back to the bare wood if you wish. When you have sanded, bare wood can be washed with a little dilute burnt umber paint to dirty and 'age' it. Buff the finished piece with a soft cloth, or wax polish if required.

Fig 34 (a) Pattern and (b) assembly for the settle

(b)

FISH TABLE (Fig 35, photograph pages 58–9)

This small table, used for the preparation of fish, game or meat, has a top made in two parts. The larger part is fixed and painted to represent marble, the smaller part is wood and is hinged to lift. The fish table is made in ⅛in wood, ⅛ × ⅜in and ⅛in square woodstrip. You will also need scraps of ¹⁄₁₆in wood and two ¼in butt hinges.

Cut four legs 2⅜in long, in ⅛in square woodstrip, and chamfer the corners of each leg as shown.

Cut two long and two short friezes in ⅛ × ⅜in strip. Using a scrap of ¹⁄₁₆in wood as a spacer, glue a long frieze between each pair of legs and leave to dry. Glue the short friezes between each leg assembly and leave to dry. Paint the leg and frieze assembly as required.

Cut the table top in two pieces in ⅛in wood. Paint the larger piece to represent white marble (see below) and the smaller piece to represent pine (see Chapter 2). Glue the marble table top on to the leg assembly to

The old painted settle makes a comfortable place to sit and clean the boots

overhang equally at back, front and side, and allow to dry.

Cut small triangular supports in ¹⁄₁₆in scrap wood and notch the corners as shown to accommodate the table legs. Glue the supports into the angle of the frieze to fit flush with the top edge.

Try the wooden table top in place and mark the outside edge of the legs on the underside of the top. Glue and pin the hinges to the underside of the wooden top on the marked line, and to the outside edge of the legs as shown.

PAINTED WHITE MARBLE FINISH

This finish is designed to imitate real marble of the type used for table or washstand tops, shelves and

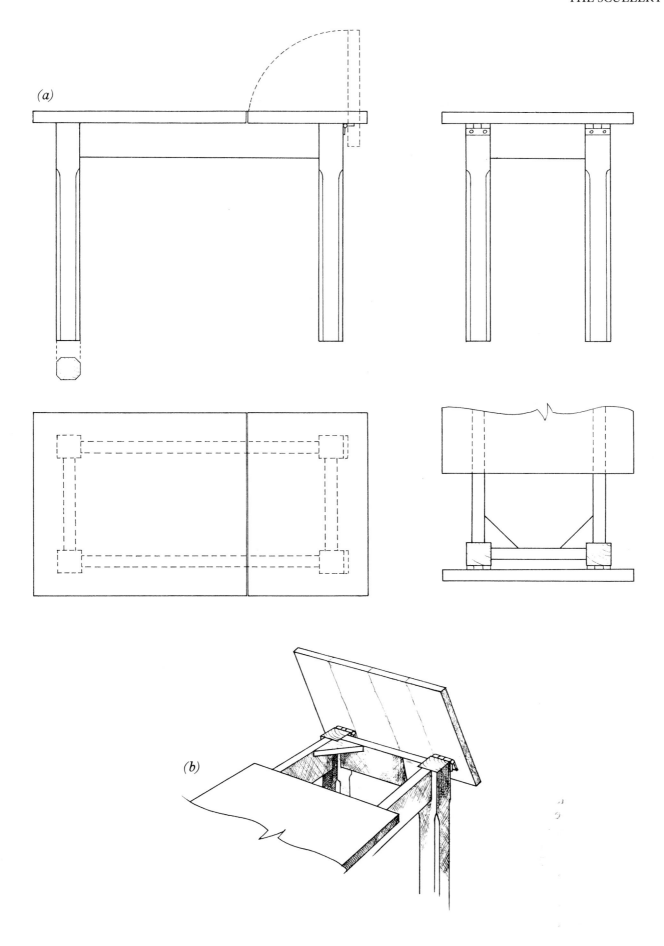

Fig 35 (a) Pattern and (b) assembly for the fish table

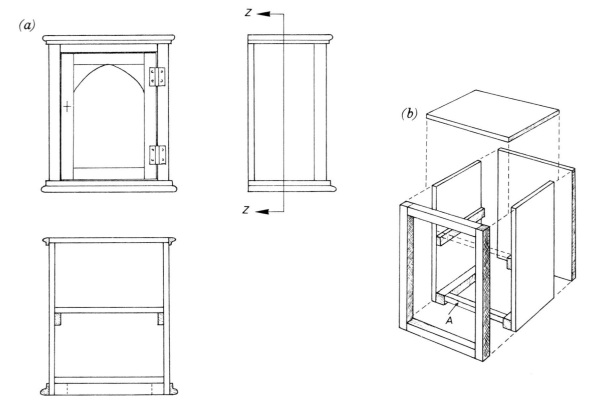

VIEW THROUGH Z-Z

Fig 36 (a) Pattern and (b) assembly for the small wall cupboard

fireplaces, so if possible, use a piece of real marble as a guide for the colour and the pattern of the veins. You will need artists' acrylic paints in titanium white, Paynes grey and crimson or brown. You will also need gesso (a fine-textured liquid plaster available from art shops), a fine-liner brush and a small piece of natural sponge.

Sand the piece thoroughly and remove all traces of dust before you begin. Dilute the gesso with water, just enough to paint a fluid coat all over the piece, and leave to dry. Sand with very fine-grade abrasive paper and apply a second coat of gesso. Sand again and repeat if necessary until you have a smooth surface.

Mix white paint with a touch of grey, paint the piece all over and allow to dry. Mix a little more grey into the white and use a piece of sponge to stipple the medium-grey colour over the painted surface.

When the stippled paint is dry, mix and apply a very dilute wash of white paint over the whole surface to create a translucent effect which does not obscure the paint underneath, and allow this to dry.

With the fine-liner brush, paint veins, fairly strongly in various shades of grey. Remember to continue the veins around the sides of the piece to imitate a slab of marble. When these veins are dry, paint a second coat of very dilute wash over them. When this is dry, paint a second layer of veins in a lighter shade of grey across the first network. Repeat the dilute wash, and paint further veins in grey and touches of crimson or brown until you have built up a realistic pattern, then apply a final dilute wash.

When the piece is thoroughly dry, apply wax polish and buff to a shine, or seal the paint with an acrylic gloss or satin varnish.

SMALL WALL CUPBOARD
(Fig 36, photograph page 54)

The cupboard is made in $1/16$in wood, $1/8 \times 1/16$in, and $1/8$in and $1/16$in square woodstrip, $3/32$in and $1/8$in mouldings with a small wooden knob, and hinges of fine leather scraps. Our cupboard was painted with blue-grey acrylic paint and 'aged' after assembly.

Cut two front-frame sides, $1 5/8$in long, in $1/8$in square woodstrip. Cut the front-frame top and bottom, 1in long, in $1/8$in square strip. Glue the top and bottom between the sides to assemble the front frame.

Cut two sides, $1 5/8 \times 5/8$in, in $1/16$in wood. Glue the sides behind the front frame.

Cut two bottom shelf-support sides in $1/8$in square strip and glue to the bottom edge of the sides to fit flush with the back edge.

Cut a bottom shelf-support front (A) in $1/16$in square strip and glue to the front frame between the side supports.

Cut two shelf supports in $1/8 \times 1/16$in strip and glue to the sides to fit flush with the back edge as shown. Cut two shelves in $1/16$in wood to fit, and glue on to the shelf supports.

Cut the back, $1 1/4 \times 1 5/8$in, in $1/16$in wood and glue on to the sides and shelves.

Cut the top, 1¼ × ¹³/₁₆in, in ¹/₁₆in wood and glue on to the assembly. Cut ³/₃₂in moulding with mitred corners and glue to the front and side edges of the top.

Cut ⅛in moulding with mitred corners and glue to the bottom edge of the front and sides as shown.

Cut the door panel in ¹/₁₆in wood to fit snugly into the door opening. Cut two door-frame sides, one door-frame top and one bottom in ¹/₁₆ × ⅛in strip. Glue the door frame on to the door panel with all edges flush.

Cut the arched door panel to fit snugly into the door frame and glue on to the door. Drill a hole to receive the doorknob.

Cut small strips of thin leather and glue on to the door and front frame with superglue to hinge the door. Paint and 'age' the cupboard as required.

SIDE-TABLE *(photograph page 54)*

The side-table is made from the pattern Fig 102 and the instructions in Chapter 7.

ACCESSORIES

WALL-SHELF *(Fig 37, photograph pages 46–7)*

The wall-shelf may be made to any size you choose, with any number of brackets to support it, and have a stained or painted finish. The shelf shown in the photograph is 4½in long with three brackets, and is made in ¹/₁₆in wood, painted with a light coat of grey-white acrylic paint.

Cut the shelf to the required size and sand the front edge and corners slightly so they are rounded.

Cut the brackets from the pattern with a fretsaw or craft knife and round the front edges as required.

Stain or paint the pieces and allow to dry.

Glue the brackets to the underside of the shelf – evenly spaced – and when dry, glue the back edge of the brackets and shelf to the wall.

The shelf above the sink in the picture on pages 58–9 is supported on small commercial metal brackets (see Acknowledgements).

off the top edges of each piece. Tape the four pieces together temporarily to drill three ¹/₁₆in diameter holes to ensure that the holes are exactly aligned on each piece.

Cut six rails in ¹/₁₆in dowelling, ensuring that they are exactly the same length.

Locate and glue three rails into the holes in each pair of sides.

Hinge the two frames together with short lengths of narrow ribbon superglued to the sides.

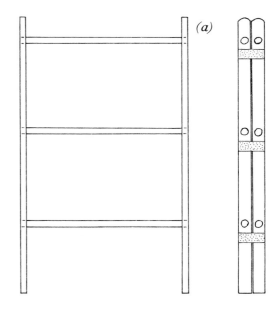

Fig 38 (a) Pattern for the clothes-horse

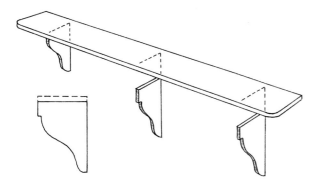

Fig 37 Pattern and assembly for the wall-shelf

CLOTHES-HORSE
(Fig 38a, photograph pages 46–7)

The clothes-horse is made in ⅛ × ¹/₁₆in woodstrip and ¹/₁₆in dowelling with hinges of narrow ribbon.

Cut four sides in ⅛ × ¹/₁₆in woodstrip and round

WASH-BOARD *(Fig 38b, photograph pages 46–7)*

Cut the wash-board in ⅛in wood, drill a hole as shown in the top and cut grooves with a small razor saw. We have painted the wash-board to represent bleached wood (see page 60).

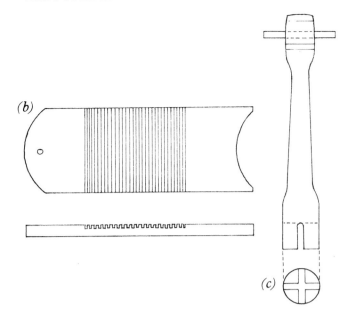

Fig 38 (b) Pattern for the wash-board and (c) the wash-paddle

WASH-PADDLE *(Fig 38c, photograph pages 46–7)*

This indispensable Victorian laundry accessory is made from ³⁄₈in square wood and ¹⁄₁₆in dowelling.

Cut a 3in blank in ³⁄₈in square wood. Use a razor saw to cut X-shaped slots, ¹⁄₄in deep in the bottom end, and a craft knife to remove slivers of wood to enlarge the slots as shown.

Use the craft knife to round off the corners of the blank and pare the shape shown on the pattern. Refine the shaping with sandpaper and score decorative rings at the top end with the craft knife.

Drill a ¹⁄₁₆in hole through the top end of the paddle and cut ¹⁄₁₆in dowelling for the handle. Push and glue the handle into the drilled hole. Paint the wash-paddle to represent bleached wood (see below).

DUCKBOARD *(Fig 39, photograph pages 58–9)*

The duckboard is made in ¹⁄₄ × ¹⁄₁₆in and ¹⁄₈ × ³⁄₃₂in woodstrip and painted to represent bleached wood.

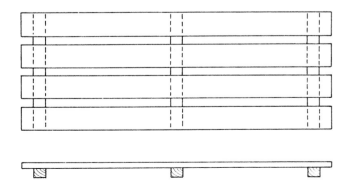

Fig 39 Pattern for the duckboard

The Victorian Scullery in the town house with a well stocked built-in larder

Cut four boards in ¼ × ¹⁄₁₆in strip and three battens in ⅛ × ³⁄₃₂in strip from the pattern.

To ensure that the boards are parallel, lay two pieces of double-sided sellotape on the work surface, approximately 2in apart. Lay the boards across the sellotape, evenly spaced and parallel.

Glue the battens across the boards as shown on the pattern and leave to dry. Remove the sellotape.

Sand the duckboard to imitate wear, and paint to represent bleached wood (see below).

BLEACHED-WOOD PAINTED FINISH

This finish can be applied to laundry accessories or any other item to represent wood which has been bleached by constant immersion in water. You will need white acrylic paint with a touch of grey and burnt umber, mixed to a very dilute wash.

Mix the colour according to the amount of 'bleaching' you require, for example, the handle end of a

Fig 40 Pattern for the apron

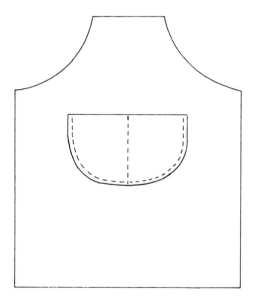

wash-paddle would be less bleached than the paddle end. Paint the colour on to the piece and leave to dry – applying further coats as necessary. Do not polish any piece painted to resemble bleached wood as the surface should be coarse and matt.

COAT RACK *(photograph pages 58–9)*

The coat rack is made of six white-metal coat hooks painted with black enamel paint and glued on to a board of ½in woodstrip painted grey.

MANGLE AND CLOTHES AIRER *(photographs pages 46–7 and 58–9)*

The mangle and clothes airer were both made from kits (see Acknowledgements), following the assembly instructions supplied. The metal parts were painted with metal primer and matt black Humbrol enamel paint, with touches of grey paint to indicate wear. The wooden rollers of the mangle and slats of the airer can be painted to represent bleached wood (see above).

APRON *(Fig 40, photograph pages 46–7)*

The apron can be made in any lightweight cotton fabric in a plain colour or small print, with ties in matching or contrasting narrow ribbon or tape.

Trace the pattern of the apron and the pocket on to the reverse of the fabric, squarely on the grain. Paint the outline with Fraycheck or a similar product and allow to dry before cutting out. Turn a small hem all round both apron and pocket, press and secure with fabric glue (or stitch).

Stitch (or glue) the pocket to the bib of the apron as shown. Stitch ribbon ties to each side of the apron and a loop to the top edge of the bib – or stitch a continuous length of ribbon around the sides of the bib, forming a loop at the top and leaving long ends as ties.

CHAPTER FOUR

The Parlour

The two parlours in this chapter, one in a Victorian cottage, and one in an Edwardian town house, demonstrate how colours and fabrics are used to create a period setting for the furniture and accessories.

Tastes in interior décor changed as new ideas became popular, thus each period has its own style. Like all new fashions, richer homes in towns were usually the first to adopt the new ideas which gradually filtered down the social scale, so that the style in a country cottage might be fifty years or more behind that in a grand town house. Re-decorating was expensive so the best and newest papers and fabrics were used where they would create the best impression – in the drawing room and the parlour.

The picture on pages 14–15 shows samples of colours, papers and fabrics which were fashionable from the eighteenth century up to the present day. In the top left-hand corner the rich crimsons and blues and small regular patterns are appropriate for grand Georgian houses. The lighter colours in the centre of the picture came into fashion in the early nineteenth century and the floral, striped patterns on the right are typically Victorian.

Moving down to the front on the right-hand side are small floral patterns in stronger shades of pink and blue which were popular in the late nineteenth century, and across to the left, the yellow, cream and brown which was fashionable earlier in the twentieth century. The accessories are typical examples of each period.

Both of our parlours are decorated in the conventional style of their day, but you might consider decorating your room in one of the more extreme but less widely popular fashions. For example, an Edwardian town house parlour might have a dado, William Morris wallpaper and an art nouveau fireplace and accessories, if the residents of your house are the artistic type; or the parlour of a 1920s house could be decorated in high art deco style.

THE ROOM BOX
(Fig 7, photograph pages 62–3)

The room box for the Victorian Parlour is made from the pattern Fig 7 and the instructions given in Chapter 2, omitting the window.

CHIMNEY BREAST *(Fig 41)*

The chimney breast is built to accommodate a 'Coalbrookdale' fireplace made from a white-metal kit. If you intend to use a different fireplace, adjust the measurements given in brackets for the chimney breast and fireplace opening as necessary. The chimney breast is built in 5mm (⅛in) Foamcore and ⅜in balsa wood.

Cut two sides, (8 × 1¹⁄₁₆in) in ⅜in balsa block, and a front (6 × 8in) in Foamcore.

Cut out the fireplace opening (shown in Fig 44) in the front and glue the sides behind the front with side edges flush.

Cut two support struts (5¼ × 1in) in Foamcore and glue on to the back of the fireplace front between the sides, above the fireplace opening as shown.

Try your fireplace in the fireplace opening and cut splayed 'cheeks' in Foamcore if necessary to fit the angle of the fireplace sides. Glue the cheeks into the fireplace opening.

Paint the inside of the fireplace opening matt black, and glue the chimney breast to the back wall (leaving an alcove 4in wide to one side, if you wish to fit the alcove shelves shown in Fig 46).

FLOORING

We have used self-adhesive wooden plank flooring for the parlour which we stained to represent oak. Cut a paper template of the floor area to use as a pattern and cut the flooring to fit. Stain the flooring and when thoroughly dry, peel away the backing and press the flooring firmly in place on the floor of the room. Apply a coat of wax polish, buffed to a soft sheen. Our rug is a piece of woven fabric, cut squarely on the grain, with the sides sealed with Fraycheck and the ends fringed by pulling threads.

The Victorian Parlour with its flamboyant faux-marbre fireplace and upholstered suite, under Her Majesty's watchful eye

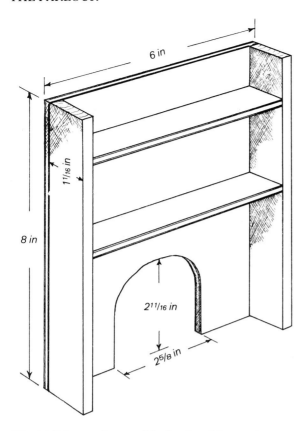

Fig 41 Plan and assembly for the chimney breast

DECORATING – VICTORIAN PARLOUR

We applied lining paper and painted the ceiling of the room with magnolia emulsion paint, and fitted an oak-stained beam across the width. The walls were papered with a dolls-house wallpaper and the paintwork is cream. Allow the wallpaper to dry thoroughly before the door and fireplace surrounds are fitted and the painted skirting-board is glued in place.

LIGHTING

We fitted a concealed light behind the beam, wired through the ceiling to a transformer.

FOUR-PANELLED DOOR *(Fig 42)*

The door described here is non-opening but the method can be used to make an opening door for a dolls-house room if the door is hinged in place. Adjust the measurements given on the pattern if necessary to fit the doorway and remember to allow clearance under the door for rugs or carpet if required. The door is made in 1/16in wood and 1/16 × 1/4in and 1/16 × 1/2in woodstrip with 3/32in moulding. The door frame is 1/4 × 1/8in woodstrip. We have used a commercial brass doorknob and a pair of fingerplates.

Cut a door panel (2¾ x 6¼in) in 1/16in wood. Cut two stiles (A) in 1/4 × 1/16in strip and glue on to each side of the panel with the edges flush.

Cut the top rail (B) in 1/4 × 1/16in strip and the centre and bottom rails (C) in 1/2 × 1/16in strip, then glue the rails on to the panel between the stiles, with the top and bottom edges flush.

Cut the centre stiles (D) in 1/4 × 1/16in strip and glue to the centre of the panels to fit between the rails.

Cut 3/32in moulding with mitred corners and glue on to the door to frame each panel.

Sand the door with fine-grade abrasive paper and paint as required – we used two coats of cream acrylic paint, allowed to dry and sanded between coats.

Drill a hole to receive the doorknob and glue knob and fingerplates in place with superglue.

Glue the door on to the wall with a slight gap under the bottom edge.

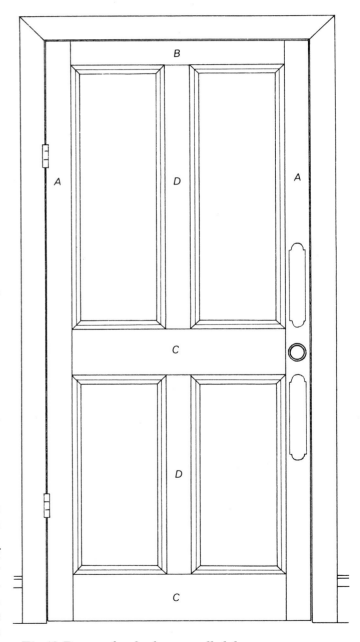

Fig 42 Pattern for the four-panelled door

Cut the door-frame top and sides with mitred corners in $\frac{1}{8} \times \frac{1}{4}$in strip to fit around the door with a very slight gap all round. Paint the pieces and glue the frame to the wall around the door.

Cut mock hinge-barrels from toothpicks, glue in place and paint, if required.

DECORATING – EDWARDIAN PARLOUR *(photograph pages 74–5)*

The Edwardian Parlour is decorated with a beige and white-striped dolls-house paper and the wooden flooring described above. The cornice, skirting-board, architrave and door are painted to represent pine (see page 34), and wax polished before fitting. The gas lights and the carpet are from specialist suppliers (see Acknowledgements).

DADO *(Fig 43, photograph page 79)*

The dado was a very popular feature of the decorating scheme through the late Victorian and Edwardian periods up to the 1930s. Our dado is made in embossed wallpaper, painted with dark green acrylic paint and polished with 'Treasure Gold' metallic wax in copper and brass colours to imitate the fashionable leather paper. The dado rail and skirting-board are painted to represent pine, and the wall above the dado rail is papered with a small-patterned paper chosen to harmonise with the dado.

In halls or kitchens the dado was often panelled with tongue and groove boards (shown in the picture

Fig 43 Pattern for the dado

on page 82), which could be polished or painted as required.

Glue the painted or stained skirting-board in place, then cut and paint the dado and paste it to the wall above the skirting-board. If you are using tongue and groove boards, make a paper template for the dado and cut, glue and butt the stained boards on to the template – then glue the paper backing to the wall. Paper the remainder of the wall to meet the edge of the dado. The rail may be commercial dado rail or narrow picture-frame moulding, stained or painted as required. Glue the rail to the wall to cover the join of dado and wallpaper.

FIXTURES

LARGE FIREPLACE SURROUND *(Fig 44, photograph pages 62–3)*

The fireplace surround is designed to accommodate a 'Coalbrookdale' arched fireplace as described above, and should be adjusted if necessary for other fireplaces. It is made in $\frac{1}{8} \times 1$in, $\frac{1}{8} \times \frac{3}{4}$in and $\frac{1}{16} \times \frac{3}{4}$in woodstrip and decorated with $\frac{1}{8}$in moulding, trimmed with skirting-board and cornice mouldings. You will also need a piece of thin, stiff card and a piece of black paper. We have painted the surround with acrylic paints to represent *faux-marbre* (see page 66), but if you prefer it could be stained or painted to represent pine or mahogany, or painted white.

Cut a backing piece $5 \times 4\frac{7}{8}$in in stiff card and cut out the fireplace opening as shown.

Cut two sides (A), and one lintel (B) 3in long, in $\frac{1}{8} \times 1$in woodstrip. Glue the sides and lintel on to the card backing. Cut two sides (C) in $\frac{3}{4} \times \frac{1}{16}$in strip and

glue centred on to sides A.

Cut two $\frac{3}{4}$in brackets in cornice moulding and two $\frac{3}{4}$in base trims in skirting-board and glue on to the top and bottom of each side as shown.

Cut the mantelshelf $5 \times \frac{3}{4}$in in $\frac{1}{8}$in wood. Cut $\frac{1}{8}$in moulding with mitred corners and glue to the front and side edges of the mantelshelf. Glue the mantelshelf on to the front assembly. Cut $\frac{1}{8}$in moulding with mitred corners and glue to the inside edges of the sides and lintel and between the lintel and mantelshelf.

Paint the fireplace surround to represent marble (see page 66).

Cut the front panel (F) in stiff black paper and glue on to the card backing to fit neatly between the painted sides and lintel.

Fit the painted white-metal fireplace and glue the completed fireplace surround to the chimney breast after the room is floored and decorated.

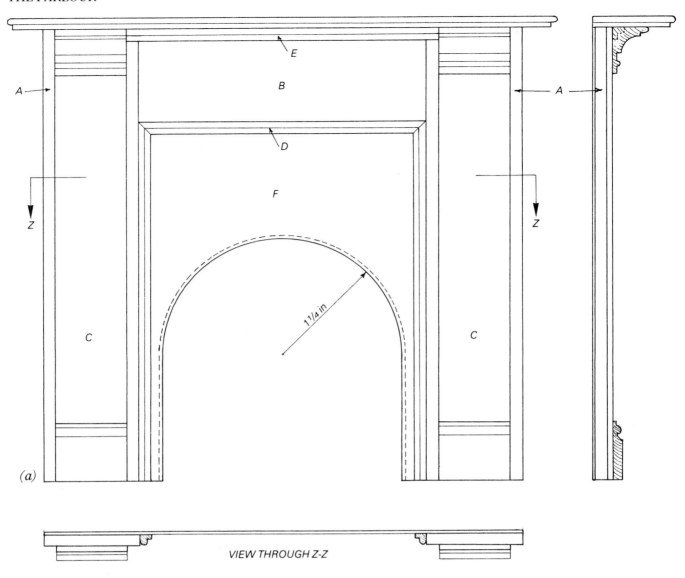

VIEW THROUGH Z-Z

Fig 44 (a) Pattern and (b) assembly for the large fireplace surround

PAINTED FAUX-MARBRE OR MARBLE FINISH

This finish can be used to imitate real marble if it is applied subtly, or to imitate the more flamboyant *faux-marbre* (fake marble), which was fashionable in Victorian houses, if it is applied more emphatically. Any appropriate colours can be used (see the Georgian room in Chapter 8) and the finish can also be applied to commercial fireplaces or kits. To make the brown marble finish shown on the fireplace in the Victorian parlour you will need artists' acrylic paints in burnt umber, Paynes grey, yellow ochre, crimson, black and white, a fine-liner brush and a small piece of natural sponge. You will also need gesso (liquid plaster) available from art shops.

Sand the piece thoroughly and remove all traces of dust before you begin. Paint a coat of gesso, slightly diluted with water, all over and when this is dry, sand thoroughly with very fine-grade abrasive paper. Re-

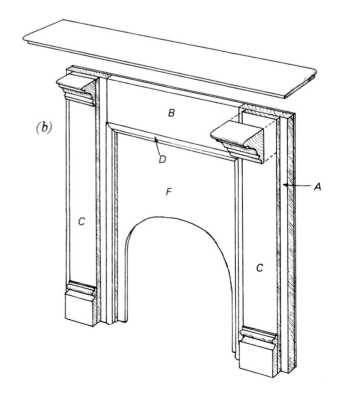

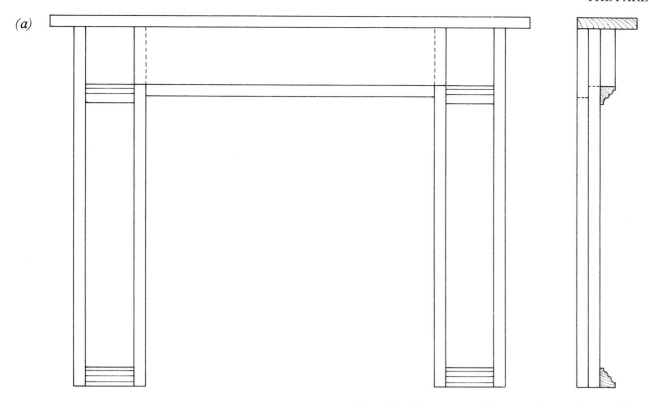

(a)

Fig 45 (a) Pattern and (b) assembly for the small fireplace surround

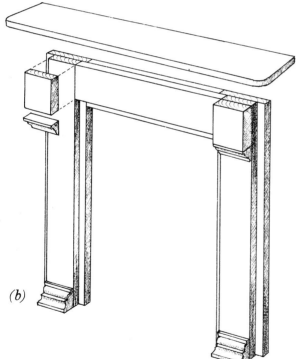

(b)

Use the fine-liner brush to paint veins in dark colours over the lighter stippled area and in light colours over the darker stippled area. Remember to extend the veins over the edges of the piece to imitate a solid slab of marble.

Apply further dilute washes and painted veins until you have a realistic pattern, then apply a final dilute wash.

Finish the piece with a coat of wax polish buffed to a shine, or seal the paint with a coat of gloss or satin acrylic varnish.

SMALL FIREPLACE SURROUND
(Fig 45, photograph pages 74–5)

The pattern is designed to accommodate a 'Coal-brookdale' tiled fireplace made from a white-metal kit. If you are using a different fireplace, adapt the measurements as necessary. We have used wood painted to represent mahogany before cutting (see page 73). You will need $\frac{1}{8}$in wood, $\frac{1}{8} \times \frac{1}{2}$in woodstrip, $\frac{3}{16}$in moulding and scraps of $\frac{5}{32}$in woodstrip.

Cut two sides $3\frac{7}{8} \times \frac{3}{4}$in and a lintel $3 \times \frac{3}{4}$in, in $\frac{1}{8}$in thick wood and glue the lintel between the sides with the top edges flush.

Cut two sides $3\frac{7}{8} \times \frac{1}{2}$in and a lintel $3\frac{1}{4} \times \frac{5}{8}$in in $\frac{1}{8}$in thick wood. Glue the lintel centred on to the first lintel with top edges flush and glue the sides centred on to the first sides.

Cut the mantelshelf $5 \times \frac{5}{8}$in, in $\frac{1}{8}$in wood, round

peat as necessary until you have a good smooth surface.

Apply a coat of white paint mixed with grey all over the piece. When this is dry, stipple yellow ochre over the surface with a piece of sponge. When this is dry, paint a very dilute wash of grey paint all over to make a translucent surface which does not obscure the stippled pattern underneath.

Stipple burnt umber mixed with a touch of crimson over the surface with the sponge and when dry, paint another very dilute wash of grey all over.

Fig 46 (a) Pattern and (b) assembly for the fitted alcove shelves

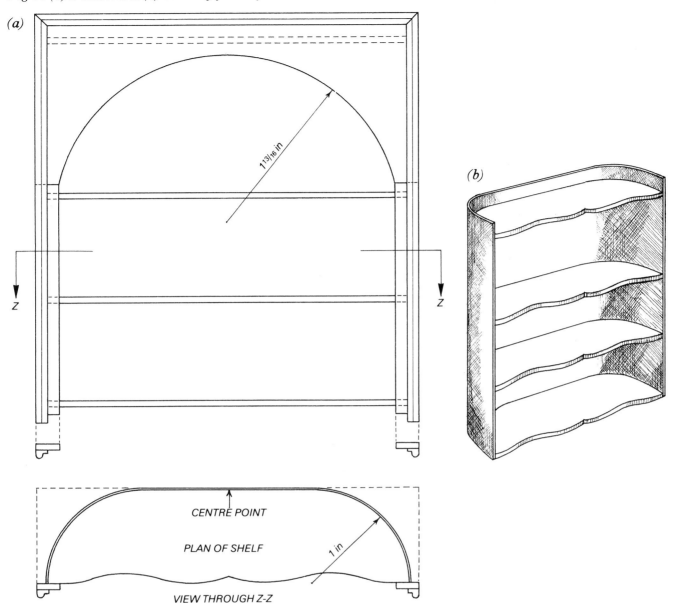

off the front corners and glue on to the sides and lintel with back edges flush.

Cut two ½ × ⅝in rectangles in ⁵⁄₃₂in scrap wood and glue on to the top end of the sides, butted under the mantelshelf. Cut four ½in pieces of ³⁄₁₆in moulding and glue on to the sides as shown.

Paint and polish the fireplace surround as required and glue to the wall.

FITTED ALCOVE SHELVES
(Fig 46, photograph pages 62–3)

The pattern is designed to fit into an alcove 4in wide and 1⅛in deep, but the method can be adapted to fit any alcove. The shelves are made in ¹⁄₁₆in wood with a curved backing of artists' watercolour paper which we have painted green to match the wallpaper. The shelves are framed with ¹⁄₁₆ × ¼in woodstrip and

⅛in moulding. Shelves and frame are painted (or stained) before assembly – we have used cream acrylic paint.

Cut four shelves in ¹⁄₁₆in wood and shape the curved edges with a fretsaw or craft knife and sandpaper. Paint as required.

Cut a paper backing 4¼ × 5in and try the piece around a shelf to check that it fits edge to edge. Rule pencil lines on the paper backing to mark the position of the shelves and mark the centre point of each line and the corresponding centre point on each shelf. Curve the backing by drawing the paper under the back of a knife.

Apply UHU or similar glue to the back edge of each shelf and when this is tacky, stick the shelves to the backing, aligning them carefully with the pencil marked lines and centres on the paper backing and gluing one shelf at a time – allowing it to dry before proceeding with the next.

Glue the back to the back wall of the alcove to leave a slight gap at each side.

Cut the frame arch in 1/16in wood to fit snugly into the alcove. Paint and then glue in place to the ceiling, top shelf and side walls.

Cut the frame sides in 1/16 × 1/4in woodstrip, paint, and glue beneath the arch to the shelves and side walls.

Cut 1/8in moulding with mitred corners, paint, and glue on to the top and side edges of the frame.

FURNITURE

BOOKCASE *(Fig 47, photograph page 82)*

The pattern is for a large bookcase, designed to house a collection of miniature books, so the shelves are fairly wide apart. If you prefer, the pattern can be adapted to accommodate another shelf or to alter the proportions.

The bookcase is made in 1/16in wood, 1/8 × 1/4in, 1/16 × 1/4in and 1/16 × 1/8in woodstrip, with 1/8in and 1/4in moulding. The back may be cut in one piece or in tongue and groove floorboarding, butted together to represent planking. We have used wood painted to represent mahogany (see page 73) before the pieces are cut. If you prefer woodstain, stain the pieces before assembly.

Cut a back in 1/16in wood (or cut, glue and butt planking) to make a panel 3⅛in × 4¹¹/₁₆in.

Cut two sides in 1/16in wood and shape the curved edges with a craft knife and sandpaper. Mark the position of the shelves on the inside of each piece and

(a)

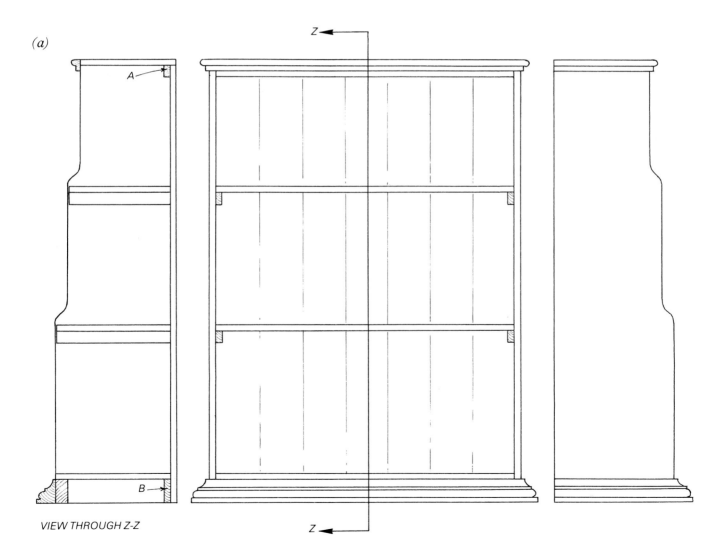

VIEW THROUGH Z-Z

Fig 47 (a) Pattern for the bookcase

(b)

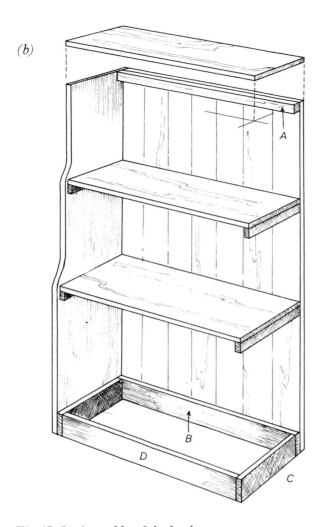

Fig 47 (b) Assembly of the bookcase

glue the sides on to the outside edges of the back.

Cut the back top support (A) in ⅛ × ¹/₁₆in woodstrip and the back bottom-shelf support (B) in ¼ × ¹/₁₆in strip. Glue the supports across the top and bottom of the back with edges flush.

Cut two side bottom-shelf supports (C) in ¼ × ¹/₁₆in strip and glue to the bottom of the sides with front edges flush.

Cut a front bottom-shelf support (D) in ¼ × ⅛in strip and glue between the side supports with front edges flush to complete the bottom-shelf support frame.

Cut four side-shelf supports in ⅛ × ¹/₁₆in strip and glue to the sides on the marked lines.

Cut three shelves in ¹/₁₆in wood and glue on to the shelf supports.

Cut the top in ¹/₁₆in wood to fit on to the back and sides with edges flush, and glue in place. Cut ⅛in moulding with mitred corners and glue to the front and side edges of the top.

Cut ¼in moulding with mitred corners and glue to the bottom front and side edges of the bookcase.

CHIFFONIER (Fig 48, photograph pages 62–3)

The chiffonier or sideboard is made in ⅛in and ¹/₁₆in wood, and ¼ × ⅛in, ⅛ × ¹/₁₆in, and ¼ × ¹/₁₆in woodstrip. You will also need ⅛in, ⁵/₁₆in and ³/₃₂in mouldings and ten turned spindles, eg, baluster spindles. The back may be cut in one piece in ³/₃₂in wood, or in woodstrip 'planks' butted together to resemble tongue and groove boards. We have painted the wood before cutting to represent mahogany (see page 73). If you prefer woodstain, stain the pieces before assembly. You will need four ⅛in offset hinges and two knobs for the doors.

Cut two front-frame sides, a top, bottom and two vertical dividers in ⅛ × ¼in woodstrip and assemble the front frame as shown in Fig 49a.

Cut two sides, 2¾ × 1⅜in, in ¹/₁₆in wood. Glue the sides behind the front frame, ensuring that they are at a right angle, and allow to dry thoroughly.

Cut the base (A) 4¹¹/₁₆ × 1½in, in ⅛in wood. Glue the assembled front frame and sides on to the base.

Cut two side bottom-shelf supports (B) in ⅛ × ¼in strip and glue the supports to the bottom edge of the sides, and to the base, leaving a ³/₃₂in gap to accommodate the back, as shown in Fig 49b.

Cut a front bottom-shelf support (C) in ⅛ × ¼in strip and glue the support behind the bottom of the front frame as shown.

Cut a bottom shelf in ¹/₁₆in wood to fit on to the bottom-shelf supports and glue in place.

Cut a pair of kennel-sides (D) in ¹/₁₆in wood the depth of the bottom shelf, to fit flush with the top of the front frame as shown. Cut a ⅛ × ¹/₁₆in notch in the top back edge of each piece to accommodate the top support.

Cut four shelf supports (E) in ⅛ × ¹/₁₆in strip the same depth as the kennel-sides. Glue supports to the kennel-sides to fit flush with the back edge. Glue supports to the sides to leave a ³/₃₂in gap to accommodate the back – ensuring that the four supports are level.

Glue the kennel-sides in place behind the front frame and to the bottom shelf. Cut two kennel-side supports (F) in ⅛ × ¹/₁₆in strip and glue to the kennel-sides and the bottom shelf as shown.

Cut two shelves in ¹/₁₆in wood to fit on to the shelf supports and glue in place.

Cut the top 4⅞ × 1⅝in, in ⅛in wood. Cut ⅛in moulding with mitred corners and glue to the front and side edges of the top. Glue the top on to the carcase to fit flush with the back edge and overhang at the front and sides.

Cut the back in ³/₃₂in wood (or cut, glue and butt planks) to fit between the sides, top and base. Cut a top support (G) (Fig 48) in ⅛ × ¹/₁₆in strip and glue the support across the top of the back with top edges flush. Glue the back on to the carcase.

Cut ⁵/₁₆in moulding with mitred corners and glue to the bottom of the front and sides.

Cut the kennel-arch in ¹/₁₆in wood to fit, shaping the curved edge with a craft knife and sandpaper, and

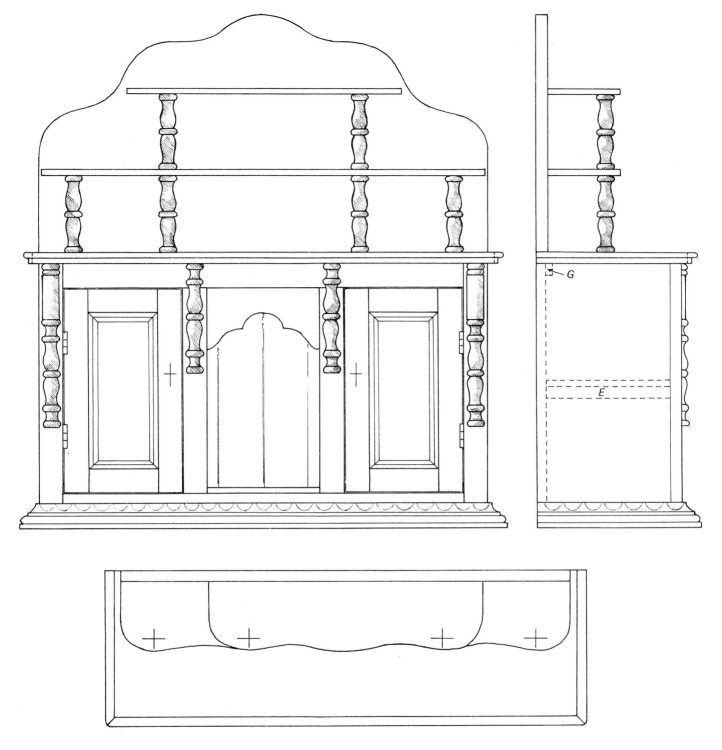

Fig 48 Pattern for the chiffonier

glue the arch into the top of the kennel with front edges flush.

Cut two door panels in ¹/₁₆in wood to fit into the door spaces. Cut a door frame top, bottom and sides for each panel ¼ × ¹/₁₆in strip and glue on to the door panels with all edges flush. Cut ³/₃₂in moulding with mitred corners and glue to the inside edges of the door frames. Cut recesses in the doors to accommodate the hinges, and drill holes to receive the knobs. Glue the hinges to the doors and front frame with superglue.

Cut two 1¾in and two 1³/₁₆in turned spindles and use a craft knife and sanding block to pare away the back half of each spindle to form a flat surface. Check that they are evenly matched and glue the half spindles to the front frame as shown.

Cut the shelf back in ¹/₈in wood and shape the curved edge with a fretsaw or craft knife and sandpaper. Glue the shelf back on to the top with back edges flush.

Cut one large and one small shelf in ¹/₁₆in wood. Cut

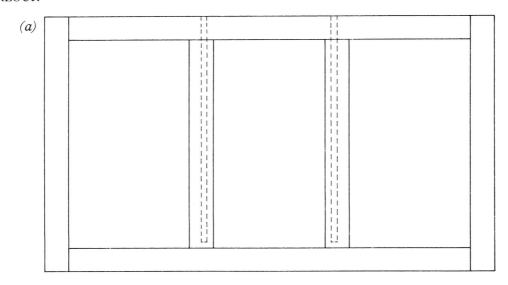

(a)

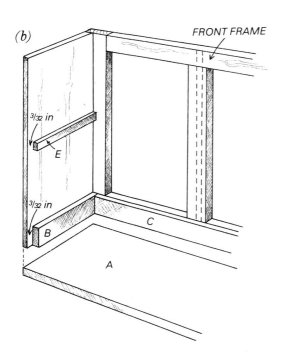

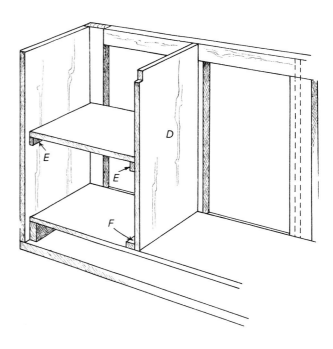

Fig 49 (a) Pattern for the front frame and (b) assembly for the chiffonier

six ¹³/₁₆in shelf spindles and check that they are exactly the same length. Glue four spindles to the underside of the larger shelf on the positions marked on the pattern and allow to dry. Glue the shelf to the shelf back and the lower end of the spindles to the top. Glue two spindles to the underside of the small shelf on the positions marked on the pattern. Glue the small shelf to the shelf back and the lower end of the spindles to the large shelf. Apply pressure and allow the glue to dry thoroughly.

Add graining detail to a painted mahogany finish (see opposite), and polish the chiffonier with a dark wax polish buffed to a soft sheen.

PEDESTAL TABLE *(Fig 50, photograph page 79)*

The table is made in ⅛in wood with a pedestal of turned wood (eg a newel-post spindle or similar). The wood is painted to represent mahogany before cutting (see opposite), or stained before assembly.

Use a compass to draw the circular table top on to ⅛in wood and mark the centre point on the underside of the top. Cut the top with a fretsaw or roughly cut with a Stanley knife and refine the shaping with a craft knife and sandpaper. Round off the edge of the table top with fine-grade abrasive paper.

Cut the pedestal from turned wood and mark the position of the legs. Pare flat areas on the pedestal to accommodate the leg ends at the marked points.

Cut three legs in ⅛in wood with a fretsaw or craft knife and round off the outer edges with abrasive paper.

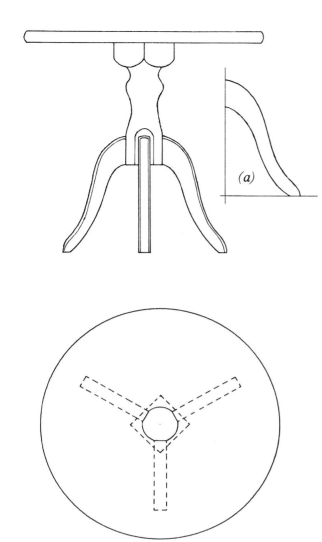

Fig 50 Pattern and assembly for the pedestal table

Glue the legs to the flattened areas on the pedestal, one at a time, holding in place as the glue dries, and check that the assembly stands square.

Glue the leg assembly to the underside of the table top on the marked centre point, apply pressure and allow to dry thoroughly.

Polish the table with wax polish buffed to a soft sheen.

MAHOGANY PAINTED FINISH

The mahogany 'stain' is a wash of burnt umber mixed with a little crimson artists' acrylic paint which should be applied to the wood (and woodstrip, mouldings and turnings) before the piece of furniture is cut and assembled. Mix the paint to a very dilute wash and paint the edges, then both surfaces of the wood and allow it to dry naturally to minimise warping.

When the furniture piece is cut, re-touch any raw edges with a little of the colour wash, applied as sparingly as possible.

When the furniture piece is assembled, mix a

thicker solution of paint so that it is opaque and fluid but not runny. Trim the bristles of an old, stiff hogs-hair paint-brush to make a 'comb' and dipping just the ends of the bristles in paint, paint grain lines on the piece, working in one direction only. Make the grain lines slightly wavy rather than straight and try to emphasise the natural grain in the wood.

When the paint is thoroughly dry, polish the piece with a dark-coloured wax furniture polish and buff to a soft sheen.

PLANT STAND *(Fig 51, photograph page 82)*

This small table is designed for displaying plants, but would be equally useful as a side-table, or with the legs shortened, as a bedside table. It is made in 1/16in wood and 1/8 × 1/4in and 1/8in square woodstrip, the pieces stained or painted before assembly.

Cut four legs and two long and two short stretchers in 1/8in square woodstrip.

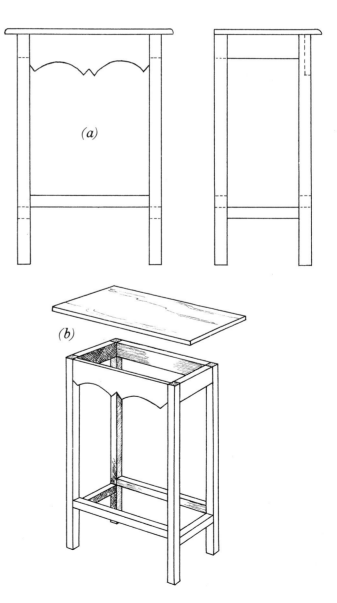

Fig 51 (a) Pattern and (b) assembly for the plant stand

Cut two side friezes and one back frieze in 1/8 ×
1/4in strip. Cut the front frieze in 1/16in wood and
shape the curved edge with a fretsaw or craft knife and
sandpaper.

Glue one side frieze and one short stretcher between each pair of legs and allow to dry. Glue the
front and back friezes and long stretchers between the
leg assemblies, check that the assembly stands square
and allow to dry.

Cut the top in 1/16in wood and round off the front
and side top edges. Glue the top on to the leg assembly
to fit flush at the back edge and overhang at the front
and sides.

WRITING TABLE *(photograph page 82)*

The writing table is made from the pattern Fig 126
and the instructions in Chapter 9 (page 169) for the
small refectory table.

UPHOLSTERED SUITE
(Fig 52, photograph pages 62–3)

The upholstered suite is made of thick art cardboard
and 1/2in balsa wood block, padded with 1/4in wadding (batting) or foam. We have covered our suite in
printed cotton, but any fabric with a very slight
stretch and a small printed or woven pattern or plain
colour would be suitable. You will also need four
wooden or plastic beads for feet for each piece.

To make the armchair, cut the back in thick art
cardboard, and in wadding (batting) or foam – trimming the padding to the dotted line shown on the
pattern. Glue the padding to the cardboard with
fabric glue.

Using the pattern as a guide, add a 3/8in seam
allowance all around, and cut two covers on the
straight grain in fabric. With right sides facing, seam
the covers together leaving the bottom edge open.
Trim the seam, clip the curves and corners and turn
through.

Ease the cover over the padded card back, pull taut
and slipstitch the bottom edge closed.

Cut two seats in 1/2in balsa block and glue one on to
the other with balsa cement. Seal the end-grain of the
balsa block with a coat of balsa cement and allow to
dry. Cut one seat in padding and glue it on to the balsa
block with fabric glue.

Using the pattern as a guide, add 3/8in all around
and cut two seats in fabric. Cover the upper and
under surfaces of the seat with fabric as shown in Fig
52b, gluing the edges of the fabric to the sides of the
seat. When the glue is dry, trim excess fabric.

Apply glue to the sides and back of the seat and fit
the back in place. Push dressmakers' pins through the
back into the seat to hold in place until the glue is dry.

To make the frill, cut a 1in wide strip of fabric on
the straight grain to fit the circumference of the chair,
and a 1 1/2in wide strip of fabric one and a half times

*The Edwardian Parlour where an elegant lady sitting
on a chaise-longue opens her birthday presents*

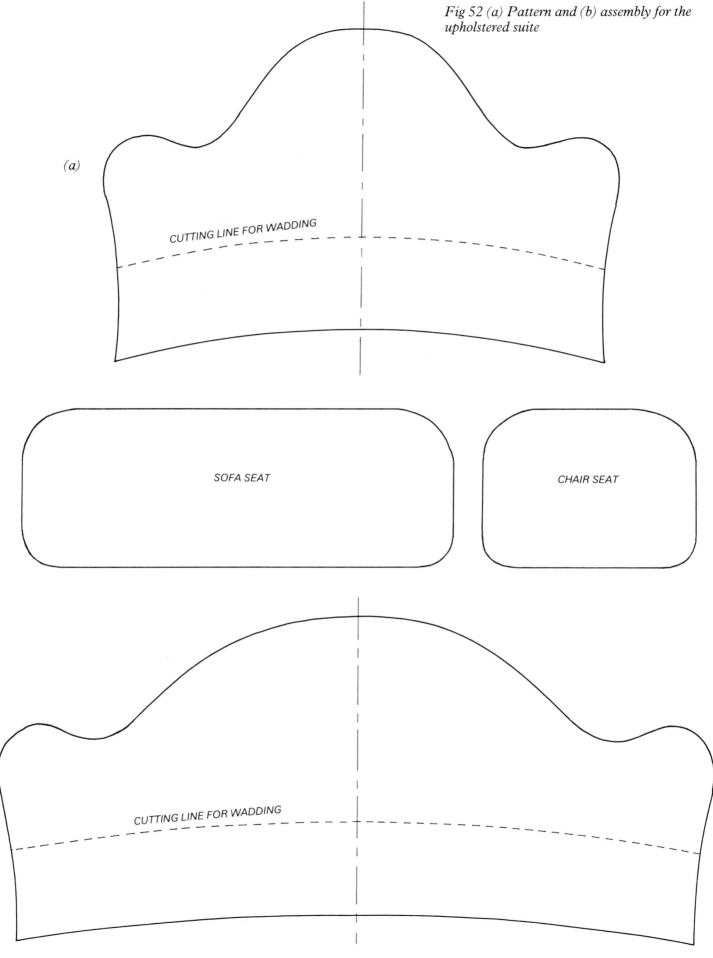

Fig 52 (a) Pattern and (b) assembly for the upholstered suite

(a)

CUTTING LINE FOR WADDING

SOFA SEAT

CHAIR SEAT

CUTTING LINE FOR WADDING

(b)

Fig 53 Pattern and assembly for the footstool

the circumference of the chair. Turn a hem on one edge of the longer strip, and gather the other edge to fit the shorter strip, then stitch the two pieces together. Turn in the top edge of the shorter strip ½in and press. Glue the frill around the chair with the join at centre back. If the frill does not hang well, run double-sided sellotape around the seat under the frill and smooth the frill down over the tape.

Glue bead feet to the underside of the seat in each corner.

The sofa is made in exactly the same way as the chair.

FOOTSTOOL (Fig 53, photograph pages 62–3)

The footstool is made in ½in balsa wood block, padded with ¼in wadding (batting) and assembled in the same way as the chair seat described above. We have covered our stool with velvet and trimmed it with fringed upholstery braid and tassels. The stool does not have feet.

CHAISE-LONGUE (Fig 54, photograph page 79)

The chaise-longue is made from stiff art cardboard and ½in balsa block, padded with ¼in wadding (batting) or foam. We have used velveteen for the cover, but any fabric with a very slight stretch in a plain colour, small print or woven pattern would be suitable. We have used four commercial turned legs, but similar legs could be whittled from dowelling, and our chaise-longue has been trimmed with fringe and narrow picot braid. The chaise-longue may be made left-handed as ours, or right-handed, by reversing the patterns for both the back and seat – just ensure that the points marked (A) and (B) on the pattern are aligned.

Cut the back in cardboard and in padding, trimming the padding to the dotted line shown on the pattern. Glue the padding to the card with fabric glue.

Using the pattern as a guide, add ⅜in seam allowance all round and cut two back covers on the straight grain of the fabric. With right sides facing, seam the covers together leaving the bottom edge open. Trim

(a)

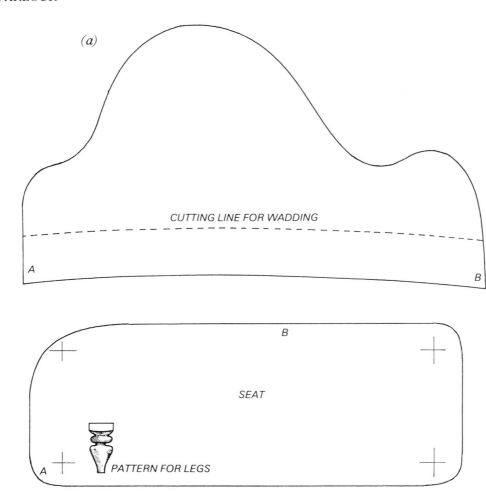

CUTTING LINE FOR WADDING

A

B

B

SEAT

A PATTERN FOR LEGS

Fig 54 (a) Pattern and (b) assembly for the chaise-longue

the seam, clip curves and turn through. Ease the cover over the padded back, pull taut and slipstitch the bottom edge closed.

Cut the seat in ½in balsa block and in padding. Glue the padding on to the upper surface of the block with fabric glue.

Using the seat pattern as a guide, add ⅜in all round and cut two covers in fabric. Cover the upper and under surfaces of the seat in fabric as shown in Fig 52b, gluing the edges of the fabric to the sides of the seat. When the glue is dry, trim excess fabric.

Apply glue to the side and back edges of the seat and position the back around the shallow curve of the seat, aligning points (A) and (B) marked on the pattern. Hold the back in place as the glue dries with dressmakers' pins pushed through the back into the seat.

Cut a strip of fabric 13½in long × 1in wide, turn in and press both long edges. Beginning at the back of the chaise-longue, wrap and glue the fabric strip around the sides of the seat and lower edge of the back, trim the end, turn in and glue in place.

Glue fringe around the seat and picot braid around the seat above the fringe and around the back. Glue the legs to the underside of the seat.

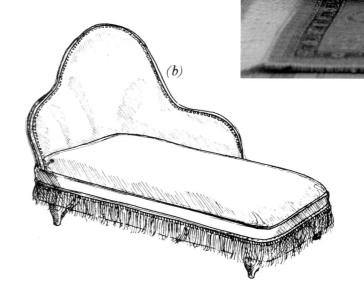

(b)

A commercial fireplace used with a dado and the appropriate accessories to make a parlour in the art nouveau style

STOOL (photograph page 79)

The stool is made in ½in balsa wood block and covered to match the chaise-longue. Cut the seat in one piece of ½in balsa, and pad and assemble the stool as shown in Fig 53 and described on page 77. Add fringe, picot braid and legs as above.

UPHOLSTERED SIDE-CHAIR
(Fig 55, photograph page 82)

The chair is made in ⅛in wood, ⅛in square and 1/16in woodstrip. It is assembled in the same way as the ladderback chair in Fig 19 and instructions in Chapter 2. Our chair is painted to represent mahogany and upholstered to match the chaise-longue.

Cut the seat and back in padding and glue the padding on to the chair with fabric glue.

Using the seat pattern as a guide, add ¼in all round and cut the seat cover in fabric, including notches to accommodate the back legs. Position the cover over the padded chair seat, apply glue to the edges of the chair seat and smooth the cover in place, easing out puckers at the corners. When the cover is firmly glued to the edges of the seat, trim away excess fabric.

Cut a piece of fabric 2½ × 1in and apply glue to one edge. Wrap the fabric around the back rail of the chair, so that the glued edge covers the padding with the short edges wrapped around the sides to the back. Fold the top of the fabric over the top of the chair, tuck the short edges in neatly and glue to hold in place.

Glue fringe and picot braid around the chair seat and the lower edge of the back to cover the raw fabric edges.

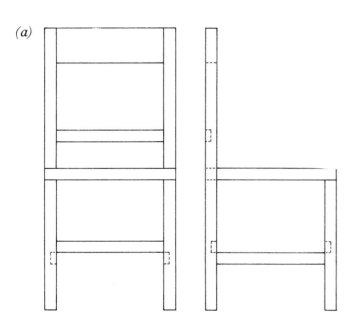
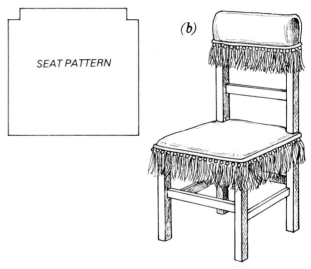

(a)

SEAT PATTERN

(b)

Fig 55 (a) Pattern and (b) assembly for the upholstered side-chair

ACCESSORIES

DOOR CURTAIN (photograph pages 62–3)

The door curtain is a piece of velvet (or other fabric), cut squarely on the grain, one and a half times the width of the door and 2in longer than the door. The curtain is hung from small commercial curtain rings (or jewellery jump-rings) on a brass pole suspended from small eyes screwed into the wall above the door. If you have an opening door, screw the eyes into the back of the door rather than the wall, make a shorter curtain and cut the pole only a fraction wider than the door.

Make narrow hems on both sides of the curtain and slightly wider hems at top and bottom. Stitch curtain rings to the top hem, evenly spaced approximately ½in apart. Thread the curtain pole through the rings and try in place to mark the position for the eyes. Screw the eyes into the wall and locate the pole. If required, screw another eye into the wall to the hinged side of the door and thread a fine cord to loop the curtain back.

TASSELLED CUSHION
(Fig 56, photograph pages 62–3)

Small scraps of fabric left over from larger projects can be used to make the cushion, with short lengths of any suitable small-scale trimmings to embellish it. We have used velvet, with cord and tassels. You will need a little cotton wool or wadding (batting) for stuffing, a gel superglue to fix the trimming, and you might find a toothpick useful for applying the glue neatly. You will also need a needle with a large eye for attaching the tassels.

Cut the cushion in one piece on the straight grain of the fabric. Fold in ¼in hem allowance at one end, secure if necessary and press.

Place the fabric right-side up and fold the hemmed end to the centre. Fold the raw end to meet the hemmed end.

Stitch seams along both sides leaving long threads at both ends. Use the long threads to secure the seams with a few stitches at both ends, then push the threaded needle through the corners to take the threads to the right side (inside) of the cushion. Trim the seams and turn through – pulling the threads gently to ease out the corners. Do not trim the threads. Stuff the cushion lightly and slipstitch the opening closed.

Seal the cut end of the cord trimming with a little glue or Fraycheck to prevent ravelling, then thread the cord into the large-eyed needle. Thread four tassels on to the cord and remove the needle.

Starting at one corner, secure the cord to the edge of the cushion with a drop of glue and make dots of glue along one edge. Press the cord on to the glued edge, slide a tassel into the corner in a loop of cord as shown and secure with a few stitches using the ends of thread. Repeat along each edge and corner and trim and secure the cord end.

POTTED PLANTS *(photographs pages 79 and 82)*

The plants are made from the pattern Fig 137 and the instructions in Chapter 10.

ANTIMACASSARS AND DOILIES
(photograph pages 62–3)

No Victorian or Edwardian parlour is complete without antimacassars on the back of chairs and sofas, and doilies under plants and ornaments. These can be cut from lace or broderie anglaise or cut from white or cream fabric with the edges sealed with Fraycheck and narrow lace or braid glued on as trimming.

DEED BOX *(photograph page 82)*

The deed box is made from the pattern Fig 129 and the instructions in Chapter 9 for the small coffer.

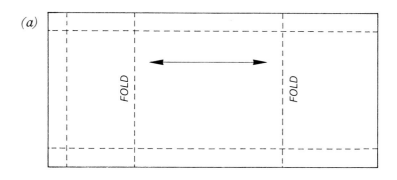

Fig 56 (a) Pattern and (b) assembly for the tasselled cushion

WHITE-METAL ORNAMENTS
(photograph page 82)

Decorating ideas, furniture and accessories from this chapter and others, brought together to make a study

The collection of ornaments shown on the bookcase, and the ink-well and quill pen are inexpensive white-metal miniatures painted with acrylic or enamel paints.

Clean any 'flashing' with a craft knife or abrasive paper and apply a coat of Humbrol (or similar) metal primer. Pieces can be spray painted or painted with a small brush using matt or satin white paint, applying several light coats and allowing each coat to dry thoroughly. This imitates marble and also makes a good base for painting colours. If you use colours, paint one at a time and allow it to dry before applying the next. A coat of gloss varnish can be applied when the paint is dry if the piece is required to resemble glazed china.

— CHAPTER FIVE —
The Bedroom

The rooms in this chapter demonstrate how similar pieces of furniture can be made to look quite different by applying alternative finishes, and can be used in different settings to create a variety of effects. The suite of furniture shown in the attic bedroom of a cottage is painted in pastel colours with a decoration of English country flowers and makes a pretty alternative to the more traditional pine finish shown in the Victorian bedroom. Both rooms, decorated with light floral papers have a feminine atmosphere, but the pine furniture can also be used with a darker wallpaper to create a very masculine bedroom.

THE ROOM BOX
(Fig 57, photograph pages 86–7)

The room box for the Attic Bedroom is made from the pattern Fig 57, and assembled in the same way as the room box in Chapter 2 except for the dormer window on the back wall.

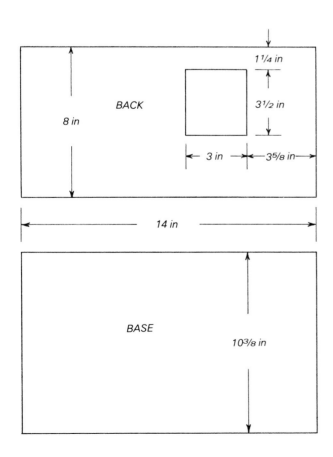

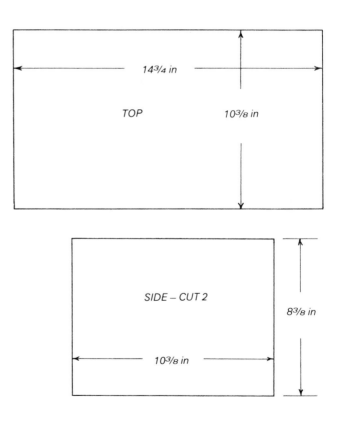

Fig 57 Plan for the Attic Bedroom room box

DORMER WINDOW (Fig 58)

The window-sill is made in ⅛in wood, with ³/₃₂in woodstrip for facing the window opening and ⅛ and ¹/₁₆in strip for glazing bars. Glazing may be glass or perspex, but should be not more than 2mm (¹/₁₆in) thick. The (non-opening) window is 2¾ × 3⅜in. Paint the woodstrip before assembling the window –

Fig 58 Pattern for the dormer window and sill

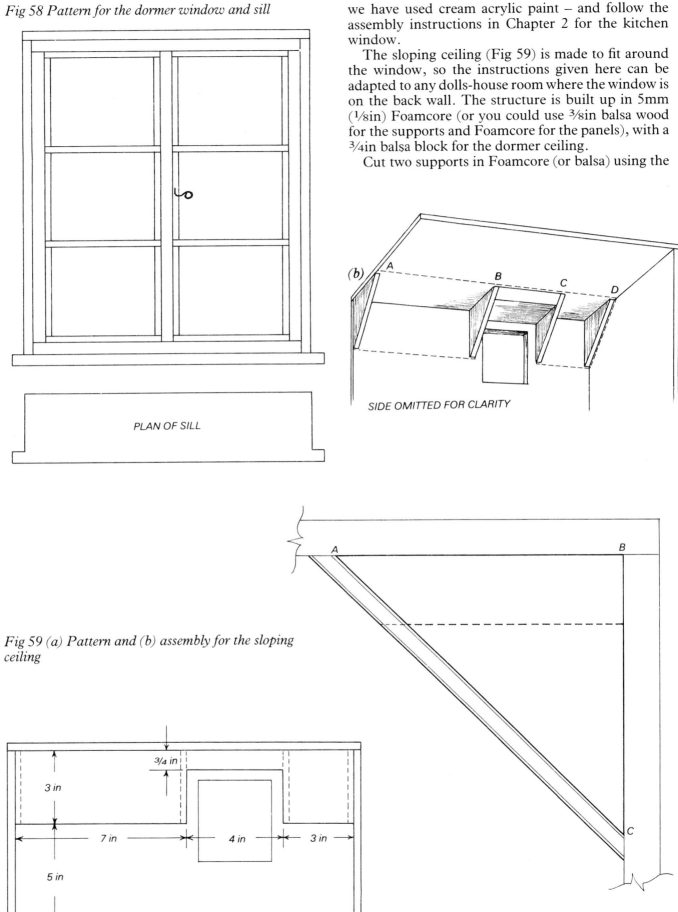

PLAN OF SILL

SIDE OMITTED FOR CLARITY

we have used cream acrylic paint – and follow the assembly instructions in Chapter 2 for the kitchen window.

The sloping ceiling (Fig 59) is made to fit around the window, so the instructions given here can be adapted to any dolls-house room where the window is on the back wall. The structure is built up in 5mm (1/8in) Foamcore (or you could use 3/8in balsa wood for the supports and Foamcore for the panels), with a 3/4in balsa block for the dormer ceiling.

Cut two supports in Foamcore (or balsa) using the

Fig 59 (a) Pattern and (b) assembly for the sloping ceiling

84

triangle (A)–(B)–(C) on the pattern as a guide. Glue one support into each back-ceiling corner of the room.

Cut the dormer ceiling in ³⁄₄in balsa block using points (A)–(B) and the dotted line on the pattern as a guide – a little wider than the window. (Our dormer ceiling is 4in wide.)

Cut two more supports, (A)–(B)–(C) on the pattern, in Foamcore (or balsa) and glue a support to each side of the dormer ceiling as shown in Fig 59b, and leave to dry.

Glue the dormer ceiling and supports to the ceiling and back wall of the room to surround the window.

Cut panels (A)–(B) and (C)–(D) in Foamcore to fit on to the triangular supports at each side of the window. Use Fig 59a as a guide to chamfer the edges of each panel, and glue the panels on to the supports.

Cut the centre panel (B)–(C) in Foamcore to fit on to the front of the dormer ceiling snugly between the two panels. Chamfer the top and bottom edges as shown and glue in place. Fill any gaps between the panels with Tetrion (or similar) rubbed in with a finger.

DECORATING

We papered the flat part of the ceiling with lining paper and applied magnolia emulsion paint. The sloping ceiling and the walls were papered with a commercial dolls-house paper. The ceiling beams are ¼ × ³⁄₈in and ¼in square woodstrip, slightly 'dis-tressed' and stained oak colour. The larger beam is glued across the centre of the ceiling and the smaller beam, cut to fit, is glued on to the sloping ceiling to one side of the window.

We used commercial wooden flooring stained oak colour and polished. This type of flooring has a self-adhesive backing, so the floor is simply cut to size (using a paper template if required) and pressed firmly in place on the plywood floor of the room. Commercial skirting-board, painted cream to match the window-frame and cut with mitred corners, was glued in place after the flooring was laid.

LIGHTING

We fitted a concealed light behind the main beam, wired through a hole in the ceiling to a transformer.

DECORATING – VICTORIAN BEDROOM
(photograph pages 94–5)

The bedroom in the dolls' house is decorated with a dolls-house wallpaper and the same wooden flooring used in the Attic Bedroom. The cornice, skirting-board, door and architrave were painted before fitting to represent pine (see page 34). The rug is from a dolls-house shop and the fireplace is a white-metal kit painted with metal primer and white gloss enamel paint. The oil lamp is wired into the copper tape system in the dolls' house.

FURNITURE

The furniture in the Attic Bedroom has been painted as a matching suite in pale blue and cream with a flower decoration. Full instructions for this painted finish can be found on page 96. It is applied to the furniture after assembly. If you prefer to paint your furniture to represent pine as shown in the Victorian bedroom, see page 34 and the wood should be painted before cutting.

SMALL WARDROBE
(Fig 60, photograph page 90)

The wardrobe is made in ¹⁄₈in and ¹⁄₁₆in wood with a back of ³⁄₃₂in wood, which can be cut in one piece or from ¹⁄₂in tongue and groove floorboarding planks glued and butted together. You will also need ³⁄₈ × ¹⁄₈in, ¼ × ¹⁄₈in, ³⁄₈ × ¹⁄₁₆in and ¹⁄₈ × ¹⁄₁₆in wood-strip. The plinth is made from ⁵⁄₈in wide commercial skirting-board, the pediment from ¼in moulding and the decoration from a pair of turned spindles (ie baluster spindles). You will also need two ¹⁄₈in offset hinges, a small doorknob and a piece of ³⁄₃₂in dowelling for the hanging rail.

Cut two front-frame sides, 6¹⁄₁₆in long, in ³⁄₈ × ¹⁄₈in woodstrip.

Cut the front-frame top and bottom, 2¼in long, in ¼ × ¹⁄₈in strip. Glue the top and bottom between the sides to assemble the front frame.

Cut two sides, 6¹⁄₈ × 1³⁄₈in, in ¹⁄₁₆in wood. Glue the sides behind the front frame and allow to dry.

Cut the base (A) 3 × 1½in, in ¹⁄₈in wood as shown on the pattern. Glue the front frame and side assembly on to the base.

Cut the floor-support front (B) in ¹⁄₈ × ¼in strip and glue behind the bottom of the front frame.

Cut two floor-support sides (C) 1in long, in ¹⁄₈ × ¼in strip and glue to the bottom edge of the sides as shown.

Cut the floor-support back (D) in ¹⁄₈ × ¼in strip and glue to the base and the floor-support sides to leave a ³⁄₃₂in gap at the back edges to accommodate the back.

The Attic Bedroom, a room under the eaves of a cottage
makes a charming bedroom for a little girl

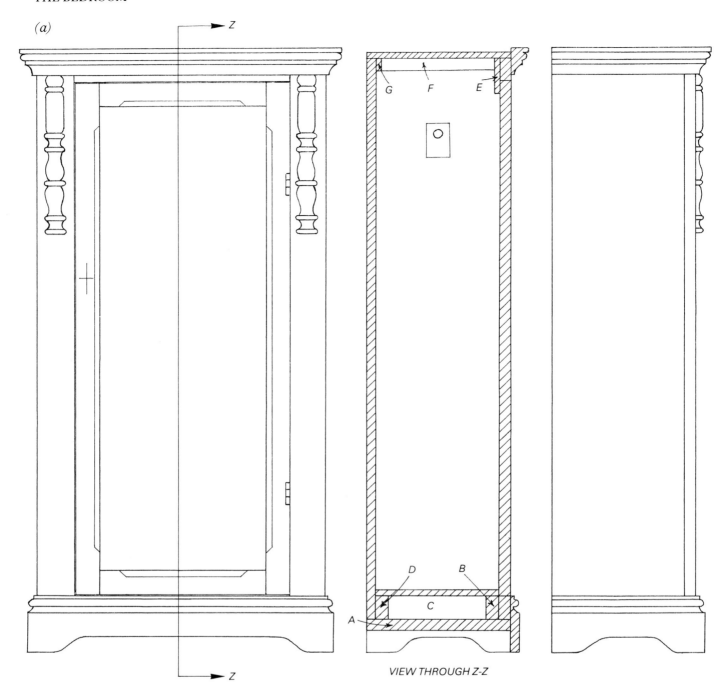

Fig 60 (a) Pattern and (b) assembly for the small wardrobe

Cut the floor in ¹⁄₁₆in wood to fit on to the floor support and glue in place.

Cut the top 3 × 1¹⁄₂in, in ¹⁄₁₆in wood and glue on to the front frame and sides.

Cut the top-support front (E) in ³⁄₈ × ¹⁄₁₆in strip and glue behind the top of the front frame to project ¹⁄₈in beneath the door opening to act as a door stop.

Cut two top-support sides (F) in ¹⁄₈ × ¹⁄₁₆in strip and glue to the top edge of the sides leaving a ³⁄₃₂in gap to accommodate the back.

Cut two hanging-rail supports ¹⁄₄ × ³⁄₄in in ¹⁄₁₆in strip. Drill holes as shown in Fig 60a to receive the hanging rail. Cut the hanging rail in ³⁄₃₂in dowelling to fit snugly between the sides. Glue supports on to each end of the hanging rail and glue the supports to the sides as shown.

Cut the back 6¹⁄₄ × 2³⁄₄in, in ³⁄₃₂in wood (or cut, glue and butt planks) to fit snugly between the sides and glue in place.

Cut the top-support back (G) in ¹⁄₈ × ¹⁄₁₆in strip and glue to the top edge of the back to complete the top support.

Cut the plinth front and sides with mitred corners in ⁵⁄₈in skirting-board. Shape the curved lower edges with a fretsaw or craft knife and sandpaper. Glue the plinth to the bottom of the front frame and sides so that the top edge of the plinth is level with the top edge of the front-frame bottom.

in the back edge of the door to accommodate the hinges and glue two offset hinges to the inside of the door and the front frame with superglue.

THE POT CUPBOARD
(Fig 61, photograph page 90)

This small bedside cupboard was originally used to house a chamber-pot and was a common feature in bedrooms before the age of indoor plumbing. The pot cupboard is made in $1/16$in wood, and $1/16 \times 1/4$in, $1/8 \times 1/4$in and $1/4$in square woodstrip. You will also need $1/8$in and $1/4$in mouldings and a pair of turned spindles (ie baluster spindles), two $1/8$in offset hinges and a small doorknob.

Cut the front-frame top in $1/8$in square woodstrip. Cut front-frame sides and bottom in $1/8 \times 1/4$in strip. Glue the top and bottom between the sides to assemble the front frame (A).

Cut two sides in $1/16$in wood and glue the sides behind the front frame.

Cut two bottom-shelf supports (B) in $1/16 \times 1/4$in strip and glue to the lower edge of the sides.

Cut two shelf supports (C) in $1/16 \times 1/8$in strip and glue to the sides as shown on the pattern.

Cut two shelves in $1/16$in wood to fit, and glue on to the bottom shelf and shelf supports.

Cut the back in $1/16$in wood and glue on to the sides and shelves.

Cut the top in $1/16$in wood and glue on to the carcase.

Cut $1/8$in moulding with mitred corners and glue to the front and side edges of the top. Cut $1/4$in moulding with mitred corners and glue to the bottom edge of the front frame and the sides.

Turn the cupboard upside-down to complete the bottom shelf support. Cut two pieces of $1/16 \times 1/4$in strip and glue them to the back and the front-frame bottom, between the side supports.

Use a craft knife and sanding block to pare away the back half from the spindles to form a flat surface. Check that they are evenly matched, trim to length and glue the spindles to the front-frame sides beneath the top moulding.

Cut the door panel in $1/16$in wood to fit into the door opening. Cut the door-frame top, bottom and sides in $1/16 \times 1/4$in strip and glue on to the door panel so that the edges are flush, and leave to dry. Chamfer the inner edges of the door frame as shown. Drill a hole to receive the doorknob. Glue offset hinges to the inside of the door and the front frame with superglue.

SINGLE BED *(Fig 62, photograph pages 86–7)*

The bed is made in $1/16$in wood, and $3/16$in square, $1/8$in square, $3/8 \times 1/16$in and $3/16 \times 1/16$in woodstrip.

Cut two legs $3\frac{1}{2}$in long and two legs $2\frac{3}{4}$in long in $3/16$in square woodstrip. Cut a small groove $3/16$in from the top with a craft knife and use sandpaper to shape rounded knobs on each leg.

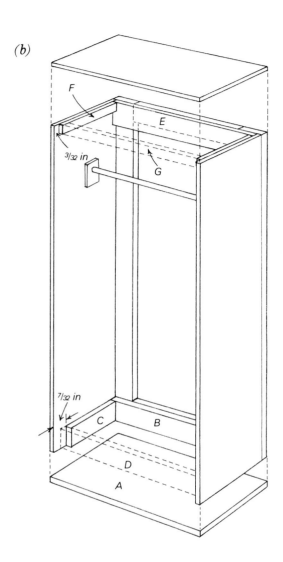

(b)

F

E

$3/32$ in

G

$7/32$ in

C

B

D

A

Cut the pediment front and sides with mitred corners in $1/4$in moulding and glue to the top of the front frame and sides.

Use a craft knife and sanding block to pare away the back half of the spindles to form a flat surface. Check that they are evenly matched, trim to length and glue the spindles to each side of the front frame beneath the pediment.

Cut the door panel in $1/16$in wood to fit into the door opening. Cut the door-frame top, bottom and sides in $1/16 \times 1/4$in strip and glue on to the door panel so that the edges are flush, then leave to dry. Chamfer the inner edges of the door frame as shown on the pattern and drill a hole to receive the doorknob. Cut recesses

*The decorative painted finish can be used to make a
matching suite of bedroom furniture*

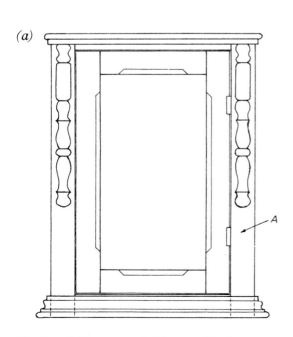

(a)

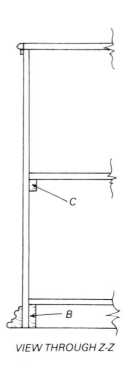

VIEW THROUGH Z-Z

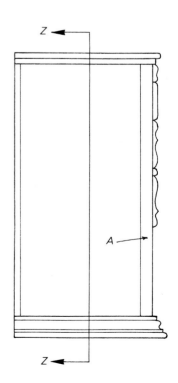

*Fig 61 (a) Pattern and (b) assembly for
the pot cupboard*

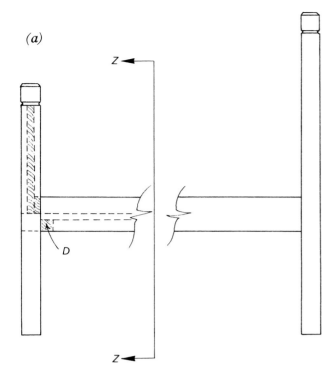

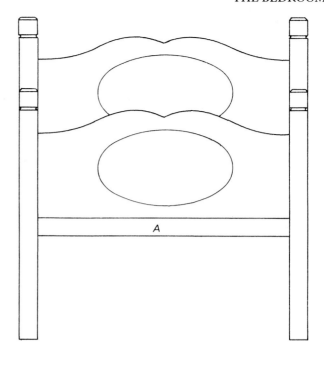

(a)

Fig 62 (a) Pattern for the single bed

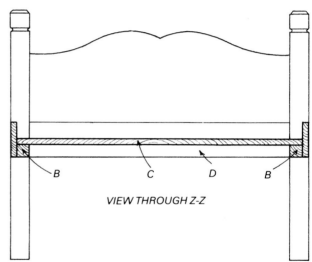

VIEW THROUGH Z-Z

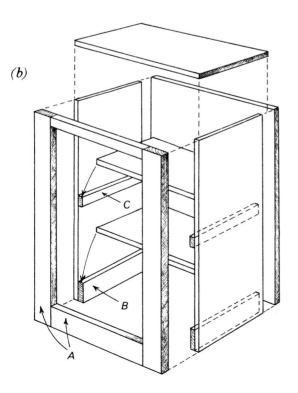

(b)

Cut the headboard and footboard in ¹/₁₆in wood. Shape the curved edges with a fretsaw or craft knife and sandpaper. Cut the headboard and footboard rails (A) in ³/₁₆in square strip.

Rest the headboard on a spacer of ¹/₁₆in scrap wood, and glue the lower edge of the headboard to the headboard rail, and the longer pair of legs to either side of the headboard and rail as shown on the pattern.

Repeat for the footboard rail and shorter pair of legs. Check that the bed legs are all of equal length and leave to dry.

Cut two side rails to the required length of the bed (6 – 6¹/₄in is usual) in ³/₈ × ¹/₁₆in woodstrip. Cut two side-rail supports (B) the same length as the side rails in ¹/₈in square strip and glue the supports to the bottom inside edge of the side rails.

Cut the bed base (C), the same length as the side rails in ¹/₁₆in wood, as shown on the pattern. Try the base on the rails to check that the rails fit flush with

Fig 62 (b) Assembly of the single bed

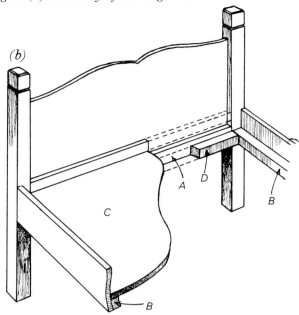

(b)

the headboard and footboard (trim the base if necessary), and glue the base on to the side rails.

Cut two base supports (D) in 1/8in square strip and glue to the underside of the base at each end to line up with the side-rail supports.

Glue the base and side-rail assembly to the headboard and footboard so that the underside of the base supports and the head- and footboard rails are flush. Check that the bed stands square, then turn on to one side and apply pressure to both ends as the glue dries.

If you wish to make a double bed, the patterns can be adapted and the same method used.

WASHSTAND *(Fig 63, photograph page 98)*

The washstand is made in 1/16in and 1/8in wood, and 3/16in square and 1/8 × 3/8in woodstrip trimmed with 1/8in moulding. The towel-rails are made of 1/16in dowelling. We used a pair of turned spindles (ie stair balusters) for the front legs, and painted the top of the washstand to represent marble before the splashback was glued in place. The splashback is made from a frame of 1/4in picture-frame moulding and decorated with five 1/2in square tiles, which may be bought from a specialist shop or made in 1/16in thick clay, by adapting the instructions on page 162 for medieval tiles.

Trim the turned front legs to length as necessary and cut two back legs in 3/16in square woodstrip.

Cut two short and two long friezes (A) in 1/8 × 3/8in woodstrip. Cut two shelf supports (B) in 1/8in square strip.

Glue the short friezes and the shelf supports between each pair of front and back legs, so that the frieze and shelf support are flush with the outside edge on each pair, then leave to dry.

Cut the shelf in 1/16in wood. Cut notches to receive the legs and shape the curved front edge with a fret-

saw or craft knife and sandpaper as shown on the pattern.

Try the shelf in place to act as a spacer, and glue the long friezes between each leg assembly. Ensure that the washstand is square then allow to dry. Glue the shelf on to the shelf supports.

Cut the top 3 1/4 × 1 1/2in, in 1/8in wood. Cut 1/8in moulding with mitred corners and glue to the front and side edges of the top. Glue the top on to the leg assembly so that the back edge of the top and the back frieze are flush. Leave the assembly under pressure to dry.

Cut four blanks for the towel-rail brackets (C) and shape the curved edges with a fretsaw or craft knife and sandpaper, as shown on the pattern. Drill holes 1/32in deep into each bracket to receive the towel-rail. Glue the brackets to each side of the washstand as shown. Cut towel-rails in 1/16in dowelling to fit, glue the ends, and ease the rails into the holes in the brackets.

Cut a backing for the splashback 3 × 1in, in 1/16in wood. Cut a frame for the backing piece with mitred corners in 1/4in picture-frame moulding and glue the frame on to the backing as shown in Fig 63b.

Spread a thick layer of wood glue inside the frame of the splashback and when the glue is tacky press the tiles into the glue and allow to dry. Grout the tiles with a little filler (Tetrion or similar) and clean up with a damp cotton bud.

Paint the washstand top to represent marble (see page 54 for instructions).

Glue the splashback on to the washstand, flush with the back edge of the top. Cut two splashback sides in 1/16in wood, shape the curved edges, and glue the sides on to the top, and to the splashback.

Our towel is a piece of cotton tape with threads pulled from each end to make a fringe.

BLANKET BOX *(Fig 64, photograph pages 86–7)*

This very useful box can be finished in a number of ways, including panelling and oak stain to make a large coffer for the Tudor house, and decorative painting to make a toy-box. The blanket box is made of 1/8in wood with a plinth of 5/8in skirting-board and trimmed with 1/4in moulding. The lid opens with two 1/4in butt hinges.

Cut a front 3 1/4 × 1 1/2in, and a base 3 1/4 × 1 1/4in, in 1/8in wood. Glue the front to the front edge of the base.

Cut two sides 1 1/4 × 1 3/8in, in 1/8in wood and glue the sides on to the base, behind the front.

Cut a back 3 1/4 × 1 1/2in, in 1/8in wood and glue the back on to the base and sides.

Cut the plinth front and sides with mitred corners in 5/8in skirting-board, shape the curved lower edge with a fretsaw or craft knife and sandpaper, and glue the plinth to the front and sides as shown on the pattern.

Cut the lid to overhang slightly at the front and

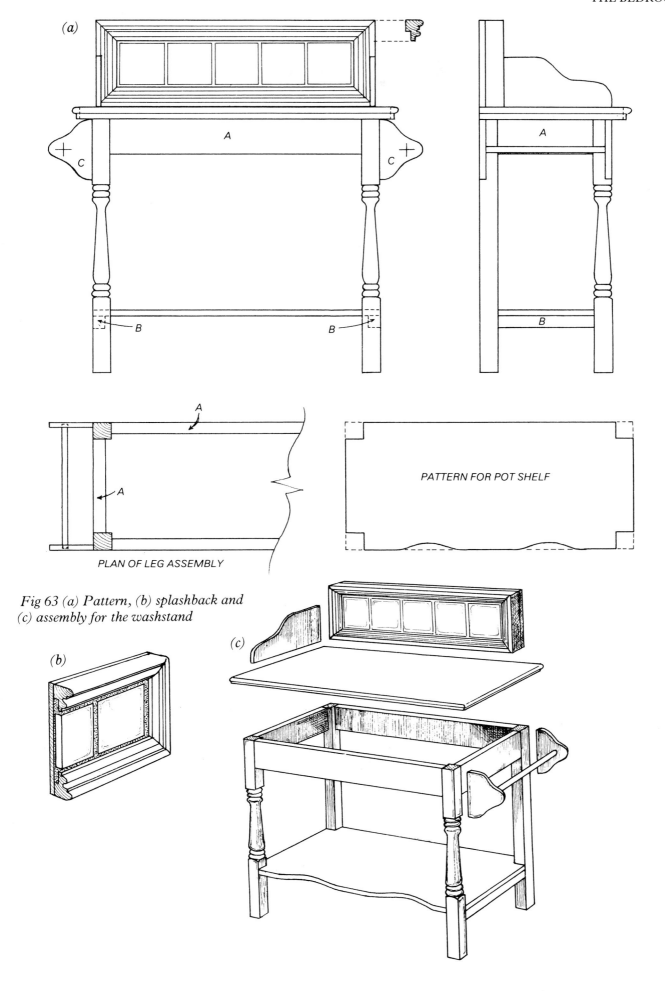

(a)

A

C C

B B

A

B

A

A

PLAN OF LEG ASSEMBLY

PATTERN FOR POT SHELF

Fig 63 (a) Pattern, (b) splashback and (c) assembly for the washstand

(b)

(c)

Fig 64 (a) Pattern and (b) assembly for the blanket box

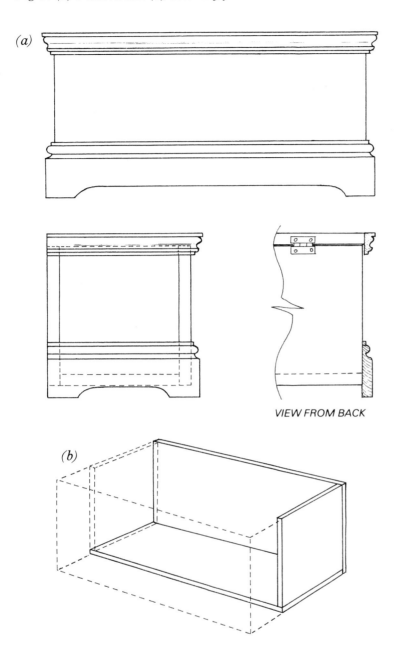

(a)

VIEW FROM BACK

(b)

sides in ⅛in wood. Cut ¼in moulding with mitred corners and glue to the front and side edges of the lid, so that the top edges are flush. Glue two hinges to the back of the lid and the box with superglue as shown.

RUSH-SEAT CHAIR (Fig 65, photograph pages 86–7)

The chair is made from ⅛in square, ¼ × ½in, ¼ × ¹⁄₁₆in and ¹⁄₁₆ × ⅜in woodstrip. The 'rush' seat can be woven after the chair is painted, with any suitable material, including soft string, cotton crochet thread or twisted raffia.

Cut two back legs in ⅛in square woodstrip and score and sandpaper the top end of each leg to shape knobs.

*The Victorian Bedroom in the dolls' house with a suite
of pine furniture and a real patchwork quilt*

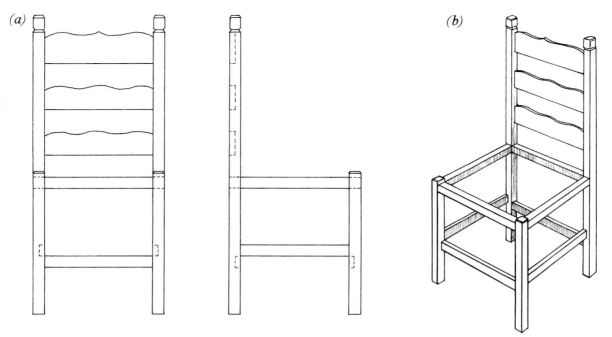

(a)   *(b)*

Fig 65 (a) Pattern and (b) assembly for the rush-seat chair

Cut two back rails in $1/4 \times 1/16$in strip, and one top back rail in $1/16 \times 3/8$in strip. Shape the curved top edges with a fretsaw or craft knife and sandpaper.

Cut the back seat rail in $1/8$in square strip, and the back stretcher in $1/16 \times 1/8$in strip.

Glue the three back rails, the seat rail and the back stretcher to one leg and allow to dry, then glue the second back leg to the rails and stretcher.

Cut two side seat rails in $1/8$in square strip. Turn the chair back on one side and glue one side seat rail in place. Allow to dry, turn to the other side and glue the second side seat rail in place.

Cut two front legs in $1/8$in square strip and chamfer the top edges as shown. Cut the front seat rail in $1/8$in square strip and one front stretcher in $1/16 \times 1/8$in strip. Glue the seat rail and stretcher between the front legs (as for the back legs).

Cut two side stretchers in $1/16 \times 1/8$in strip and glue to the back assembly. Glue the front leg assembly to the side rails and stretchers. Check that the chair stands square and support as the glue dries. Paint the chair before weaving the seat.

To weave the seat use as long a length of string as you can comfortably work with, threaded through a short darning needle. Secure the end of the string to the left side of the front seat rail with glue or a slip-knot and weave the string following the guide in Fig 66, under and back over the front seat rail, under and back over the left side rail, across and under and over the right rail, under and over the back rail etc. Continue working around the square until the space is filled. The string should be pulled taut, but gently. Join new lengths of string as necessary with knots on the underside of the seat and fasten off when the weaving is complete by threading the loose end into the underside of the seat, secured with a little glue.

Fig 66 Method for weaving the chair seat

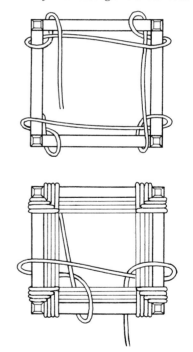

DECORATIVE PAINTED FINISH
(Fig 67, photograph page 90)

The painted finish described here has been used for the furniture in the Attic Bedroom but it could be applied to other furniture in the book. The methods can also be used to 'customise' inexpensive commercial furniture and turn a very ordinary item into some-

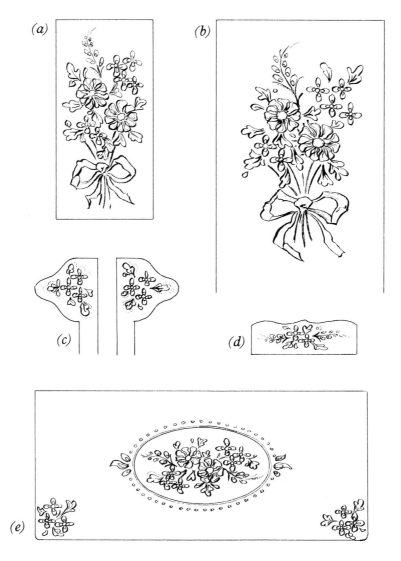

*Fig 67 Patterns for the decorative painted finish for the
Attic Bedroom furniture*

thing special, simply by sanding the piece thoroughly to remove the original finish, and adapting the instructions to the individual piece as appropriate. You might also consider using this finish for a kit as an alternative to the recommended woodstain.

You will need fine-grade abrasive paper, good quality artists' brushes (we recommend sable detail and liner brushes in sizes 3–5), acrylic paints in your choice of colours (instructions are given for the colours shown in the photograph) and wax polish to finish.

Sand the furniture piece thoroughly and remove all traces of dust before you begin painting.

Paint an undercoat (we have used pale blue) all over the outside of the piece, excluding the back and underside, the top of the wardrobe and the door edges. Allow the undercoat to dry thoroughly, then sand with fine-grade abrasive paper.

Paint all parts (except door panels and spindles) with a second coat of pale blue. Paint the door panels and spindles cream. Allow to dry thoroughly and sand again. Trace the outline of the oval 'panels' on to the bed headboard and footboard and the blanket box lid and paint the ovals cream.

Apply a second coat of cream to the door panels, spindles and the oval panels, and pale blue to the other parts. (If necessary, sand again and repeat until you have a smooth surface.)

Define the detail on the mouldings and spindles with fine lines in cream and medium blue.

Trace the pattern (Fig 67) lightly on to the piece in pencil. The small panel (a) is for the pot cupboard; the larger panel (b) for the wardrobe; the sprig (c) is for the towel-rail brackets on the washstand; (d) is for the top rail of the chair; the oval panel (e) is for the bed headboard and footboard and (with the corner sprigs) for the lid of the blanket box.

Using the photograph on page 90 as a guide, paint the centres of the two main flowers (in patterns a, b and c) in yellow, and paint feathery petals in medium lilac. Paint the centres of the smaller flowers pale yellow and the round petals in medium blue. Define the base of each petal with a deeper shade of the same colour and the edges with a paler shade. Add a touch

A comfortable bed, a good book and his cat for company help to make a poorly old gentleman feel better

of white to the flower centres. Paint the bows in shades of medium blue and cream.

Use a fine-liner brush to lightly draw the curved stem of the tiny flower sprays in green. Paint yellow florets decreasing in size towards the tip. Touch in a little black at the base of each floret and a little white at the tip. Finish the florets with a few dots of yellow.

Paint the flower stems and leaves in green, check that the design is well balanced and add leaves if necessary. Touch in dark green veins on the leaves and add a touch of pale green to the edges. Outline the oval panels, and add the dots and leaves in medium blue.

When the painted finish is thoroughly dry, apply a coat of wax polish and buff with a soft cloth. Glue the doorknobs in place with superglue – we have used brass knobs painted cream.

LARGE WARDROBE
(Fig 68, photograph pages 94–5)

The wardrobe is made in ⅛in and 1/16in wood, ¼ × ⅛in, ⅜ × 1/16in and ⅛ × 1/16in woodstrip. You will also need ⅝in skirting-board for the plinth, ¼in moulding for the pediment, 3/32in dowelling for the hanging rail, four ⅛in offset hinges and two small handles. The back may be cut in one piece in 3/32in wood, or made from ½in floorboarding butted together to resemble tongue and groove planking. Our wardrobe is painted to represent pine (see page 34) and if you choose a similar finish the wood should be painted before cutting. If you prefer woodstain, the pieces should be stained before assembly. Use the assembly diagram Fig 60b as a guide to assemble the large wardrobe.

Cut two front-frame sides 6in long, in ¼ × ⅛in woodstrip. Cut the front-frame top and bottom 3½in long, in ¼ × ⅛in strip. Glue the top and bottom between the sides to assemble the front frame.

Cut two sides 6 × 1⅜in, in 1/16in wood. Glue the sides behind the front frame and allow to dry thoroughly.

Cut the base (A) 4 × 1½in, in ⅛in wood, and glue the front frame and sides on to the base.

Cut the floor-support front (B) in ⅛ × ¼in strip and glue behind the bottom of the front frame. Cut two floor-support sides (C) 1in long, in ⅛ × ¼in strip and glue to the bottom edge of the sides as shown. Cut the floor-support back (D) in ⅛ × ¼in strip and glue to the base and support sides to leave a 3/32in gap at the back edge to accommodate the back.

Cut the floor in 1/16in wood to fit on to the floor support and glue in place.

Cut the top 4 × 1½in, in 1/16in wood and glue on to the front frame and sides.

Cut two top-support sides (F) in ⅛ × 1/16in strip and glue to the top edge of the sides, leaving a 3/32in gap to accommodate the back.

Cut two shelf supports (H) in ⅛ × 1/16in strip and glue to the sides as shown, leaving a 3/32in gap to

accommodate the back. Cut the shelf in 1/16in wood to fit on to the supports and glue in place.

Cut two hanging-rail supports (I) in 1/16in wood and drill holes as shown to receive the hanging rail. Cut the hanging rail in 3/32in dowelling to fit snugly between the sides. Glue supports on to each end of the hanging rail, and then glue the supports to the wardrobe sides as shown. Cut the back in 3/32in wood (or cut, glue and butt planks) to fit snugly between the sides and glue in place.

Cut the top-support back (G) in ⅛ × 1/16in strip and glue to the top edge of the back to complete the top support.

Cut the plinth front and sides with mitred corners in ⅝in skirting-board. Shape the curved lower edges with a fretsaw or craft knife and sandpaper. Glue the plinth to the bottom of the front frame and sides so that the top edge of the plinth is level with the top edge of the front-frame bottom.

Fig 68 (a) Pattern for the large wardrobe

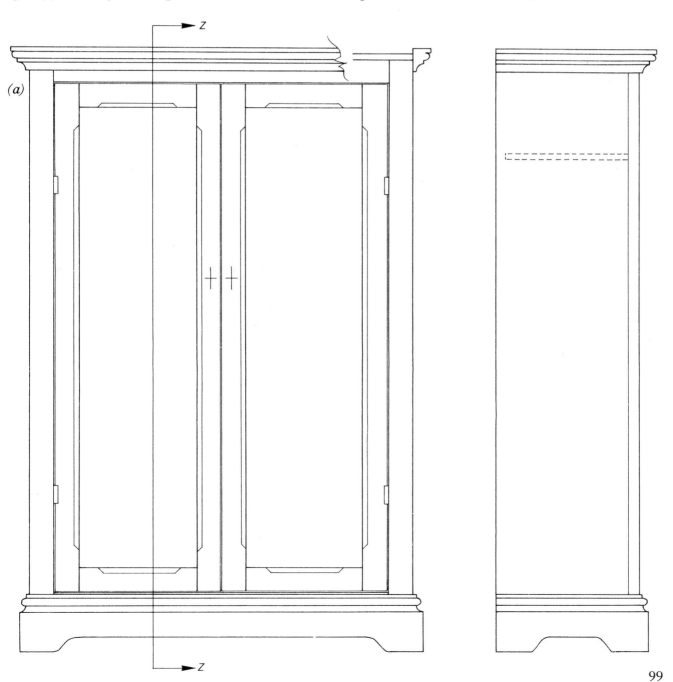

(a)

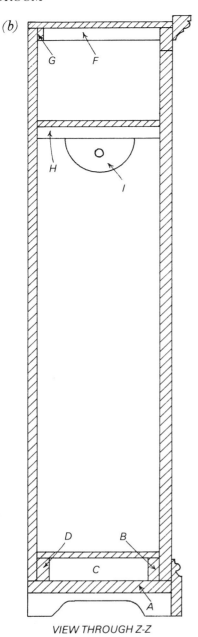

(b)

VIEW THROUGH Z-Z

Fig 68 (b) Assembly for the large wardrobe

Cut the pediment front and sides with mitred corners in ¼in moulding and glue to the top of the front frame and sides as shown.

Cut two door panels in ¹⁄₁₆in wood to fit snugly into the door opening. Cut door-frame top, bottom and sides for each panel in ¼ × ¹⁄₁₆in strip and glue on to the door panels with edges flush. Allow to dry thoroughly. Chamfer the inner edges of the door frames as shown and drill holes to receive the door-knobs.

Cut recesses in the back edge of each door to accommodate the hinges, and glue and pin two offset hinges to each door and to the front frame with superglue.

Apply wax polish to the front and sides of the wardrobe and buff to a soft sheen.

ACCESSORIES

PATCHWORK QUILT
(Fig 69, photograph pages 94–5)

Our patchwork quilt is a traditional pattern, made authentically in blocks of sixteen patches. To make a single quilt you will need twenty blocks; to make a double you will need twenty-five blocks. Four blocks could be used to make a cushion cover, backed with plain fabric.

To make the patchwork quilt, you will need ⅓yd (or metre) of fine cotton fabric in a plain colour, and scraps of tiny print fabrics in toning colours. We have used Liberty Tana lawn in cream and shades of pink and blue prints. If you want the quilt to look old, use old fabrics or soften the colours of new fabric by soaking in a mild solution of household bleach and rinsing thoroughly. Iron all fabric before cutting and use the smallest possible needles (size 10 sharps) and fine cotton sewing thread.

Using the actual size pattern Fig 69a, trace (or photocopy) the appropriate number of blocks on to stiff paper. Cut the paper blocks into individual templates using a craft knife and metal ruler.

Using the individual paper templates as a guide, cut the fabric pieces ⅛in larger all the way round, squarely on the grain of the fabric. Fold the extra fabric carefully around each template and tack (baste) to hold in place – as shown in Fig 69b. Prepare eight print diamond-shaped patches, four plain triangular and four plain square patches for each block.

With right sides facing, stitch the patches together with the smallest possible oversewing stitches to form a block as shown in Fig 69a. Begin with an eight-pointed star formed by joining two sets of four print diamonds. Complete the block by adding the plain triangles and squares.

With right sides facing, oversew the completed blocks together to form the quilt.

To prepare the border, cut four strips of scrap fabric on the straight grain ⅝in wide × 1in longer than the side of the quilt. Cut strips of paper (templates) ⅜in wide, the same length as the fabric strips. Fold each fabric strip in half, lengthwise (right side out) and press. Insert a paper strip against the fold and tack to hold in place.

Place the folded edge of each strip to the patchwork edge, right sides facing, and oversew together, beginning with each side of the quilt, then the top and bottom. Open out the quilt, right side uppermost, and overlap the borders at each corner – hemming to hold in place. Trim the excess fabric at the border ends.

Remove the paper templates. Cut a lining to fit the quilt in plain fabric, and tack the quilt and lining together with wrong sides facing.

Bind the quilt edges with matching print bias bind-

(a)

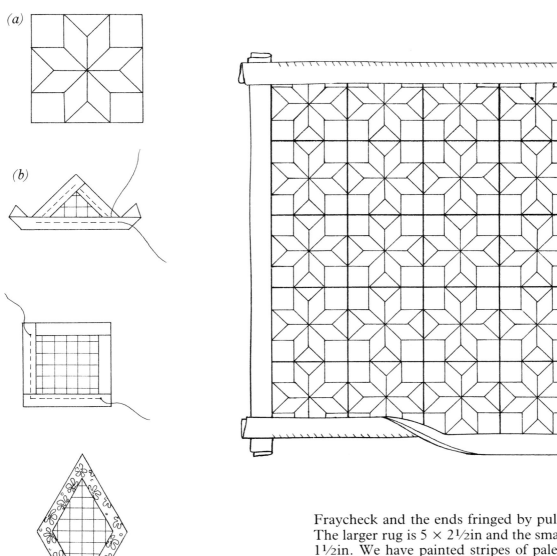

(b)

Fig 69 (a) Pattern and (b) plan and method for the patchwork quilt

ing or bias-cut fabric strip. Beginning in the middle of one side, with right sides facing, stitch the binding to the quilt so that it completely covers the border strips. Stitch binding all round the quilt, mitring the corners. Trim the border if necessary, then fold and hem the binding to the quilt lining.

Remove all tacking (basting) threads, and if required, press lightly by hovering a steam iron above the quilt, taking care not to flatten the patchwork.

COTTON RUGS *(photograph pages 86–7)*

The rugs are made from rectangles of heavyweight woven cotton fabric (we have used cream calico), cut squarely on the grain with the sides sealed with Fraycheck and the ends fringed by pulling threads. The larger rug is 5 × 2½in and the smaller is 3½ × 1½in. We have painted stripes of pale blue acrylic paint at each end of the larger rug and used the pattern in Fig 67e (with sprigs in each corner) painted on to the smaller rug, as described for the painted furniture. If the fabric does not have sufficient weight to lie flat on the floor, iron Vilene (or similar) on to the back.

CURTAINS *(photograph pages 86–7)*

The lace curtain is a strip of 2in wide cotton lace edging cut to fit the window, with the ends sealed with Fraycheck. It is glued lightly to the window-frame at each side to hang just clear of the window-sill. The curtains are made in lightweight cotton fabric, on a pole of fine dowelling suspended from two small pins.

Cut two curtains to fit the window, with narrow hems at each side, a deeper hem at the bottom, and long enough to make a casing at the top. Fold the hems, secure with fabric glue and press. Fold the top and stitch a casing to fit the dowelling. Thread the dowelling through the casing and pull up the curtains to each side. Steam, by hovering the iron above the curtain, to set the folds. Suspend the pole on fine pins or small eyes, screwed into the wall above the window-frame.

— CHAPTER SIX —

The Sitting Room

As a change from the more old-fashioned parlour shown in Chapter 4, the rooms in this chapter represent the 1950s and 60s.

The 1950s Sitting Room is decorated and furnished in the post-war 'contemporary' style and represents a small house on one of the new estates which were built in the surburbs. The large picture-window, plain door and gas convector heater are typical of these houses and the furniture and accessories are all in the latest fashion.

The 1960s room is furnished as a teenagers' 'bed-sit' complete with a curtained 'kitchenette' in the corner of the room – all in the style of the time.

The furniture patterns in this chapter are very simple and are designed especially for beginners but if you want to create a real atmosphere of the period then colours, patterns and accessories must be chosen carefully. In most homes, people could not afford to completely re-decorate and furnish in the new style so modern wallpaper and a new 'free-form' coffee table might be found with the old upholstered suite, perhaps disguised with new covers in a modern print. It is this uncomfortable blend of old and contemporary which is so evocative of the period.

The 1950s Sitting Room

THE ROOM BOX

(Fig 70, photograph pages 106–7)

The pattern in Fig 70 will make a room box 16in wide, 10in deep and 8in high, which is a typical size for the sitting room in a small modern house. Our sitting room has a large (non-opening) picture-window, a (non-opening) flush door and a tiled fireplace with a gas convector heater.

The measurements given in brackets in the following text are for the room box shown in the photograph, but the methods can be adapted to any dolls-house room.

To make the room box, you will need good quality ³⁄₈in plywood, an all-purpose saw, and a fretsaw to cut the window opening. You will also need a small plane and sandpaper. The room box is assembled with wood glue and veneer pins. The front edge of the box may be faced with a frame of woodstrip after the room is decorated.

Draw the pattern on to the wood with a sharp pencil and cut the base, back, top, and two sides. For the best results, saw fractionally outside the drawn lines and use a small plane to smooth the edges back to the line. Sand each piece thoroughly.

Draw the window opening on the back wall and cut out with a fretsaw on the drawn line. Clean the edges of the window opening with sandpaper.

Glue and pin the back on to the base, ensuring that the pieces form a right angle.

Glue and pin one side on to the back and base, then the other side.

Glue and pin the top on to the back and sides as shown in Fig 71.

If you wish, the outside of the room box can be stained or painted. To frame the front edge, cut woodstrip with mitred corners and glue in place with contact-adhesive (eg Evostick or similar) after the interior of the room is decorated.

PICTURE-WINDOW (Fig 72)

The window in the room box projects beyond the outside wall to accommodate a realistic window-sill. The window-frame is made in ¹⁄₂ × ¹⁄₈in woodstrip, with an inner frame and glazing bars of ¹⁄₈in square strip. The window-sill is ³⁄₄in deep, made in ¹⁄₈ × ⁵⁄₈in woodstrip. The glazing may be glass or perspex, but should be 1¹⁄₂mm (¹⁄₁₆in) thick – our window is 4¹⁄₂ × 8in. It is easier to stain or paint the window-frame and sill before assembly – we have used teak woodstain.

Cut the window-sill a little wider than the window opening, with notches at each end so that it fits into the opening and projects ¹⁄₈in (see Fig 72).

Face the top and sides of the window opening with ¹⁄₂ × ¹⁄₈in woodstrip, to fit flush with the inside wall

and project on the outside wall as shown.

Make a frame of ⅛in square woodstrip, glued into the opening and flush with the outside edge.

Fit the glass against the frame, and glue a second frame of ⅛in square strip to the opening, butted against the glass.

Cut and glue the horizontal glazing bar to the inside of the glass, using a 1in wide cardboard spacer to ensure that it is level. Cut and glue the vertical glazing bars in place as shown on the pattern.

FLUSH DOOR (Fig 73)

The simple flush door can be made and glued in place before or after decorating, as you prefer. It is made in thin, stiff cardboard (posterboard), faced with self-adhesive wood veneer to represent teak – we have used Microwood. The door frame is ¼in woodstrip, sanded to round off the outside edge and painted

The tiled fireplace with gas convector heater and the sideboard with sliding doors were both the latest fashion in the 1950s

white before gluing in place.

Cut a piece of card (3 × 6in), face one surface with self-adhesive veneer cut to fit, and glue the door to the wall (1⅛in from the front edge of the room box). Cut the door frame with mitred corners and glue around the door, leaving a slight gap all round. Note, if you fit the door before the floor is carpeted, allow clearance under the door for the floor covering.

The door handle is cut from wood scrap, with a thin slice of ³⁄₃₂in dowelling, on a plate of thin card. Glue the pieces together as shown and paint the door handle and plate with metallic silver paint. Paint the keyhole in matt black and paint mock hinges on the door frame. Allow the paint to dry thoroughly, and glue the door handle to the door.

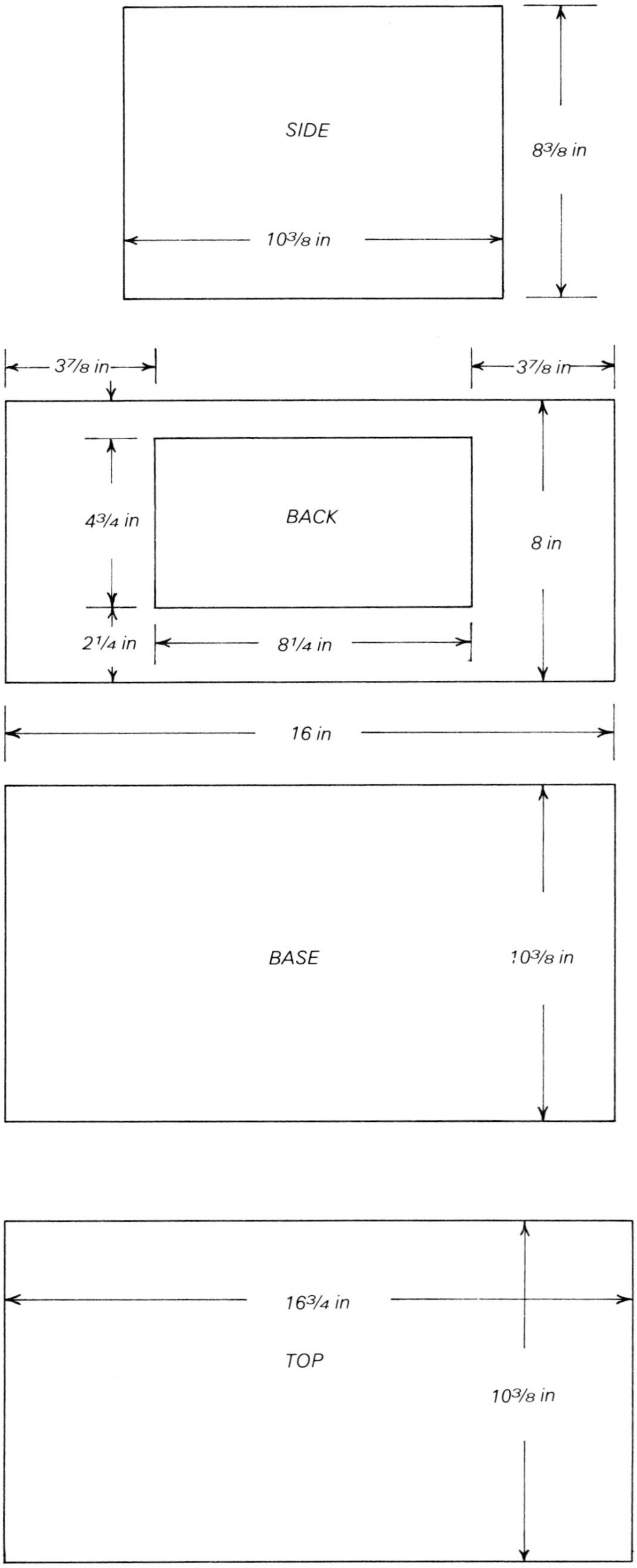

SIDE

8³/₈ in

10³/₈ in

←— 3⁷/₈ in —→ ←— 3⁷/₈ in —→

4³/₄ in   BACK   8 in

2¹/₄ in ←— 8¹/₄ in —→

←———— 16 in ————→

BASE   10³/₈ in

←———— 16³/₄ in ————→

TOP

10³/₈ in

Fig 70 Plan for the 1950s Sitting Room room box

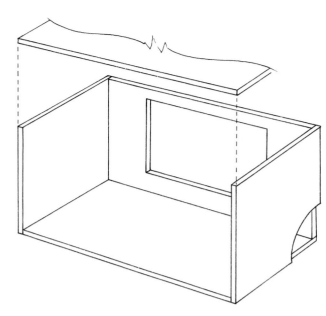

Fig 71 Assembly for the room box

DECORATING

We papered the ceiling with dolls-house ceiling paper (lining paper and white emulsion paint would be equally appropriate), and two walls with a commercial dolls-house wallpaper. The fireplace wall, in typical 1950s fashion, contrasts with the other walls – we have used lining paper painted with beige emulsion. The skirting-boards are white-painted 5/16in wide woodstrip, glued in place after the carpet is fitted, and the cornice is white-painted ¹/₄in moulding, glued to the wall and ceiling with mitred corners. In a room of this period, you might also fit a picture-rail.

FITTED CARPET

The carpet in the 1950s room is grey furnishing velvet but any heavyweight fabric in a plain colour or suitable pattern could be used.

Measure the floor area carefully, (or make a paper template) and mark, squarely on the grain, on the back of the piece of fabric. If you are using a fabric which frays badly, seal the edges with Fraycheck or glue on the cutting line, and allow to dry before cutting.

Fix the carpet to the floor with double-sided sellotape around the outside edge, or fabric glue around the edge or all over the floor, as you prefer. Smooth the carpet carefully over the floor so there are no wrinkles and press it firmly in place around the edges of the room. The raw edges will be covered by the skirting-boards, and if you wish, the front edge can be concealed by a piece of narrow woodstrip glued in place.

Fig 72 Pattern and assembly for the picture-window   *Fig 73 Plan for the flush door and door handle*

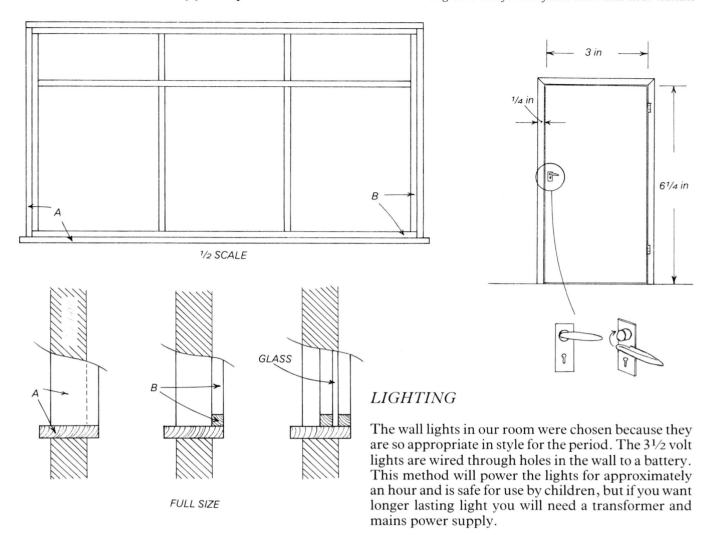

½ SCALE

FULL SIZE

GLASS

LIGHTING

The wall lights in our room were chosen because they are so appropriate in style for the period. The 3½ volt lights are wired through holes in the wall to a battery. This method will power the lights for approximately an hour and is safe for use by children, but if you want longer lasting light you will need a transformer and mains power supply.

FIXTURES

TILED FIREPLACE
AND CONVECTOR HEATER
(Fig 74, photograph page 103)

The fireplace surround is made in ⅛in wood, faced with self-adhesive veneer – we have used Microwood in a light colour for the inner surface and front edges, and a dark colour for the outer surface. The fireplace is tiled with air-drying clay tiles, painted with acrylic colours applied with a small piece of natural sponge, on a backing of 5mm (⅛in) Foamcore. The convector heater is made in thick paper of the type used for watercolour painting and a scrap of ¼in balsa wood. The fireplace is assembled on a backing of thin card (postcard is ideal) and glued on to the wall when complete.

Cut a fireplace front 4⁵⁄₁₆ × 3⅝in, in Foamcore and cut out the heater space as shown on the pattern. Use strips of dark grey paper glued in place to face the cut edges of the heater space.

To make the tiles, roll out air-drying clay to an even ¹⁄₁₆in thickness, cut a piece (slightly larger to allow for shrinkage) to fit the Foamcore front and cut out the heater space. Allow the clay to dry leather-hard, and score the tiles with a pointed tool as shown on the pattern. When the clay is dry, glue it on to the Foamcore front with UHU or a similar tacky craft glue.

Paint the tiles with light-beige acrylic paint and allow to dry. Mix a darker shade of colour and use a small piece of natural sponge to dab paint on to the tiles in a mottled effect. When the paint is dry, redefine the lines between the tiles with a wooden toothpick or similar tool to imitate grouting. Apply a coat of acrylic sealer if required. Glue the assembled fireplace front on to a backing of thin card and trim the card around the outside edge.

*The 1950s Sitting Room is a great place to spend a
winter afternoon 'swooning' to the latest records*

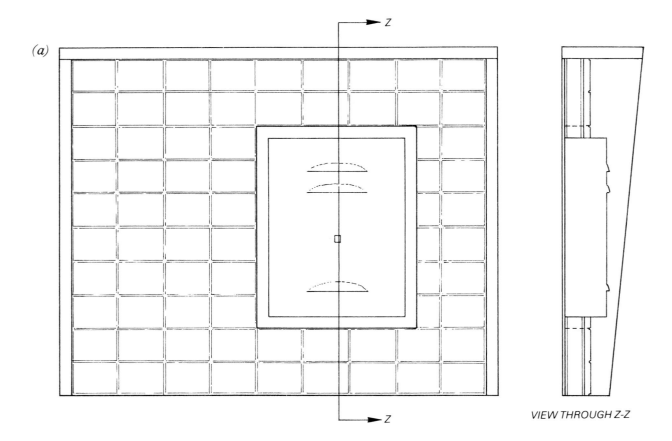

(a)

Z

Z

VIEW THROUGH Z-Z

Fig 74 (a) Pattern and (b) assembly for the tiled fireplace and convector heater

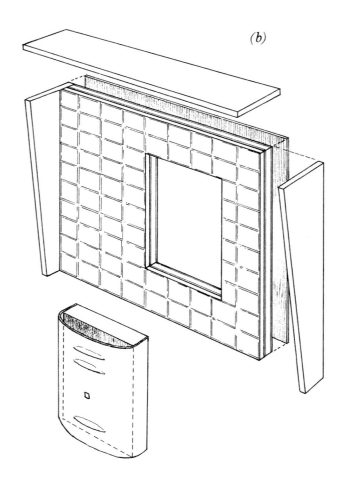

(b)

Cut two surround sides in ⅛in wood and veneer the inside face and front edges of each piece. Glue the surround sides to each side of the fireplace front.

Cut the surround top in ⅛in wood and trim the front edge to follow the line of the sides. Veneer the underside face and front edge and glue the top on to the front and sides.

Cut veneer to fit and apply to the outside faces of the surround sides and top. Polish the outside of the surround with wax polish if required.

To make the convector heater, cut a support 1⅜ × 1⅞in, of ¼in balsa and paint it matt black.

Cut a strip 1⅞ × 2in of watercolour paper and mark the three ventilators shown on the pattern. Draw the paper strip under a ruler or the back of a knife to curve it. Cut slits in the paper with a craft knife at the lower edge of the ventilators and ease the paper outwards, stretching it to form flaps. Note, that a gentle touch is required to stretch the paper without tearing it. Glue the sides of the paper strip to the balsa block as shown, and paint the paper matt grey, reshaping the ventilators as necessary.

Cut a tiny rectangle of silver paper for the makers' label, paint a logo in red paint, and glue the label to the front of the heater as shown.

Apply glue to the back of the balsa block, and fit the convector heater into the heater space. Glue the assembled fireplace to the wall.

The 1960s Bed-Sitting Room
THE ROOM BOX
(Photograph pages 118–19)

The room box is made from the pattern in Fig 7 and the instructions in Chapter 2, with a window in the side wall but no chimney breast.

DECORATING

The Bed-Sitting Room has a white-painted ceiling and is papered with a commercial dolls-house wallpaper. The fitted carpet is a self-adhesive flocked paper. The skirting-board, painted white, is fitted after the room is decorated and carpeted.

LIGHTING

The lights are the same inexpensive fittings used in the 1950s sitting room, 'customised' with matching shades made in printed cotton trimmed with narrow braid, glued over the original shades.

FIXTURES

KITCHENETTE CORNER
(photograph pages 118–19)

We have fitted a pelmet of 1/2in woodstrip, veneered with Microwood self-adhesive veneer and glued to the ceiling. A printed cotton curtain is gathered and glued behind the pelmet to screen a 'kitchenette' corner of the bed-sitting room, which contains a cupboard unit.

The double cupboard unit is made from the pattern Fig 90 and instructions in Chapter 7, in 1/8in wood veneered with Microwood and omitting the door frames. The worktop is covered with patterned Fablon (or similar self-adhesive plastic) and has a cut-out to accommodate a sink made from a small plastic butter or jam container. A piece of matching patterned plastic is stuck to the wall behind the cupboard as a splashback.

FURNITURE

DISPLAY-SHELF UNIT
(Fig 75, photograph pages 118–19)

The display shelves are made in 1/8in wood faced with self-adhesive veneer – we have used Microwood – in a light colour for the inner faces of the sides and the shelves, and a darker colour for the outer faces of the sides.

Cut a pair of sides and veneer both faces. Paint (or veneer) the front edges as required – we have used acrylic paint to match the lighter veneer.

Cut five shelves, ensuring that they are exactly the same width. Veneer both surfaces and paint (or veneer) the front edges of each shelf.

Cut three shelf dividers, veneer both surfaces and paint (or veneer) the front edges. Cut the shelf back and veneer the inside surface.

Assemble the shelf unit from the bottom upwards. Glue the bottom two shelves to one side. Glue the divider and the shelf back in place. Glue the next shelf, divider, shelf, divider and top shelf in place.

Then glue the second side on to the assembly. (Note, that you may find it helpful to cut cardboard spacers from the pattern to assemble the shelves accurately.)

When the glue is thoroughly dry, polish the shelf unit as required.

SIDEBOARD *(Fig 76, photograph pages 118–19)*

The sideboard is made in 1/8in wood with sliding doors made in 1/32in wood and a back in 1/16in wood. The carcase and doors are faced with self-adhesive veneer – we have used Microwood – in a dark colour for the carcase and a light colour for the doors. The doors have small wooden doorknobs and slide in a frame of 1/4in double-grooved reeded moulding.

Cut four front door-frame pieces in double-grooved moulding with mitred corners as shown in Fig 76a. Glue and assemble the top, bottom and one side of the front door frame ensuring that the assembly is absolutely square and allow to dry.

Cut two doors from the pattern in ¹/₃₂in wood (note, that the doors are not the same size). Veneer the front face of each door and paint the edges to match if required. Cut two support strips for each door in ¹/₃₂in woodstrip and glue on to the back of the door as shown. Drill holes in the front of each door and glue doorknobs in place.

Fit the smaller door (A) into the front groove of the door frame, and the larger door (B) into the back groove. Ensure that both doors slide easily. Glue the second side of the door frame in place and allow to dry.

Cut the sideboard base, top and two sides in ¹/₈in wood.

Glue the assembled door frame to the front edge of the base. Glue the sides on to the base to fit behind the door frame. Glue the top on to the sides to fit behind the door frame.

Cut the back in ¹/₁₆in wood and glue on to the assembly as shown.

Cut veneer to fit and apply to the sides and top of the carcase. If required, paint a wash of colour on the back and underside of the carcase.

Cut two legs and one stretcher in ¹/₈in wood. Paint if required and glue the stretcher between the legs. Glue the legs and stretcher to the underside of the carcase as shown. Finish the sideboard with a coat of wax polish.

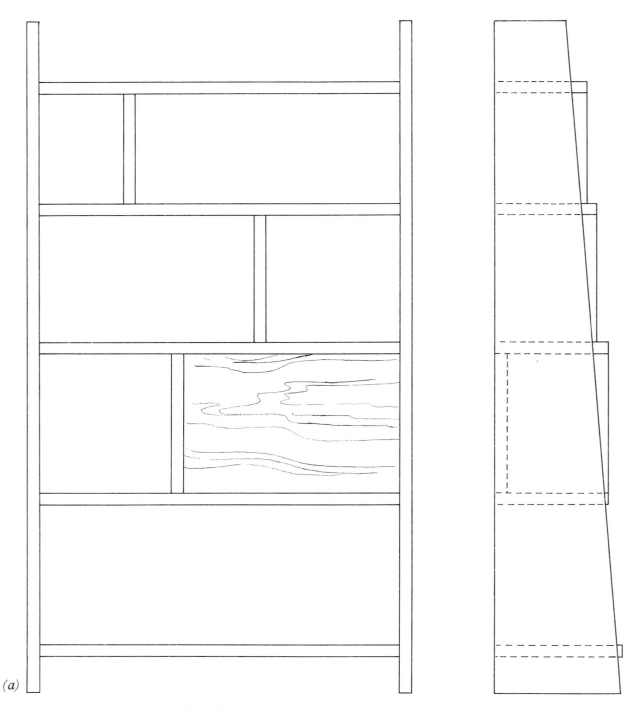

(a)

Fig 75 (a) Pattern and (b) assembly for the display-shelf unit

The sofa could belong to any time in the twentieth century, but the coffee table is unmistakably '50s

(b)

111

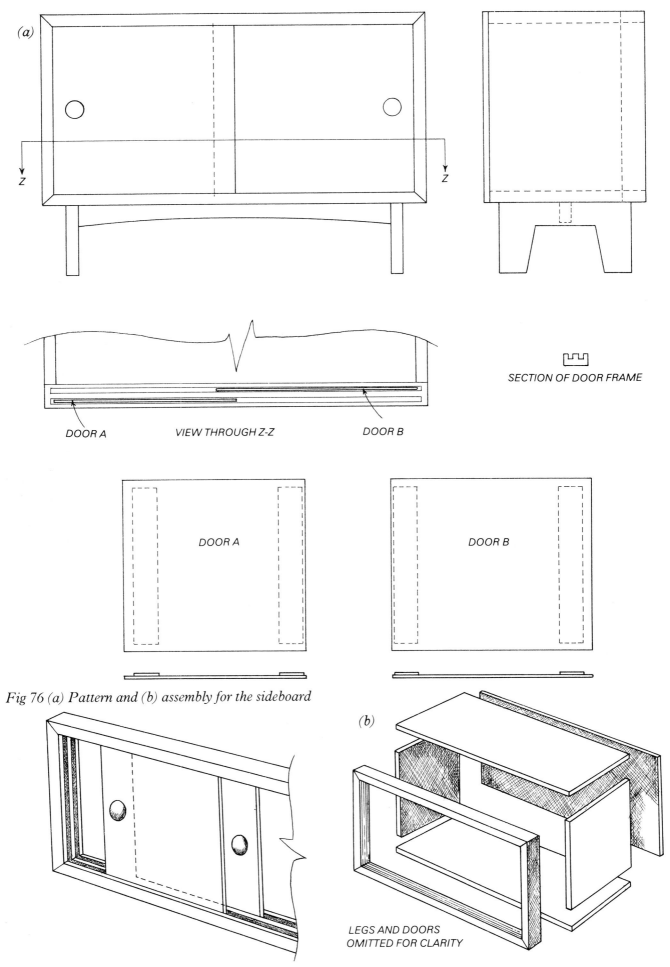

SECTION OF DOOR FRAME

DOOR A

VIEW THROUGH Z-Z

DOOR B

DOOR A

DOOR B

Fig 76 (a) Pattern and (b) assembly for the sideboard

LEGS AND DOORS
OMITTED FOR CLARITY

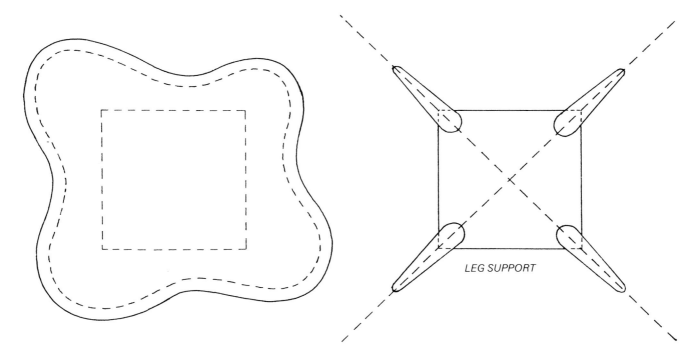

Fig 77 Pattern and leg-assembly guide for the free-form coffee table

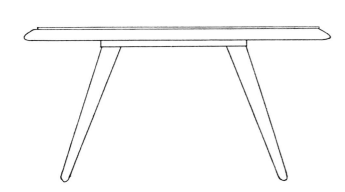

LEG SUPPORT

FREE-FORM COFFEE TABLE
(Fig 77, photograph page 111)

The top of the coffee table is made in 1/8in wood and faced with self-adhesive veneer – we have used Microwood. The legs can be sanded to shape from 1/4in diameter dowelling, or made from any suitable oddments of turned wood – we have used sections cut from inexpensive lace bobbins.

Trace the pattern for the table top on to the wood and cut out the shape roughly with a razor saw. Trim the curves with a Stanley knife and refine the shaping with sandpaper to form a bevelled edge as shown on the pattern.

Cut the leg support as a 1 1/2in square of 1/16in wood. Paint (or stain) the table top and the leg support – we used dark grey acrylic paint allowed to dry slowly to prevent warping.

Cut the veneer table top using the dotted line on the pattern as a guide. Position carefully and press firmly in place on the table top.

Cut four legs in dowelling and use a craft knife and sandpaper to shape the taper and round off the lower ends. Trim the top end of each leg to an angle of 10°,

so that the finished length of the leg is 1 5/8in. Check that the legs are the same length and the angle is uniform on all four. Paint or stain if required.

To assemble the table, make a guide for the leg alignment by drawing a cross on a sheet of paper and tape the leg support on to this cross with a corner angle on each line (see Fig 77). Sighting from above, glue the legs in place in each corner of the leg support, aligning with the guide, and allow to dry thoroughly.

Glue the leg assembly to the underside of the table top, centred as shown on the pattern, check that the table stands square and allow to dry. Finish the table with a coat of wax polish.

UPHOLSTERED SUITE
(Figs 78 and 79, photograph page 111)

The sofa and chair shown in the photograph have covers in a blue-green woven fabric which resembles moquette and is typical of the 1950s. These patterns, however, can be used with different fabrics to make upholstered furniture suitable for any sitting room from the 1920s to the present day.

You will need 1/2in and 1/4in thick balsa wood block for the basic construction, and 1/8in foam and 1/4in wadding (batting) for the upholstery. Fabric for the covers should be light or medium weight, woven with a slight stretch so that the covers will fit smoothly, and something which does not fray badly, eg cotton, fine wool, or fine velour. Edges can be sealed with Fraycheck (or similar) before cutting if necessary. To make matching covers for a sofa and two armchairs you will need approximately 1/2yd

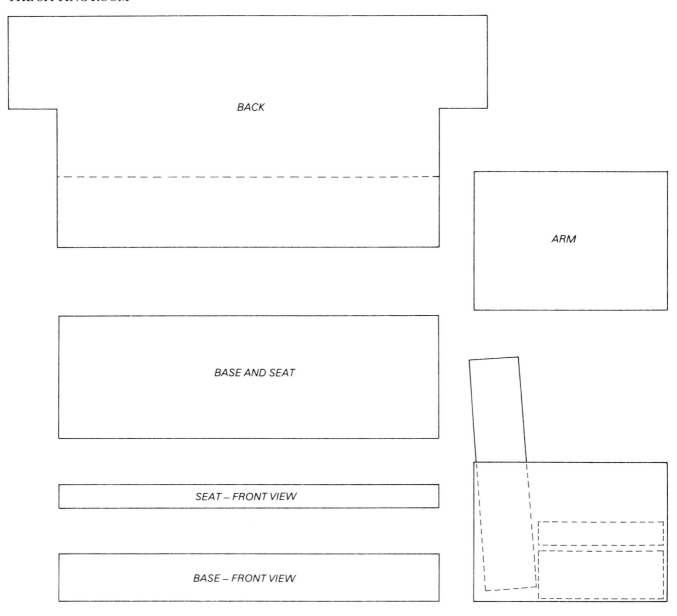

*Fig 78 Pattern and assembly guide for the
upholstered sofa*

(metre) of fabric. You will also need approximately
2yd of bonding tape (eg Wondaweb) and scraps of
medium-weight iron-on interfacing (eg Vilene), and a
fabric glue. Feet for the sofa and chairs are wooden or
plastic beads, and you will need four for each piece.

To make the sofa (Fig 78), cut one back, two arms
and one base in ¼in balsa. Seal the end-grain of each
piece with balsa cement or glue and allow to dry.

Cut two backs, four arms, one base and one base
front in foam. Cut one back and one seat in wadding
(batting). Trim the back piece to the dotted line
shown on the pattern.

Glue the foam pieces to each face of the corresponding balsa blocks with fabric glue. Glue the wadding
(batting) over the foam on one face of the back and
seat and allow to dry thoroughly.

Cut the back cover (Fig 80), on the straight-grain of
the fabric – noting the folded edge – and snip into the
corners (A) as shown on the pattern.

Using Fig 78 as a guide, add a seam allowance of
¼in all round, and cut covers in folded fabric (with
the fold at the bottom edge of each piece) for the arms,
base and seat on the straight-grain of the fabric.

Cover the padded balsa blocks, wrapping the fabric
so that it fits tightly. Apply glue sparingly to the balsa
and secure the long edges first, and allow to dry. Fold
mitred corners, as if wrapping a parcel, and glue the
remaining edges in place. Secure with dressmakers'
pins or elastic bands until the glue is dry, as shown in
Fig 81.

Cut three 9 × 1in strips of fabric on the straight-
grain. Cut three 9 × ½in strips of Vilene. Centre
each Vilene strip on a fabric strip (wrong side), turn
in the long edges, press and secure the raw edges with
Wondaweb. Seal one short end of each strip with
Fraycheck and trim square.

Secure the sealed end of a fabric strip to one arm of
the sofa with pins and, beginning at the centre of one

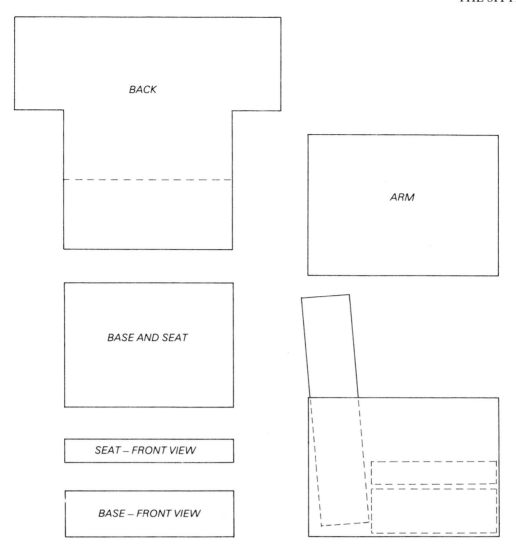

Fig 79 Pattern and assembly guide for the
upholstered chair

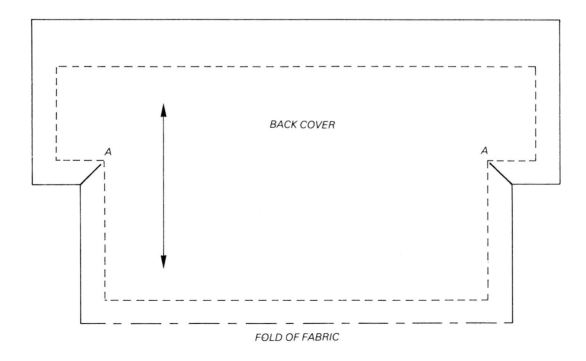

Fig 80 Pattern for the back cover for the sofa

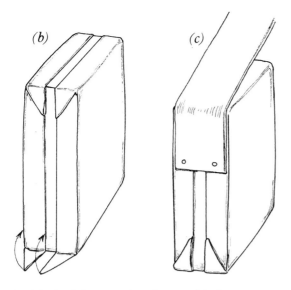

Fig 81 Method for covering the seat block

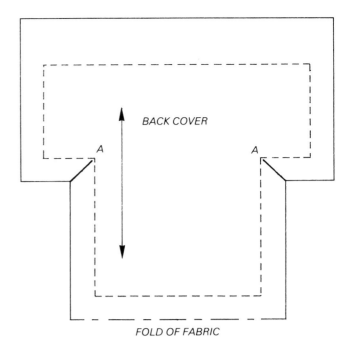

BACK COVER

A   A

FOLD OF FABRIC

Fig 82 Pattern for the back cover for the chair

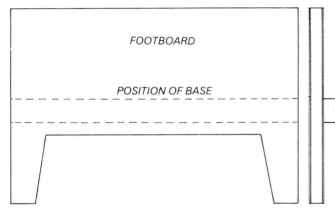

FOOTBOARD

POSITION OF BASE

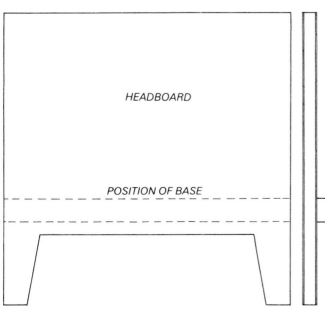

HEADBOARD

POSITION OF BASE

Fig 83 Pattern for the divan bed footboard and headboard

side, stretch and glue the strip around the edges of the arm (Fig 81c). Trim the end, secure with pins, seal the cut end and allow to dry. Repeat for the other arm.

Glue the third fabric strip to the back, in the same way as the arms, with the ends secured at points (A) shown on the pattern.

To assemble the sofa, glue the seat on to the base, matching the fabric joins to the back. Check that the ends of both pieces are aligned and leave to dry.

Following the guide in Fig 78, glue one arm to the seat assembly. When the glue is almost dry, apply glue to the back and side of the seat assembly and position the back and the second arm. Check that the assembly is square and the back slopes slightly away from the seat as shown. Secure temporarily with pins pushed into the balsa and allow to dry thoroughly.

Glue (and pin) bead feet to the underside of the arms in each corner of the sofa.

The chair (Fig 79 and back cover Fig 82) is made in the same way as the sofa.

DIVAN BED *(Fig 83, photograph pages 118–19)*

The bed is made in ⅛in wood, faced with self-adhesive veneer (Microwood) and has a base of ¼in balsa wood block.

Cut a base 6 × 3in in ¼in balsa block.

Cut the headboard and footboard in ⅛in wood with a small razor saw and craft knife. Face both sides of each piece with veneer and paint the edges if required to match.

Mark the position of the base on both headboard and footboard and glue the base to the headboard, ensuring that the pieces form a right angle. Apply pressure as the glue dries.

Glue the footboard to the base, ensuring that the bed stands square and apply pressure as the glue dries. Polish the headboard and the footboard as required.

SMALL COFFEE TABLE
(Fig 84, photograph pages 118–19)

The coffee table is made in 1/8in wood veneered with Microwood self-adhesive veneer.

Cut one top 2¾ × 1½in, and two legs with a razor saw and craft knife and veneer both sides of each piece. Paint the edges of each piece to match if required.

Glue the legs to the underside of the top as shown and apply pressure as the glue dries.

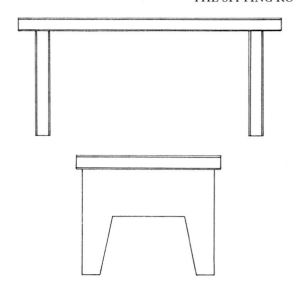

Fig 84 Pattern for the small coffee table

ACCESSORIES

CURTAINS AND BOX PELMET
(Fig 85, photograph pages 118–19)

The curtains and fabric-covered box pelmet shown in the 1950s sitting room are made in hand-printed cotton (see page 118 for instructions on printing fabrics) – any lightweight cotton fabric would be suitable, and you will also need thin, stiff cardboard and ½ × ¼in and ½ × 3/16in balsa wood for the pelmet. We have added a piece of sheer net curtain, hung from the pelmet behind the (non-closing) cotton curtains. The measurements on the pattern and given below in brackets are for the window in our sitting room, but the method can easily be adapted to fit any window.

Cut two curtains to fit the window, taking care to

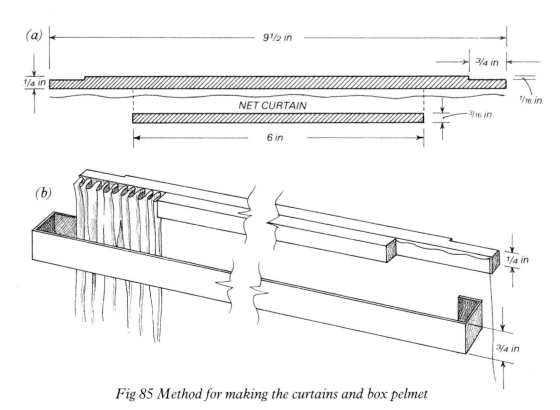

Fig 85 Method for making the curtains and box pelmet

match any horizontal pattern. Fold narrow hems on both sides and a slightly larger hem at the bottom end of each curtain, press and secure the hems with fabric glue. Run two or three gathering threads through the top of each curtain and draw up to an even (1¾in) width. Pin the curtains on the ironing board, set the folds by hovering a steam iron above them and leave to dry.

Cut a piece (9½in long) in ½ × ¼in balsa and cut ¾in long slots on the back edge, ¹/₁₆in deep, as shown on the pattern.

Cut net curtain if required, seal the edges with Fraycheck, and glue the top edge to the front of the balsa strip.

Cut a (6in long) piece of ½ × ³/₁₆in balsa and glue to the centre front of the longer balsa strip, sandwiching the top edge of the net curtain.

Glue the top edge of each curtain to the balsa strip, either side of the centre strip, as shown in Fig 85b and leave to dry.

Cut a piece of stiff card (12½ × ¾in) and a piece of fabric (12½ × 1½in). Centre the card on the fabric, and fold and glue the long fabric edges to the back of the card.

Score the back of the fabric-covered card ¾in from each end, and again ¾in from the first line, to bend each end to fit around the balsa strip, forming the box pelmet.

Glue the back of the pelmet and fit it in place over the curtains and around the balsa strip, securing the ends in the slots in the back of the strip, and allow to dry.

Glue the back of the pelmet to the wall above the window.

PRINTED FABRIC (photograph pages 118–19)

The following method for printing with acrylic paint has been used to pattern the fabric for the curtains in the 1950s sitting room and is particularly useful if you cannot find a suitable period pattern or the colours you want. It can also be used to print wallpaper or heavier fabrics for rugs and carpets. You will need sufficient fabric for the curtains or other items you may wish to make, with a little extra allowed for waste, and you may find it helpful to practise on some scrap fabric. The type of acrylic paints which are sold for fabric painting are the best to use and you will need several small potatoes to use as printing-stamps. We have used cotton curtain-lining fabric, printed with two pattern elements in turquoise and coral-pink, and added detail with a black felt pen. Scraps of fabric have been used to make cushions.

Tape the fabric squarely on to a drawing or cutting board with masking tape, so that it is taut. Cut the potatoes in half and cut a simple pattern into the potato with a craft knife. Remove the area of potato around the pattern so that you have a raised 'stamp' on the cut end of each piece. Each stamp will be a different element of the pattern and you can make as

The 1960s Bed-Sitting Room was every teenagers' dream of independence – but it was not usually this tidy!

many of them as you wish, but effective patterns can be made with just two or three shapes.

Mix the paint colours in individual saucers, then dip the potato in paint and press it on to the fabric using a level up-and-down movement to apply the pattern.

If you want a regular pattern, mark lines on the fabric with a ruler and Fadeaway vanishing marker pen and apply the first (largest) shape in the first colour, evenly spaced on the marked lines. Stamp the second pattern in the second colour evenly in the spaces.

When the painted patterns are dry, use felt pens to add detail to the shapes and extra detail to the pattern. Iron the fabric on the wrong side to set the colours when the paint is dry.

PRINTED RUG *(Fig 86, photograph page 111)*

The rug is made in plain-coloured heavyweight woven fabric, or medium-weight fabric backed with iron-on interfacing, eg Vilene, and the pattern is painted with acrylic paints. Our rug is made in cream calico with a pattern in coral-pink, turquoise and black.

Draw the outline of the rug squarely on the grain of the fabric and seal the long edges with Fraycheck, allowed to dry before cutting out. Pull threads to fringe both short ends of the rug.

Trace the design lightly in pencil and paint with acrylic colours, using the paint as dry as possible and allowing each colour to dry before applying the next. If the rug does not have sufficient weight to lie flat, iron interfacing (or carpet tape) on to the underside.

FUR RUG *(photograph pages 118–19)*

The fur rug is made from a scrap of fur fabric with a medium-length pile.

Trace the pattern for the coffee table top (Fig 77) on to the back of the fur fabric and cut out with small sharp scissors, taking care to snip through the backing fabric only and not the pile. Seal the edge with Fraycheck if necessary and brush the pile smooth with an old toothbrush or similar.

ELECTRIC FIRE AND RECORD PLAYER *(photograph pages 118–19)*

The electric fire and record player are made from white-metal kits, painted with metal primer and enamel paints. The element of the fire was painted bright orange and we glued a fine plastic-covered wire to the back to represent the flex. We cut covers for the records (supplied with the kit) from magazine illustrations.

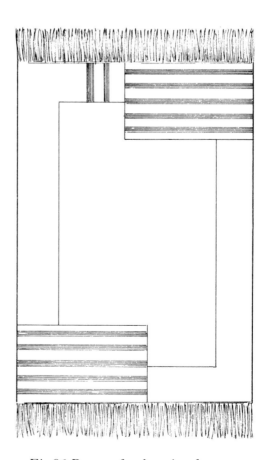

Fig 86 Pattern for the printed rug

CHAPTER SEVEN

The Town Kitchen

The two rooms in this chapter demonstrate how furniture with a similar painted finish can be used for very different period kitchens.

The 'designer' kitchen is completely modern with its bright yellow walls, vinyl flooring and automatic washing machine; while the dolls-house kitchen is firmly set in the nineteenth century, dated by its open range and oil lighting. The furniture in both rooms is painted blue with an 'aged' finish and looks completely appropriate in both settings.

In the Modern Kitchen, fitted units are built in along one wall to accommodate the sink, the washing machine and the Aga cooker, and painted to match the furniture. Modern accessories such as the eco-friendly washing powder and the cork notice board give the room character. The Victorian Kitchen is also used as a dining-room and the atmosphere, though cosy, is more formal.

THE ROOM BOX

(Fig 87, photograph pages 122–3)

The room box is made from the pattern in Fig 87, as for the 1950s Sitting Room in Chapter 6, except for the window on the back wall.

WINDOW (Fig 88)

The window projects ⅛in beyond the back wall to create a realistic impression of depth. The window opening is faced with ½ × ⅛in and ⅛in square woodstrip and framed with ¼in moulding. The window can be glazed with glass or perspex which should be 2mm (¹⁄₁₆in) thick, or less. Our window is 3¼ × 3¾in. It is easier to assemble the window-frames in pre-painted wood, and neater to decorate the room before the window-frame is glued in place.

Face the top, bottom and sides of the window opening with ½ × ⅛in woodstrip to fit flush with the inside and project on the outside wall.

Make a frame of ⅛in square strip, glued into the opening to fit flush with the outside edge.

Fit the glazing in place and glue a second frame of ⅛in square strip into the opening, butted against the glass (see Fig 88b).

After the room is decorated, cut a window-frame of ¼in moulding with mitred corners, paint and glue the window-frame to the wall around the window opening butted against the inner frame (see Fig 88c).

DECORATING: MODERN KITCHEN

We papered the ceiling of the Modern Kitchen with lining paper and applied a coat of white emulsion paint.

The walls were papered with golden-yellow artists' watercolour paper, pasted with household wallpaper paste, and an area of tiles cut from a magazine illustration was glued to the wall behind the Aga. The skirting-boards, painted to match the furniture, were glued in place after the fitted furniture units.

VINYL FLOORING

The floor in the Modern Kitchen is made from a self-adhesive vinyl floor tile. There are several types of these floor tiles available from DIY shops, which can be bought individually in a fairly wide range of colours. Choose the thinnest type you can find – these are usually the cheapest brands.

The floor can be made all in one piece, though if it is an awkward shape you may find it easier to make a paper template of the floor area to use as a pattern. Alternatively, the tile can be cut into strips using a craft knife and metal ruler, and laid to represent vinyl flooring from the roll.

If you use two tiles in different colours they can be cut into 1in or 1½in squares, and laid in a chequer-board pattern. The self-adhesive backing will stick to any clean dry surface so the tiles can be laid directly on to the floor, but if you find this awkward cut a paper template and stick the tiles on to the paper and when the floor is complete, glue the paper backing to the floor with UHU or similar tacky craft glue.

*A Modern Kitchen in 'designer' style with all the
desirable clichés, including an Aga and carefully 'aged'
painted furniture*

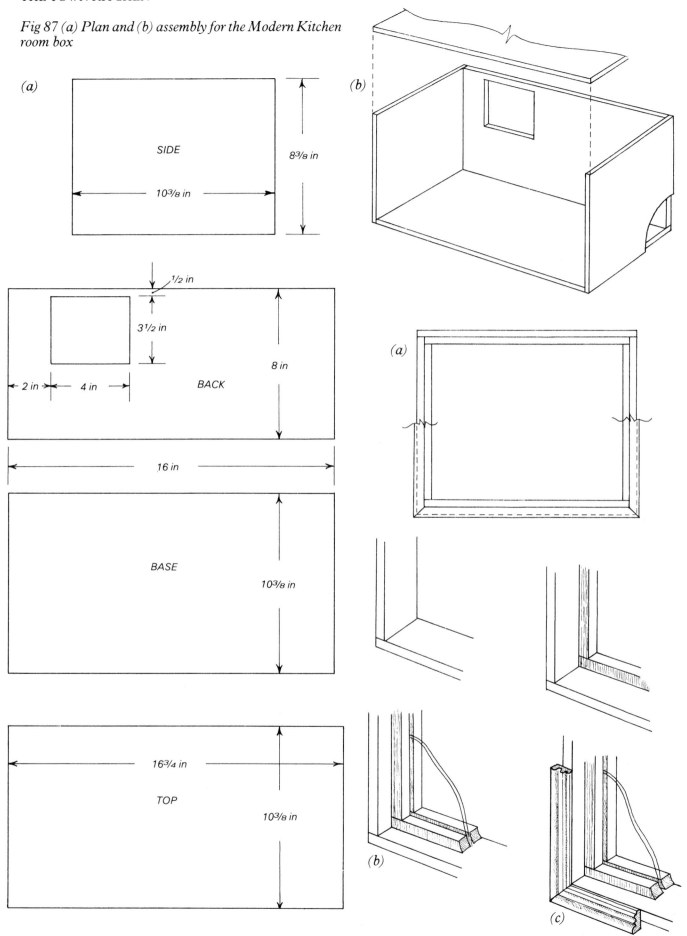

Fig 87 (a) Plan and (b) assembly for the Modern Kitchen room box

(a)

SIDE

$8^{3}/_{8}$ in

$10^{3}/_{8}$ in

$^{1}/_{2}$ in

$3^{1}/_{2}$ in

8 in

2 in   4 in   BACK

16 in

BASE

$10^{3}/_{8}$ in

$16^{3}/_{4}$ in

TOP

$10^{3}/_{8}$ in

(b)

(a)

(b)

(c)

Fig 88 Pattern and assembly for the window

LIGHTING

The pendant light is wired through a hole in the ceiling to a transformer.

DECORATING: VICTORIAN KITCHEN
(photograph pages 134–5)

The Victorian Kitchen in the dolls' house has a built-in cupboard made as the larder in Chapter 3. It is fitted into the alcove beside the chimney breast, be-hind a partition wall with a hinged door. The room is papered with a dolls-house wallpaper and floored with a tile-patterned floor paper. The picture-rail, skirting-board, doors and architrave were painted to represent pine before fixing in place (see Chapter 2 page 34).

The oil lamp is wired into the copper tape system in the house. The shelf on brackets (see Chapter 3 page 57) is painted cream and glued to the wall above the fireplace opening which houses a kitchen-range made from a white-metal kit. The kitchen-range is shown on pages 26–7.

FIXTURES

The fitted cupboard and drawer units in the Modern Kitchen are made individually and assembled on a common plinth, cut to fit the required space. The worktop, with a hole to accommodate the sink, is cut to fit on to the assembled units. In our kitchen there are single cupboard, double cupboard and drawer units and a slot for trays (and a washing machine), with a common plinth and worktop to the left of the Aga cooker and a separate double cupboard to the right of the Aga.

We have painted the units with blue acrylic paint and fitted small white-painted brass knobs. If you intend to use a similar painted finish, it can be applied after assembly as only the outside surfaces of each unit are painted. If you prefer woodstain or an acrylic-paint wash to resemble pine (see Chapter 2 page 34), the wood should be stained or painted before cutting to avoid warping. The plinth was painted black and the worktop paint-washed to represent pine.

We have used an Aga cooker (see Acknowledgements), which is available in all Aga colours as a kit (or ready-made to order) in the type illustrated and in an older style. We chose dark green to complement the blue and yellow colour scheme in this kitchen. Instructions for the washing machine are given below. It is designed to fit between two units and is assembled on the common plinth.

SINGLE CUPBOARD UNIT
(Fig 89, photograph pages 122–3)

This cupboard is made in 1/16in wood, and 1/8in square, 1/8 × 1/4in, 1/8 × 1/16in and 1/4 × 1/16in woodstrips. The door opens with two 1/4in butt hinges and has a small knob.

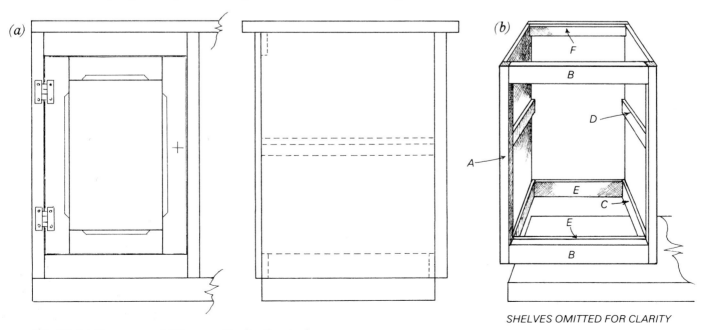

SHELVES OMITTED FOR CLARITY

Fig 89 (a) Pattern and (b) assembly for the single cupboard unit

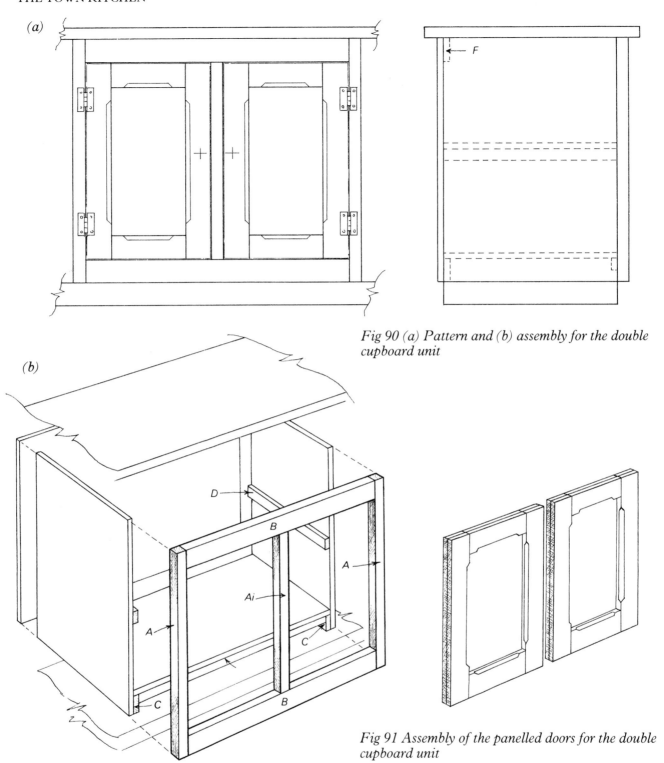

(a)

Fig 90 *(a) Pattern and (b) assembly for the double cupboard unit*

(b)

Fig 91 *Assembly of the panelled doors for the double cupboard unit*

Cut two front-frame sides (A) in 1/8in square woodstrip, and a front-frame top and bottom (B) in 1/8 × 1/4in strip. Glue and assemble the front frame as shown.

Cut two sides in 1/16in wood and glue the sides behind the front frame.

Cut two bottom-shelf supports (C) in 1/4 × 1/16in strip and glue to the bottom inside edges of the sides.

Cut two shelf supports (D) in 1/8 × 1/16in strip and glue to the sides as shown on the pattern.

Cut two shelves to fit in 1/16in wood and glue on to

the shelf supports.

Cut the back in 1/16in wood and glue on to the sides and shelves.

Cut two bottom-shelf supports (E) and glue in place under the bottom shelf.

Cut the top back support (F) and glue in place across the top edge of the back.

Cut the door panel in 1/16in wood to fit into the front frame. Cut the door-frame top, bottom and sides in 1/4 × 1/16in strip, glue the door frame on to the door panel and leave to dry.

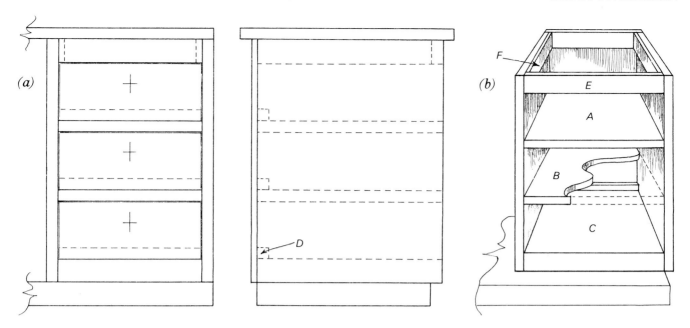

Fig 92 (a) Pattern and (b) assembly for the drawer unit

Measure ⅛in from each corner and chamfer the inner edges of the door frame as shown. Drill a hole to receive the doorknob.

Paint the cupboard, fit the doorknob and hinge the door on to the front frame with superglue.

DOUBLE CUPBOARD UNIT
(Fig 90, photograph pages 122–3)

Materials are as for the single cupboard, with four butt hinges and two knobs.

Cut two front-frame sides (A) and one vertical divider (Ai) in ⅛in square strip. Cut the front-frame top and bottom in ¼ × ⅛in strip. Glue and assemble the front frame as shown.

Cut two sides in 1/16in wood and glue the sides behind the front frame.

Cut two bottom-shelf supports (C) in ¼ × 1/16in strip and glue to the bottom inside edge of the sides.

Cut two shelf supports (D) in ⅛ × 1/16in strip and glue to the sides as shown on the pattern.

Cut two shelves to fit in 1/16in wood and glue on to the shelf supports.

Cut the back in 1/16in wood and glue on to the sides and shelves.

Cut two bottom-shelf supports (E) and glue in place under the bottom shelf.

Cut the top back support (F) and glue in place across the top edge of the back.

Cut two door panels in 1/16in wood to fit into the front frame. Cut the door-frame pieces in ¼ × 1/16in strip, glue the door frames to the doors as shown in Fig 91 and leave to dry.

Measure ⅛in from each corner and chamfer the inner edges of the door frames as shown. Drill holes to receive the knobs.

Paint the cupboard with acrylic paint, fit the doorknobs and hinge the doors on to the front frame with superglue.

DRAWER UNIT *(Fig 92, photograph pages 122–3)*

The drawer unit is made in ¼in, ⅛in and 1/16in wood. You will also need ¼ × ⅛in, ¼ × 1/16in woodstrip and ⅛in square woodstrip, and three drawer knobs.

Cut two sides and two drawer dividers (A and B) in ⅛in wood. Cut the base (C) in ¼in wood.

Cut three drawer stops (D) in ⅛in square strip and glue to the back edges of the drawer dividers and base as shown.

Glue the base to the inside bottom edge of one side, ensuring that it is at a right angle, and allow to dry.

Turn the assembly on to one side, and using a spacer cut from scrap wood, glue the drawer dividers to the side and allow to dry.

Glue the other side to the base and the drawer dividers.

Cut the back in 1/16in wood and glue on to the sides, drawer dividers and base.

Cut the top front (E) in ¼ × ⅛in strip and glue between the sides, flush with the top edge.

Cut two drawer slides (F) in ¼ × 1/16in strip and glue to the inner sides, flush with the top edge.

Cut three drawer fronts in 1/16in wood to fit the drawer openings. Cut the bottom, back and sides for each drawer in 1/16in wood.

Glue the drawer bottom behind the front. Glue the drawer sides on to the bottom behind the front. Glue the back to the sides and bottom as shown in Fig 93.

Drill holes to receive the drawer knobs, paint the drawer unit and fit the knobs.

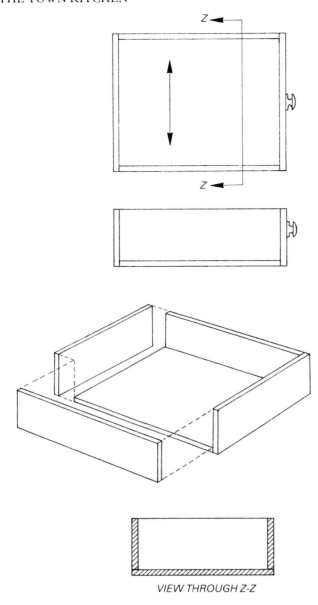

VIEW THROUGH Z-Z

Fig 93 Assembly of the drawers for the drawer unit

PLINTH

The assembled cupboard and drawer units are glued on to a common plinth, cut in ¼in thick wood to fit. In our kitchen the plinth is 9¼in long to accommodate the units, the washing machine and a slot for trays. The washing machine is assembled between two units and requires a gap of 2in. Our tray slot is ¾in wide.

Cut the plinth to the required size and paint the front and side edges. Glue the units on to the plinth, to overhang at the front by ⅛in and at the back by ¹⁄₁₆in.

WASHING MACHINE
(Fig 94, photograph page 130)

The washing machine is designed to fit into a 2in gap between fitted units, and is glued on to the common plinth. It is supported on a frame of ⅛ × ¼in and ⅛in square woodstrip glued to the units at either side. (If you prefer to make the washing machine free-standing, adapt the method by adding side panels.) The front and back panels (and sides if required) are made in Plasticard – a rigid, white plasticised card which is ¹⁄₃₂in thick. Plasticard is available from most craft suppliers. The washing-machine drum is a plastic bottle cap or similar with a diameter of approximately 1½in – we used the cap from a bottle of washing liquid. The (non-opening) door is made from a 1⅛in diameter washer painted white, with a window cut from rigid transparent plastic (eg the lid from a margarine tub). The control panel is cut from a magazine illustration.

To make the support frame (Fig 95), cut two sides (A) and the top and bottom (B) in ¼ × ⅛in woodstrip. Glue the frame pieces to the units at either side of the gap, set back ¹⁄₁₆in from the front, as shown.

Cut the washing machine front panel in Plasticard to fit snugly into the gap. Cut out the window hole, following the dotted line on the pattern.

Paint the washer with white gloss (acrylic or enamel paint) and glue it on to the front of the panel to frame the cut-out. Cut the window in transparent plastic to fit into the cut-out and glue it on to the back of the panel.

Tuck fabric scraps into the drum to represent washing and glue the drum to the back of the panel as shown.

Glue the control panel in place on the front of the panel and varnish or cover with transparent Fablon (or a similar self-adhesive plastic), if required.

Paint a plastic or cardboard scrap grey or silver and glue on to the door to represent a handle. Draw the outline of the filter-door in pen, or glue on a Plasticard cut-out as required.

Glue the assembled front on to the support frame.

Cut four back support pieces in ⅛in square strip and glue to the units at either side of the washing machine, set back ¹⁄₁₆in from the back. Cut a back panel in Plasticard (or ¹⁄₁₆in wood scrap) to fit and glue on to the back support frame.

TRAY SLOT *(Fig 96)*

The tray slot is made to fit into a gap left between fitted units glued on to a common plinth. The method can be adapted to make a slot of any width required to store trays or fit a wine-rack – ours is ¾in wide.

Cut and glue supports of ⅛in square woodstrip to the sides of the units at either side of the slot, set back ¹⁄₁₆in from the back edge.

Cut a back panel to fit in ¹⁄₁₆in wood, paint as required. Apply glue to the supports and slide the back panel into place against the supports.

Cut a base to fit in ¹⁄₁₆in wood, paint as required and glue the base on to the plinth.

Cut a front arch to fit, and glue between the units, flush with the front edges.

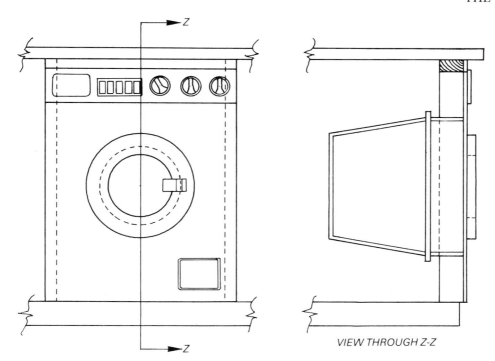

Fig 94 Pattern for the washing machine

VIEW THROUGH Z-Z

Fig 96 Assembly for the tray slot

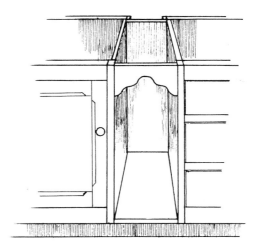

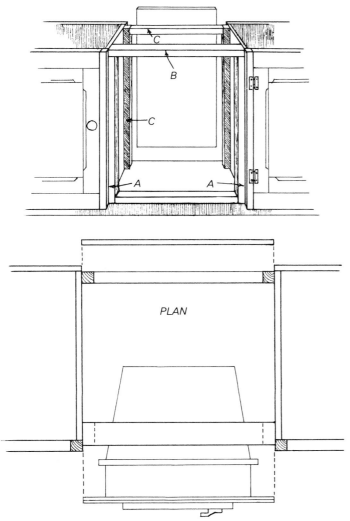

PLAN

Fig 95 Assembly for the washing machine and support frame

WORKTOP

The worktop is made in 1/8in wood, painted as required, to fit on to the assembled units with an overhang of 1/8in at the front edge. Where the worktop fits against the wall, the side is flush with the unit – the side abutting the Aga overhangs the unit by 1/8in. The worktop has a cut-out hole over the double cupboard unit to accommodate the sink. Our sink is a white plastic container of the type used for individual portions of butter or jam (from hotels or service stations etc). If you wish, the container can be painted with silver enamel paint to represent stainless steel. We have used a pair of commercial brass taps.

Cut the worktop in 1/8in wood to fit and sand the front and overhanging side edges so they are slightly

129

Simple crockery and accessories for the Modern Kitchen, including eco-friendly powder for the washing machine

rounded. Paint as required (we have used a pine acrylic-paint wash) and mark the cut-out for the sink to fit the container. Cut out the hole with a fretsaw or Stanley knife and glue the container in place.

Glue the worktop on to the units. Drill holes in the back corners of the sink into the worktop, and glue the taps in place.

COOKER HOOD *(Fig 97, photograph pages 122–3)*

The cooker hood is made in one piece with a flue, cut to fit the height of the kitchen ceiling. Measurements given below and on the pattern are to fit the ceiling in our kitchen which is 8in high – the pattern should be adjusted as necessary for other heights. You will need 1/16in wood, 1/16 × 1/4in woodstrip and 5/16in moulding

for the cooker hood and flue, and 5mm (1/8in) balsa wood block (or Foamcore) for the support. We have painted the cooker hood with blue acrylic paint and papered the flue to match the kitchen wall.

Cut a front panel (A) 3 1/8in wide × 1 3/4in high, in 1/16in wood. Shape the curved lower edge with a fretsaw or craft knife and sandpaper.

Cut two front sides (B) in 1/16 × 1/4in woodstrip and shape the lower ends as shown. Glue the front sides to the front panel.

Cut a support (C) 3 1/8 × 3/4in, in balsa (or Foamcore) and glue to the back of the front assembly as shown by the dotted line on the pattern.

Cut two sides in 1/16in wood and glue behind the front and to the support.

Cut moulding with mitred corners and glue to the front and sides as shown on the pattern.

Paint the assembly from the moulding downwards as for the cooker hood, and wallpaper above the moulding as for the flue. Glue the completed cooker hood to the wall above the Aga.

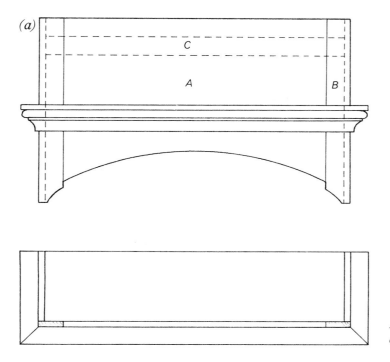

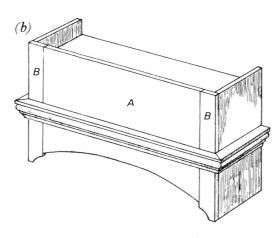

Fig 97 (a) Pattern and (b) assembly for the cooker hood and flue

FURNITURE

DRESSER (Fig 98, photograph pages 122–3)

The kitchen dresser is made in two parts, top and base, which are glued together after assembly. Both parts are made in 1/8in and 1/16in wood with planked backs made from 1/2 × 3/32in woodstrip – we have used tongue and groove floorboarding. Woodstrip should be chamfered along one edge to resemble tongue and groove boards when butted together and you will need approximately 6ft to make the dresser. (If you prefer, the backs may be cut in 3/32in wood and scored to represent planking.) You will also need 1/8 × 1/16in, 1/8 × 1/4in, 1/8 × 3/16in and 1/16 × 1/4in woodstrip, 1/8in and 1/16in square woodstrip, and 1/8in and 3/16in mouldings. We have painted the outside of the dresser with blue acrylic paint, and the inside of the top to represent pine. If you use a similar finish, the dresser can be painted after assembly but you could paint pieces as you go along. If you prefer woodstain or a painted pine finish (see page 34), the wood should be stained before assembly or painted before cutting. We have used five small brass knobs, painted white to resemble china, for the cupboards and drawers. We hung the doors with four 1/4in butt hinges and fitted ten commercial cup hooks on the shelves.

THE DRESSER TOP (see assembly Fig 15a)

Cut, glue and butt ten planks of woodstrip to make a back panel 3 3/4in high × 4 5/8in wide.

Cut a top 3/4in deep and the same width as the back in 1/16in wood. Glue the top on to the back.

Cut two sides in 1/16in wood. Shape the curved front edges with a fretsaw or Stanley knife and sandpaper. Glue the sides to the back and top.

Cut back and side supports (A) in 1/16 × 1/4in woodstrip and glue to the bottom edge of the back and sides as shown.

Cut shelf supports (B) in 1/16 × 1/8in strip (and spacers in scrap wood) and glue to the sides as shown.

Cut two shelves in 1/16in wood, round off the front corners, and glue on to the shelf supports and to the back. (Note, that the bottom shelf is slightly deeper than the top shelf.)

Cut the top support (C) in 1/8 × 1/16in strip and glue to the top edge of the back.

Prepare a blank for the frieze in 1/8 × 1/4in strip, shape the curved edge and glue the frieze to the underside of the top, between the sides.

Cut 3/16in moulding with mitred corners and glue to the front and sides of the top. Drill holes into the front edge of the shelves and fit cup hooks (if required) with superglue after painting or polishing.

THE DRESSER BASE (Fig 98b)

Cut the front-frame top (D) in 1/8in square woodstrip. Cut the front-frame sides (E), bottom (F) and horizontal divider (G) in 1/8 × 1/4in strip.

Cut two short and two long vertical dividers (H and J) in 1/8 × 1/4in strip.

Assemble the front-frame pieces as shown and allow the glue to dry thoroughly.

Cut supports K and L as shown. Turn the front

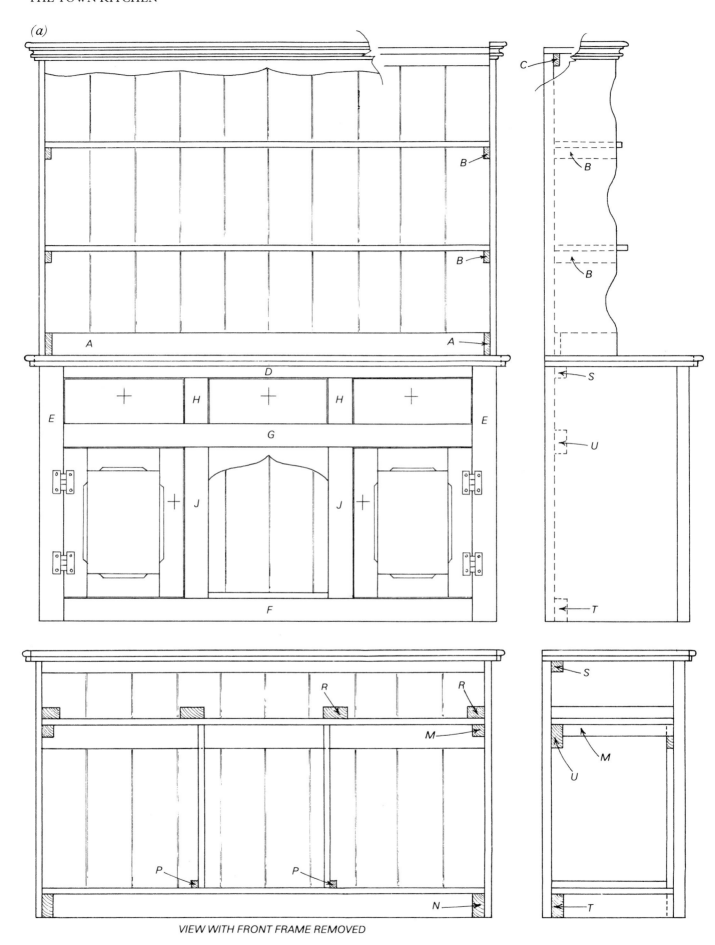

VIEW WITH FRONT FRAME REMOVED

Fig 98 (a) Pattern and (b) assembly for the dresser

(b)

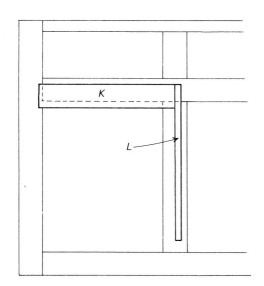

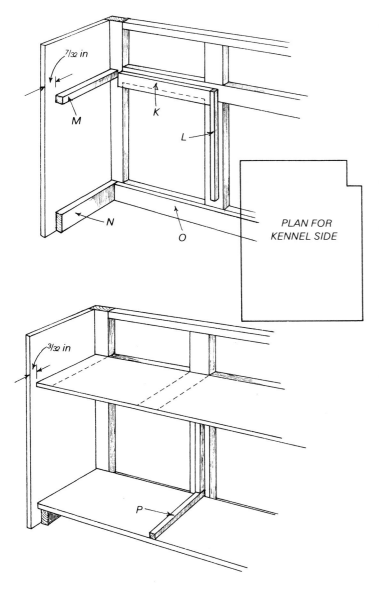

PLAN FOR
KENNEL SIDE

frame on to its face and glue the supports on to the back of the front frame at either side as shown in Fig 98b. (Note, that these pieces will support the drawer shelf and the front of the kennel.)

Cut two sides, $1\frac{3}{8} \times 2\frac{3}{4}$in, in $\frac{1}{16}$in wood and glue the sides on to the back of the front frame as shown in Fig 98b.

Cut two side drawer shelf supports (M) $1\frac{1}{4}$in long, in $\frac{1}{8}$in square strip and glue to the sides, with the top edge level with the front shelf support – to leave a gap of $\frac{7}{32}$in at the back edge.

Cut two side bottom-shelf supports (N) in $\frac{1}{8} \times \frac{1}{4}$in strip, and glue to the bottom edge of the sides, to leave a gap of $\frac{7}{32}$in at the back edge.

Cut the front bottom-shelf support (O) in $\frac{1}{16} \times \frac{1}{4}$in strip and glue behind the bottom edge of the front frame.

Cut two shelves $1\frac{3}{4}$in deep, in $\frac{1}{16}$in wood to fit on to the shelf supports leaving a gap of $\frac{3}{32}$in at the back edge. Glue the shelves on to the shelf supports.

Cut two kennel side supports (P) in $\frac{1}{16}$in square strip and glue on to the bottom shelf to finish flush at the back edge.

Using the pattern as a guide, cut a pair of kennel sides in $\frac{1}{16}$in wood and glue in place against the side supports, with notched edges to the back.

Cut two outer drawer dividers (R) in $\frac{1}{8} \times \frac{3}{16}$in strip, and two inner drawer dividers (R) in $\frac{1}{8} \times \frac{1}{4}$in strip. Glue the drawer dividers to the drawer shelf to line up behind the front frame as shown by the dotted line in Fig 98b.

Cut, glue and butt ten planks of woodstrip to make a back panel $2\frac{3}{4}$in high $\times 4\frac{5}{8}$in wide – checking that this fits perfectly between the sides.

Cut the top support (S) in $\frac{1}{8}$in square strip to fit across the back and glue to the inside top edge of the back.

Cut the bottom support (T) in $\frac{1}{8} \times \frac{1}{4}$in strip to fit across the back and glue to the inside bottom edge of the back.

Cut a back drawer shelf support (U) in $\frac{1}{8} \times \frac{1}{4}$in strip to fit across the back, and glue to the back to fit beneath the drawer shelf.

Glue the back in place between the sides and against the shelves. Cut a top $4\frac{7}{8} \times 1\frac{9}{16}$in, in $\frac{1}{8}$in wood and glue the top on to the carcase. Cut $\frac{1}{8}$in moulding with mitred corners, and glue to the front and side edges of the top.

Cut the kennel-arch in $\frac{1}{16}$in wood. Cut a support in $\frac{1}{8}$in square strip to fit and glue to the top back edge of the kennel-arch. Glue the kennel-arch in place to fit flush with the front frame. Cut a piece of $\frac{1}{8} \times \frac{1}{16}$in strip to fit and glue into the bottom front edge of the kennel.

Cut three drawer fronts in $\frac{1}{16}$in wood to fit the drawer spaces. Cut bottoms and sides for each drawer in $\frac{1}{16}$in wood. Glue the drawer bottom behind the front. Glue the drawer sides on to the bottom behind the front. Glue the back to the bottom and sides as shown in Fig 99. Drill holes in the fronts to receive the drawer knobs.

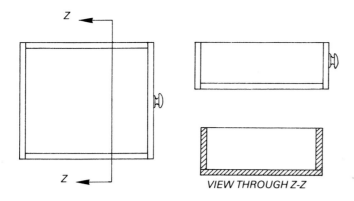

Z

Z

VIEW THROUGH Z-Z

Fig 99 Pattern and assembly for the dresser drawers

Cut two door panels in 1/16in wood to fit into the front frame. Cut door-frame pieces in 1/16 × 1/4in strip, glue the door frames on to the door panels and leave to dry. Measure 1/8in from each corner and chamfer the inner edge of the door frames as shown on the pattern. Drill holes to receive the doorknobs and glue the hinges to the doors and the front frame with superglue.

Glue the dresser top on to the base.

WALL-SHELVES
(Fig 100, photograph pages 134–5)

The wall-shelves are made in 1/16in wood with a back of 1/2 × 3/32in woodstrip planks – we have used tongue and groove floorboarding. Woodstrip should be chamfered along one edge to resemble tongue and groove when butted together and you will need approximately 3ft to make the shelves. You will also need 1/16 × 1/8in and 1/16 × 1/4in woodstrip, 3/16in moulding, and eight cup hooks if required. We painted the outside of the shelves with blue acrylic paint, and the inside to represent pine (see page 34). If you plan to use a similar finish, the shelves can be painted after assembly. If you prefer woodstain or an acrylic-wash pine finish, the wood should be stained or painted before cutting.

Cut, glue and butt seven planks of woodstrip to make a back panel 3 3/8in wide × 3 1/4in high.

Cut the top and bottom (both 3 3/8 × 3/4in), in 1/16in wood. Glue the top and bottom to the back with back edges flush.

Cut the back top support (A) in 1/16 × 1/8in strip and glue to the back and underside of the top.

Cut the back bottom support (B) in 1/16 × 1/4in strip and glue to the back and upper side of the bottom.

Cut the sides in 1/16in wood. Shape the curved edges with a fretsaw or Stanley knife and sandpaper. Glue the sides on to the back, top and bottom.

Cut the side bottom supports (C) in 1/16 × 1/4in strip and glue to the sides and bottom with front edges flush.

Cut four shelf supports (D) in 1/16 × 1/8in strip (and a spacer from scrap wood) and glue the shelf supports

*The Victorian Kitchen in the dolls' house, where the
fashion for painted furniture began and the 'ageing'
occurred naturally*

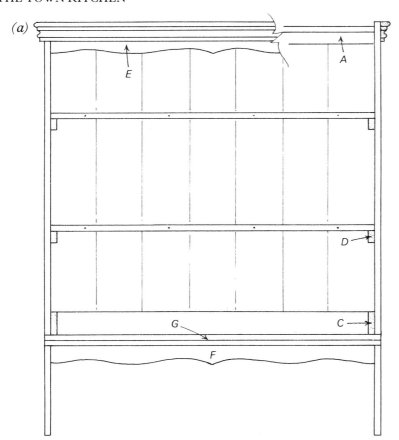

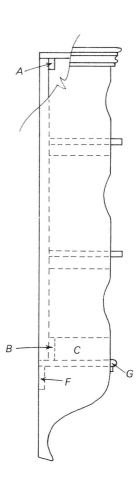

(a)

(b)

Fig 100 (a) Pattern and (b) assembly for the wall-shelves

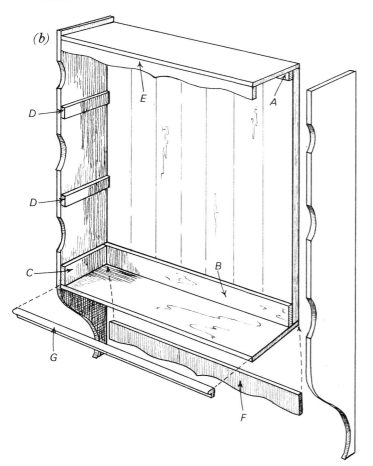

to the sides.

Cut two shelves ¾in deep in ¹⁄₁₆in wood and round off the front corners. Glue the shelves on to the supports and to the back.

Cut a blank for the frieze (E). Shape the curved edge with a fretsaw or craft knife and sandpaper, and glue the frieze beneath the front edge of the top, between the sides.

Cut a blank for the bottom frieze (F), shape the curved edge and glue the frieze beneath the back edge of the bottom, between the sides.

Cut ³⁄₁₆in moulding, with mitred corners, and glue to the front edge of the top, and top edge of the sides.

Cut ³⁄₁₆in moulding to fit (G), and glue across the full width of the bottom front edge.

Drill holes as required and fit cup hooks with superglue.

KITCHEN TABLE
(Fig 101, photograph pages 122–3)

Our table top is made from ⅛ × ⅜in woodstrip planks butted together – but the top can be cut as one piece in ⅛in wood if you prefer. We have used a set of commercial turned legs which are available from most dolls-house suppliers. The table top was painted with an acrylic wash to resemble pine before cutting (see Chapter 2 page 34), and the frieze and legs were painted blue after assembly.

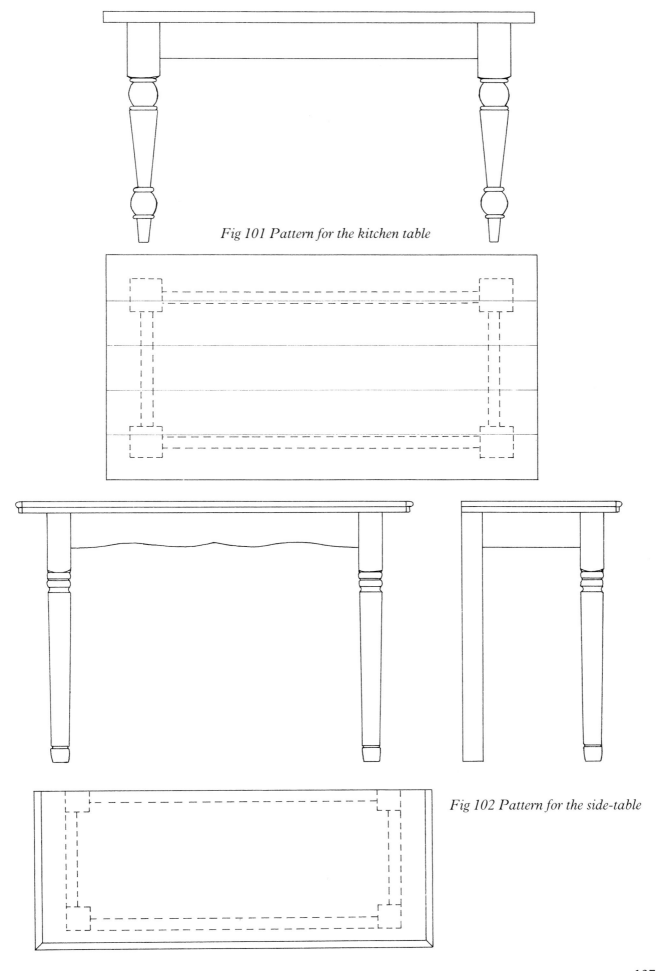

Fig 101 Pattern for the kitchen table

Fig 102 Pattern for the side-table

Cut, glue and butt five planks (or cut one piece) to make a table top $2^{7}/_{16} \times 4^{1}/_{2}$in.

Cut two short and two long friezes in $^{1}/_{8} \times {}^{3}/_{8}$in woodstrip. Using spacers of $^{1}/_{8}$in scrap wood (see Fig 18), glue the short friezes between pairs of legs and leave to dry.

Stand the assembly upright and glue the long friezes in place – support as necessary and leave to dry. Paint the leg and frieze assembly.

Place the table top face down on the work surface, and glue the leg and frieze assembly in place. Apply pressure as the glue dries.

SIDE-TABLE *(Fig 102, photograph pages 122–3)*

The table top and frieze are made in $^{1}/_{8}$in wood, and the top is edged with $^{1}/_{8}$in moulding. The back legs are $^{1}/_{4}$in square woodstrip, and the front legs are a pair of commercial turned legs (available from dolls-house suppliers) with $^{1}/_{4}$in square section top ends. Note, that this side-table is rather higher than an ordinary table – if you prefer the legs may be shortened. Our table top was painted to represent pine before cutting, and the legs and frieze were painted blue after assembly.

Cut the table top in $^{1}/_{8}$in wood. Cut $^{1}/_{8}$in moulding with mitred corners and glue to the side and front edges of the table top and allow to dry.

Cut two back legs in $^{1}/_{4}$in square woodstrip, and trim the front legs if necessary to ensure that all four legs are exactly the same length.

Cut two short and two long friezes in $^{1}/_{8}$in wood. Shape the curved edge on the front frieze with a fretsaw or craft knife and sandpaper.

Glue the two short friezes between pairs of legs (one back and one front), and flush with the outside edges of the legs.

Stand the assembly upright and glue the long friezes in place, support as necessary and allow to dry. Paint the leg and frieze assembly.

Place the table top face down and glue the leg and frieze assembly to the underside of the top, with the back edge of the legs flush with the back edge of the top. Apply pressure as the glue dries.

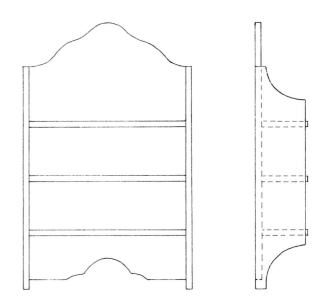

Fig 103 Pattern for the small wall-shelves

SMALL WALL-SHELVES
(Fig 103, photograph pages 122–3)

The small wall-hanging shelves are made in $^{1}/_{16}$in wood, and painted blue to match the other kitchen furniture. If you use woodstain or a paint-wash finish, the wood should be stained or painted before cutting.

Cut a back, two sides and three shelves in $^{1}/_{16}$in wood. Shape the curved edges with a fretsaw or craft knife and sandpaper.

Glue one side to the back. Glue the shelves to the back and side – using a spacer of scrapwood if required to align the shelves.

Glue the second side to the back and shelves. Apply pressure to the assembly as the glue dries. Paint as required. Glue the shelves to the wall.

RUSH-SEAT CHAIR

The chair is cut and assembled in the same way as the chair in Chapter 5, using the pattern Fig 65, and painted before the seat is woven.

ACCESSORIES

TOY KITCHEN FURNITURE
(photograph page 139)

The toy dresser, table and chair are made from patterns in the book, reduced by 50% via photocopying. Make the furniture in wood and woodstrip half the thickness described in the instructions, $^{1}/_{32}$in and $^{1}/_{16}$in rather than $^{1}/_{16}$in and $^{1}/_{8}$in. Most of the patterns in the book can be reduced to $^{1}/_{24}$ scale in this way, but we recommend that you start with something simple if you have not worked in this scale before.

PAINTED TRAY *(Fig 104a, photograph pages 122–3)*

The tray is made in $^{1}/_{16}$in wood and can be stained or painted as you prefer, with or without the painted flower decoration.

Cut a paper template for the handle ends in folded paper to ensure symmetry.

Cut a base, two sides and the two handle ends in $^{1}/_{16}$in wood. Use a craft knife to shape the curved handles and refine the shaping with sandpaper wrapped around a pencil or piece of dowelling.

Glue the handle ends on to the base, ensuring they are vertical, and allow to dry. Fit the sides, trim if necessary and glue on to the base butted to the handle ends.

When the glue is dry, round off the top edge slightly with fine-grade abrasive paper.

Paint the tray with acrylic paints in the colour of your choice, or to represent pine.

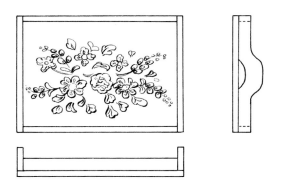

Fig 104 (a) Pattern for the painted tray

Toy furniture in ¹/24 scale can be made for your doll's tea party from the patterns in the book reduced by photocopying

If required, trace the flower pattern on to the tray and paint with fine-liner and fine-detail brushes and acrylic paints. If you wish to 'age' the tray, apply a dilute wash of burnt umber paint, and while the paint is wet, lift most of it off with a piece of sponge, leaving darker areas in the corners of the tray.

Finish the tray with a coat of wax polish on the top and sides, buffed to a soft sheen.

PAPER-TOWEL HOLDER
(Fig 104b, photograph pages 122–3)

The towel holder is made from scraps of ¹/16 × ¹/2in woodstrip and ¹/16in dowelling.

Cut two ends in woodstrip and shape the curved edges with a craft knife. Mark the position on each piece and drill $\frac{1}{16}$in holes into, but not through each.

Cut a back $1\frac{3}{16} \times \frac{1}{2}$in, in woodstrip and glue the back between the ends. Paint the towel holder as required.

Cut a piece of dowelling to fit snugly into the holes. Cut a strip of paper kitchen towel, slightly narrower than the dowelling. Mark coloured borders with felt pen if required and roll the paper tightly around the dowelling. Spring and glue the dowelling into the holes in the sides.

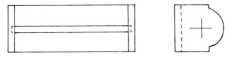

Fig 104 (b) Pattern for the paper-towel holder

RUGS *(photographs pages 122–3 and 130)*

The rugs shown in the Modern Kitchen were made by colour laser printing (see page 173) on thick cotton fabric from a magazine illustration. We glued cotton fringe to the ends of the rug, and folded and glued a hem on each side.

ROLLER BLIND *(photograph pages 122–3)*

The roller blind is a rectangle of cotton fabric, cut to fit the window with a small folded and glued hem – or the edges may be sealed with Fraycheck or similar. Stiffen the fabric if necessary with Fraycheck or spray-on starch and glue the top end of the blind to a length of $\frac{1}{8}$in dowelling, cut to fit the width of the window. Roll the fabric around the dowelling, add a thread and tiny bead-pull, and glue the blind in place at the top of the window.

NOTICE BOARD *(photograph page 130)*

The notice board is a rectangle of $\frac{1}{16}$in cork, framed with woodstrip cut with mitred corners, and glued on to a backing of thin stiff card. The board is dressed with tiny pictures cut from magazines and glued in place.

SIMPLE CROCKERY *(photograph page 130)*

Inexpensive white-metal 'crockery' is painted with white gloss enamel paint to represent china, and decorated with a simple pattern in enamel colours.

Paper plates are decorated with 'transfers' made from magazine illustrations with 'Decal It' and 'Decal Cote' (available from craft suppliers), following the instructions supplied with the Decal products.

MODELLED CROCKERY
(photograph pages 134–5)

Simple jugs, bowls and plates can be modelled in 'Real Clay' or a similar air-drying clay, using pencils, the ends of tools or spoons etc as moulds.

To make a bowl, knead a small ball of clay and press it into a thin pancake. Grease the end of a small screwdriver handle or similar shaped mould with a smear of vaseline, and press the clay pancake over the mould. Make a fine roll of clay and join it to the bowl with slip (clay mixed with water) to form a foot for the bowl, and press a flat base. Leave the clay on the mould until it is leather-hard, then remove it and trim the top edge with a craft knife and allow to dry thoroughly.

Make a teapot with a rolled ball of clay, trimmed to make a flat base and indented with a pen lid or similar tool at the top to indicate a lid. Add a spout made from a rolled cone of clay, cut at an angle; a handle made from a fine roll of clay; and a tiny rolled ball for a knob on the lid, joined to the pot with slip.

Make a mug by shaping the clay over the end of a pencil and adding a tiny rolled handle; or a jug by shaping the clay over a pencil and adding more clay to round out the shape, and a rolled handle.

Paint the dry pieces with acrylic paints and seal the colours with gloss or satin acrylic varnish.

PACKAGES *(photograph page 130)*

Packages for washing powder, cereals, coffee and other items are made by cutting suitable labels from magazine illustrations and wrapping them around small blocks of scrap wood or dowelling or around small pieces cut from the life-size item, eg bin-liners etc.

CHAPTER EIGHT

The Georgian Room

The Georgian period (known as Colonial in America) roughly spans the eighteenth century and is a very popular style with miniaturists. It represents a taste in architecture and decoration brought back to Britain by aristocratic young men from their 'grand tours' of Europe. At first only the wealthy had new houses built in this style, but by the end of the century the fashion had worked its way down the social scale. Georgian features include sash windows, six-panelled doors and marble or white-painted fireplace surrounds in symmetrically planned rooms which were light and elegant and decorated in bright strong colours. Painted panelling or the newly fashionable wallpapers, moulded plaster cornices, panelled dados and polished wooden floors were popular. Grand houses were often decorated and furnished very elaborately giving an impersonal atmosphere, and perhaps the style is most attractive in the diluted form in which it was used in more modest homes.

The Georgian Room in this chapter is shown furnished as both a drawing room and a bedroom, in the elegant and uncluttered style of the time. The 'Chippendale' drawing-room furniture is made from kits customised with a painted decoration, and a pattern is given to make the grand four-poster bed.

THE ROOM BOX
(Fig 105, photograph pages 146–7)

The pattern in Fig 105 will make a room 15½in wide, 10in deep and 11½in high, which is a realistic size for a small room in a grand Georgian house, or an average room in a more modest house. The methods described in this chapter can all be adapted to a dolls' house – the measurements given should be amended to suit the individual room.

Our room box is framed with a commercial picture-frame, and is supported behind the frame on wooden battens (see Fig 106). If you intend to frame a similar room box, check that the measurements will fit into the rebate of your frame and adjust if necessary, or choose a frame to fit your room box.

To assemble the room box you will need ³⁄₈in plywood, a saw, (a fretsaw for door and window openings), whitewood glue and veneer pins.

Cut a base, a back, a top and two sides in plywood. (Cut a doorway if you wish to use an opening door and a hole to accommodate the window if you wish to use one.) Glue and pin the back on to the base, ensuring that the pieces are at right angles. Glue and pin one side on to the back and base, then the other side.

If you intend to fit a frame around your room box, drill ¹⁄₈in countersunk holes through the base, approximately 2in from the front and back edges as shown. Cut two 14in long wood battens to fit under the box so that the frame will clear the work surface. Screw the battens to the underside of the box through the drilled holes, ensuring that the screws are countersunk below floor level.

Glue and pin the top on to the back and sides. Sand the box thoroughly inside and out.

We have fitted a false wall of 5mm (¹⁄₈in) Foamcore (or plywood) to the back wall of the box to accommodate the fireplace without a chimney breast. To make a similar wall, cut the Foamcore to fit and cut out the fireplace opening. Glue support battens of ³⁄₄in wide Foamcore (or balsa wood) to the back of the box, across the ceiling, down each side and across the base at either side of the fireplace opening. Cut vertical supports to fit and glue to the back wall at either side

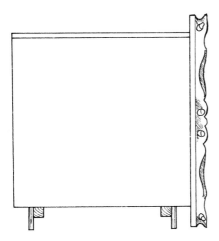

Fig 106 Method for battens and framing the room box

(a)

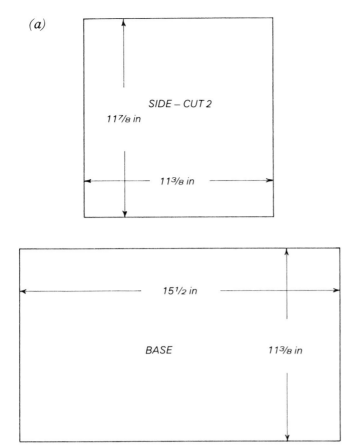

SIDE – CUT 2

11⁷/₈ in

11³/₈ in

15½ in

BASE

11³/₈ in

15½ in

BACK

11½ in

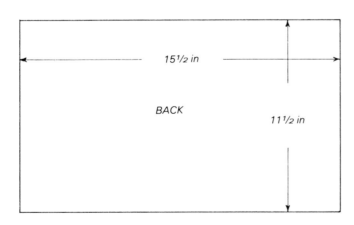

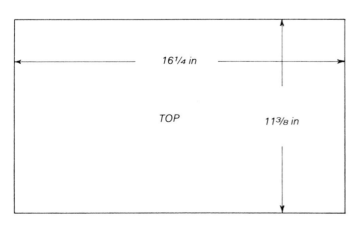

16¼ in

TOP

11³/₈ in

(b)

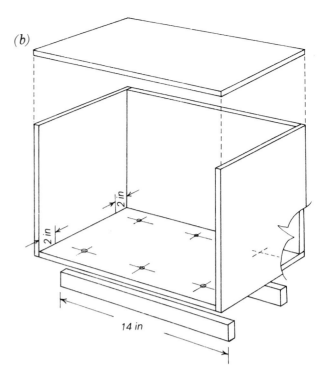

2 in

2 in

14 in

Fig 105 (a) Plan and (b) assembly for the Georgian room box

of the fireplace. Glue the false wall on to the battens so that it is supported ¾in away from the back wall of the room.

DECORATING *(Fig 107)*

We have decorated our room in the grand fashion with an elaborately moulded cornice and silk-covered walls as an interpretation of the Georgian style rather than a strictly authentic copy. We have used kits to make the (non-opening) door and the fireplace surround, and floored the room with self-adhesive wooden planking. If you wish, a commercial Georgian window could be fitted into the right wall. The 'moulded' ceiling is made from embossed wallpaper with a commercial ceiling rose (medallion).

CORNICE *(Fig 108)*

We made an elaborate cornice built up from three different mouldings (see Acknowledgements) and painted cream with the details picked out in two tones of gold and blue-green. To make a similar cornice choose ¾in and ⅝in decorative wood mouldings and a moulded frieze. Paint sufficient wood mouldings and frieze to make the cornice – apply two or three coats of acrylic paint, and pick out the detail with a fine-detail brush in the colours required.

Cut ¾in moulding with mitred corners and glue it to the top of the walls and the ceiling. Cut the moulded frieze and glue it on to a backing of painted woodstrip if necessary to add depth, so that the profile of the frieze follows the cornice. Glue the frieze to the wall, butted beneath the cornice. If you intend to cover the walls with silk panels as we have done, do

A hand-painted finish can turn simple kits into furniture
which will complement the grandest houses

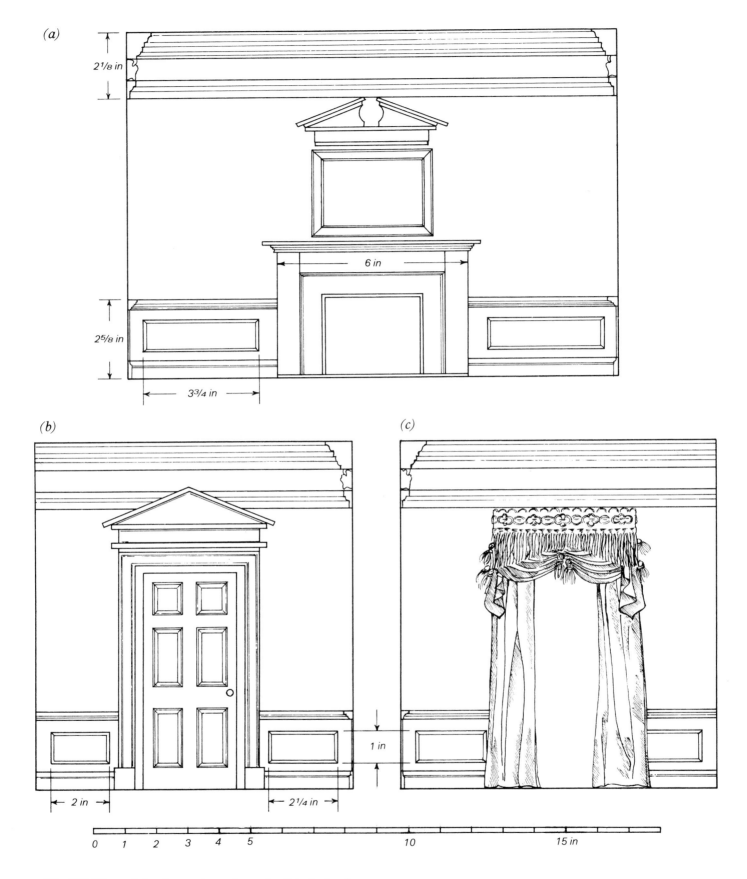

(a)

2⅛ in

6 in

2⅝ in

3¾ in

(b)

(c)

1 in

2 in

2¼ in

0   1   2   3   4   5   10   15 in

*Fig 107 Plan of the decorating scheme for (a) the back
wall, (b) the left-hand wall and (c) the right-hand wall
of the Georgian Room*

Fig 108 Pattern for the cornice

not glue the ⁵⁄₈in moulding in place beneath the frieze until the walls are covered.

CEILING

The ceiling in the Georgian room is covered with a white embossed-pattern wallpaper which we have painted in dark and light shades of blue-green to emphasise the pattern.

Measure and cut the ceiling paper to fit so that the pattern is squarely centred. Paint the pattern with fine brushes in the colours required and allow the paint to dry. Paste the paper on to the ceiling to butt against the top edge of the cornice. Paint the ceiling rose if required, centre it carefully and glue to the ceiling. (If you intend to fit a ceiling light, ensure that there is a hole in the rose and ceiling through which to feed the wire.)

SILK WALL PANELS

Cut a panel for each wall in stiff drawing paper or very thin card, to fit from the lower edge of the frieze to 2⁷⁄₈in above the floor. Cut silk for each panel on the straight-grain of the fabric, ½in larger at both sides and the bottom edge, but fitting flush at the top edge. Glue the top edge of the silk on to the paper – or spray the paper with Spray Mount adhesive (available from art shops) and smooth the silk on to it. Turn under the bottom edge of the silk and glue it to the back of the paper panel. Turn under both sides of the silk and glue to the back of the paper panel.

Trim the back wall panel to fit around the fireplace opening and secure the cut edges with glue. (If you are making an opening door (and window) trim the side wall panels as necessary and secure the cut edges with glue.) Glue the silk-covered paper panels to the walls – back wall first – to fit ³⁄₈in below the cornice frieze so that the bottom edge is 2½in above the floor.

Cut ⁵⁄₈in painted moulding with mitred corners and glue to the walls, butted below the frieze, to cover the raw top edge of the silk panels. Note, that if, like ours, your door pediment is tall enough to reach the cornice, then the cornice on the left wall should be cut to fit around it after the door is in place.

FLOOR

We have used a sheet of self-adhesive wooden flooring, cut to fit the room. Make a paper template if required, and peel off the backing and press the flooring firmly on to the plywood floor. Polish the floor with wax furniture polish.

DOOR AND WINDOW *(Fig 107b)*

We have used an exterior Georgian door with door frame and pediment assembled from a kit which is larger than a conventional interior door but looks very imposing. We assembled the door frame and painted it to resemble white marble as described in Chapter 3 (see page 54). The door was assembled and painted to represent *faux-marbre* in the same way as the fireplace surround in Chapter 4 (see page 66), using darker shades of blue-green on the stiles and rails, and lighter shades on the panels. The panel mouldings were painted pale blue-green *faux-marbre* before being glued on to the door. Fit (or hinge) the door into the door frame and glue the door handle in place. Glue the door frame and door on to the wall. Trim the cornice moulding to fit around the pediment and glue in place.

Georgian windows are available ready-made or as kits with fixed or opening sashes from most dolls-house suppliers. If you choose to use one, paint the window-frame to complement the door, and fit the window in place – either into the window hole cut in the wall, or glued on to the wall with an illustrated 'view' behind the window. Glue the window-frame to the wall to cover the cut edges on the silk panels.

FIREPLACE *(Fig 107a)*

Our fireplace surround was assembled from a Georgian fireplace kit and painted to represent white marble (see Chapter 3 page 54). We fitted splayed 'cheeks' cut from 5mm (¹⁄₈in) Foamcore into the fireplace opening, and papered the opening with embossed brick 'cladding', painted black to resemble soot.

The hearth is a piece of ¹⁄₁₆in wood (or card), painted grey and glued to the floor. Glue the fireplace surround to the wall, and, if required, trim the opening with ¹⁄₁₆in square section brass tubing (available from model shops). This can be cut to fit with a small saw and glued to the edges of the opening with UHU or similar glue.

DADO PANELLING *(Fig 107)*

The dado panelling is made from stiff, thin art cardboard trimmed with ¹⁄₈in moulding and a ³⁄₈in dado rail and ⁵⁄₈in skirting-board.

Cut 2½in deep cardboard panels to fit the back

The Georgian Drawing Room, where 'dangerous liaisons' are conducted over the tea cups in very elegant surroundings

wall at either side of the fireplace, the left wall at either side of the door and the right wall.

Paint sufficient ⅛in moulding to make panel frames for each panel – we have used pale blue-green *faux-marbre* to match the door-panel frames.

Cut and assemble the panel frames in painted ⅛in moulding for each panel, as shown on the pattern. Trace the outline of each panel frame on to the cardboard panels and draw a second line, ¹⁄₁₆in inside the traced outline. Using a craft knife and metal ruler, cut out the centre panel from each panel on the inner marked line.

Paint the panels and centre panels – we have used darker and lighter shades of blue-green *faux-marbre* to match the door – and allow to dry.

Glue the panels to the walls, trimmed as necessary, to fit butted against the lower edge of the silk panels, down to the floor. Glue the centre panels into the cut-out spaces in the panels, and glue the panel frames in place to cover the cut-out lines.

Paint the dado rail and skirting-board – we have used a pale shade of blue-green *faux-marbre* to match the panel frames. Glue the dado rail (cut with mitred corners) to the wall to cover the join between the silk panels and the dado panels. Glue the skirting-board (cut with mitred corners) – trimmed to fit at each side of the door and fireplace – to the bottom of the dado panels.

LIGHTING

We have used a pair of candle lights glued to the wall at each side of the door, and a chandelier hung from the ceiling rose (medallion) with wires fed through holes in the wall and ceiling to a transformer.

FRAMING

If you are framing your room box, glue the front edges of the box into the rebate in the back of the picture-frame with contact-adhesive – with the box lying on its back – and apply pressure as the glue dries.

FURNITURE

DRAWING-ROOM SUITE
(photograph pages 146–7)

The furniture in the Georgian drawing room is made from kits. We have used a pair of Chippendale chairs, a settee and a tea-table, and assembled them following the instructions supplied with the kits. Rather than using the recommended mahogany stain, we have 'customised' the furniture with a decorative painted finish (see page 148).

DECORATIVE PAINTED FINISH
(Fig 109, photograph page 143)

This decorative painted finish can be applied to furniture pieces made from patterns in the book or to any commercial piece or kit. If you intend to apply it

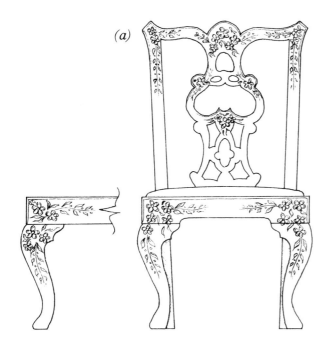

Fig 109 Pattern for the decorative painted finish (a) for the chair and settee and (b) for the tea-table

148

to a piece of ready-made commercial furniture, sand the piece thoroughly to remove all trace of the original finish before you begin.

You will need fine-grade abrasive paper, such as 320- to 400-grit, acrylic paints in the base colour and detail colours of your choice (we used pale cream with details in gold, blue and green), a good quality ¼in soft flat brush, and fine-detail and liner brushes.

Sand the piece thoroughly with very fine-grade abrasive paper and remove all traces of dust before painting.

Apply three or four light coats of acrylic paint in the base colour, allowing each coat to dry thoroughly. Sand with very fine-grade abrasive paper before applying the next coat, until the surface is as smooth as possible and the grain of the wood is covered.

With a fine-liner brush, paint the outlines of the chair and settee backs and seats, and the moulded edge of the tea-table with a fine line in gold.

Trace the flower patterns on to the piece very lightly in pencil, or use the drawings as a guide and paint the flowers and leaves as delicately as possible. We have used blue for the flowers and green for the leaves, with a darker shade at the edge and a lighter shade at the centre of each petal and leaf. Add dots of blue to each side of the leaf sprays and add flower centres and leaf stems in gold.

Allow the paint to dry thoroughly, then polish the piece with clear wax furniture polish buffed to a soft sheen.

Cover the seat pad with fabric – we used silk – and glue the fabric to the underside of the pad, and the pad into the recess in the chair or settee with craft glue.

FOUR-POSTER BED
(Fig 110, photograph pages 150–1)

The measurements shown on the pattern and given in brackets below will make a very large four-poster bed but the method can easily be adapted to make a smaller double or single bed. We have used a set of commercial turned bed-posts – similar posts can be found in dolls-house shops or could be whittled from dowelling. We have painted the posts cream. You will also need ⅜in balsa wood block and ⅛ × ⅜in and 3/16in square woodstrip.

Cut the bed base (6⅜ × 5⅜in) in ⅜in balsa, and cut ⅛in square notches in each corner to accommodate the posts (see Fig 110b).

Cut ⅛ × ⅜in woodstrip to fit both end and side edges of the base and glue in place to enlarge the notches to ¼in as shown.

Cut canopy-support ends and sides (A) in 3/16in square strip to correspond with the end and side edges of the base.

Using a canopy-support side as a spacer, glue a pair of posts into the notches in one side of the bed base and allow to dry.

Turn the assembly on to one end and using a canopy-support end as a spacer, glue the third post

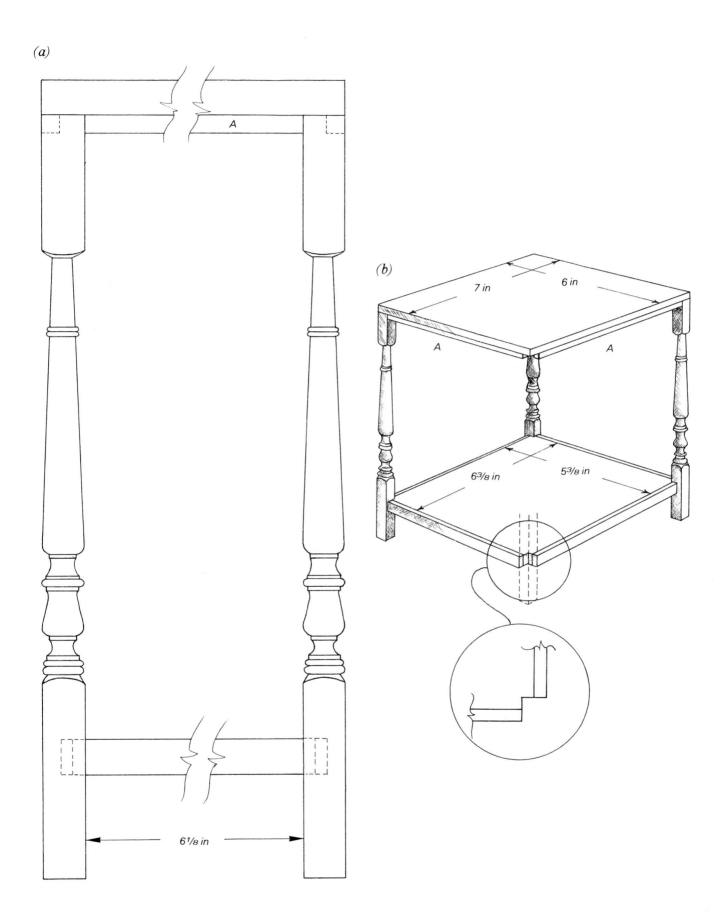

(a)

A

(b)

7 in

6 in

A

A

6³/₈ in

5³/₈ in

6¹/₈ in

*Fig 110 (a) Pattern and (b) assembly for the
four-poster bed*

into its notch and allow to dry. Turn the assembly and glue the fourth post in place.

Cut the canopy (7 × 6in) in ⅜in balsa and glue it on to the top of the posts. Glue the canopy supports to the underside of the canopy between the posts with the edges flush.

Paint the bed posts as required and apply wax polish.

BED TESTER AND HANGINGS (Fig 111)

The tester and hangings on our bed are made in silk, trimmed with self-fringing and braid, but any light-weight fabric in a plain colour, small print or woven pattern would be suitable. You will also need ½in wadding (batting), thin, stiff art cardboard and fabric glue to make the tester. If your bed is a different size, amend the pattern in Fig 111 as necessary.

Working with the bed upside-down, cut a piece of wadding (batting) to fit and glue it to the underside of the canopy. Cut a canopy lining 1in larger than the canopy in fabric (we have used white silk) and place it over the wadding (batting). Snip the corners to accommodate the bed posts and glue the edges of the lining over the canopy supports on to the side edges of the canopy, smoothing the lining taut over the wadding.

Turn the bed right way up and cut a (1½in wide) strip of fabric one and a half times the circumference of the canopy to make the frill. We have fringed the bottom edge of the frill by pulling threads and added a trimming of fine picot braid, glued in place above the fringe.

Gather the top edge of the frill and glue it around the canopy with the cut ends overlapping slightly at a back corner.

Cut the bed hanging (14 × 8½in) on the straight-grain of the fabric. Turn in and glue hems on both short sides, and fringe and trim the bottom edge. We have lined the centre part of the hanging, behind the head of the bed, with a panel of white silk. Gather the top edge of the hanging and glue it around the back of the canopy, and part of the sides, over the canopy frill.

Cut two tester sides, and two ends (one with curved edges and one without) in cardboard. Score the card on the dotted lines shown on the pattern to bend. Using the pattern as a guide, cut fabric ½in larger all around and cover each card tester piece with fabric, snipping the curves and corners and folding and gluing the fabric edges to the back of the card.

Glue the tester pieces to the edges of the canopy over the frill and hanging so that the bend in the tester is level with the top of the canopy. Allow the glue to dry, then gently splay the sides and ends of the tester forward along the bend and secure the corners with a little tape glued in place inside the tester. Glue braid trimming around the tester on the line of the bend.

We have added a matching bedspread and cushions trimmed with frilled braid, fringing and tassels in fabric to match the bed hangings.

The Georgian Bedroom, with a grand four-poster bed and hand-painted 'Chinese' wall panels

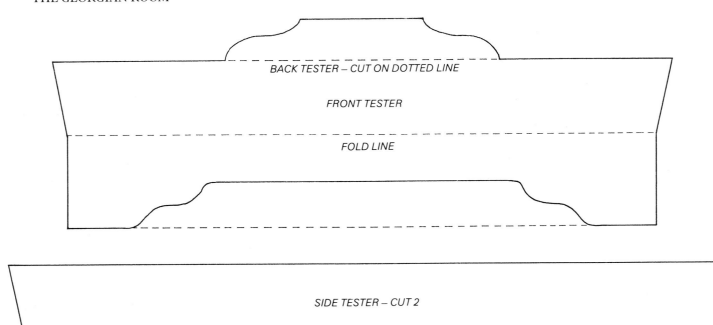

BACK TESTER – CUT ON DOTTED LINE

FRONT TESTER

FOLD LINE

SIDE TESTER – CUT 2

Fig 111 Pattern for the tester for the four-poster bed

ACCESSORIES

FORMAL CURTAINS
(Fig 112, photograph page 143)

The curtains (drapes) in the Georgian drawing room are fixed to the wall, to create the illusion of a window behind them, but the method can also be used to make curtains for a real window. The curtains, swag and tails can be made in any lightweight fabric – though natural fabrics, such as cotton or silk, usually hang and drape better than man-made fibres. We have used silk, trimmed with narrow picot braid. The pelmet is made of wide upholstery braid trimmed with tassels. Our curtains are hung over an opaque muslin curtain to disguise the absence of a window. The measurements given on the pattern should be adjusted if necessary to fit individual windows.

Cut a batten in 1 × ³⁄₈in balsa wood scrap, 2in wider than the window. Cut a piece of ¹⁄₈ × ⁵⁄₈in woodstrip scrap the same length, and glue it on to the front of the balsa batten so that the top edges are flush, leaving a recess at the lower edge, as shown in Fig 113.

Cut two curtains on the straight-grain of the fabric as shown in Fig 112c. Hem or trim the bottom edge of each curtain – we have made a small fringe by pulling threads and added a trimming of narrow picot braid glued above the fringe. Turn in and glue hems on

both sides of each curtain and add trimming if required. Gather the top edge of the curtains and glue them into the recess in the batten (over a gathered muslin curtain if required).

Cut the swag on the straight-grain of the fabric as shown in Fig 112a. Fringe and trim or hem the lower edge and gather the swag on the dotted lines shown on the pattern. Pull up and adjust the gathers to make folds, and glue the top edge of the swag on to the batten over the curtains. Push dressmakers' pins through the fabric into the balsa if necessary to secure the folds.

Cut the tail piece (Fig 112b) on the straight-grain of the fabric and fringe the edges all round. Fold the piece to make three or four pleats at each side of centre, then press and tack (baste) to hold the pleats in place. Cut the tail piece in half across the centre on the dotted line shown on the pattern, to make two matching tails. Glue the tails on to each end of the batten over the swag (see Fig 113) and tack (baste) to secure the pleats.

Cut a pelmet of wide, fringed upholstery braid to fit around the batten and glue the braid in place with the cut ends lapped on to the back of the batten. Trim the fringe to shape a curve and add tassels if required. Glue the batten to the wall (above the window) so that the curtains hang just clear of the floor.

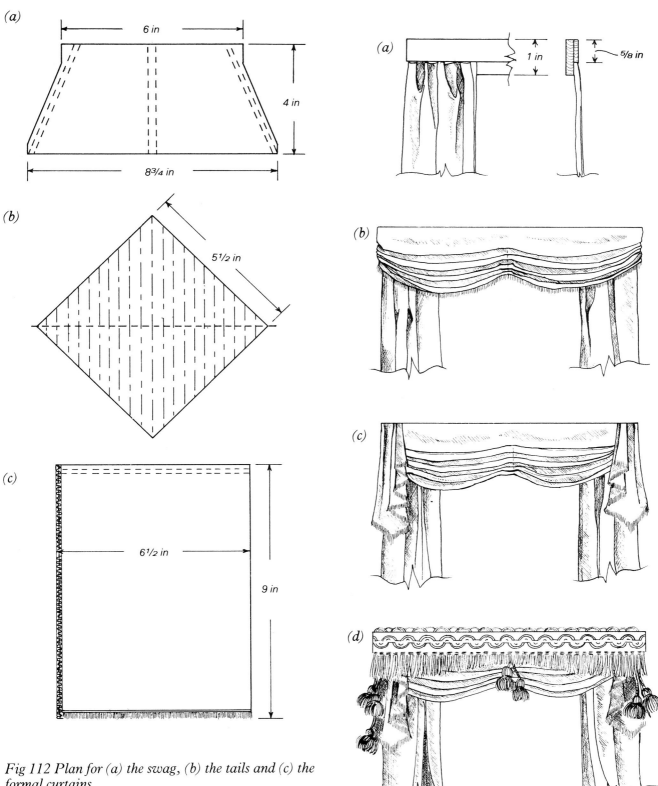

Fig 112 Plan for (a) the swag, (b) the tails and (c) the formal curtains

Fig 113 Assembly for the formal curtains and pelmet

PAINTED FLOORCLOTH (photograph page 143)

The floorcloth (or rug) is made by colour laser copying a suitable magazine or catalogue illustration on to heavyweight white or cream cotton fabric (see page 173). We folded and glued a hem around the cloth and backed it with iron-on interfacing on the underside.

PAINTED WALL PANELS
(Fig 114, photograph pages 150–1)

The panels are designed to represent the painted silk or silk-paper panels which were imported from China in the eighteenth century and used as wallpaper in grand houses of the period. We have framed two panels with narrow picture-frame moulding painted with a pale blue-green *faux-marbre* effect, but if you prefer the patterns could be used to make wallpaper panels which can be pasted on to the walls of the room. To make wallpaper, trace or photocopy the pattern and paint sufficient pieces to decorate the room, making each piece slightly different, as the hand-painted originals; or more simply paint two panels and colour photocopy them to make the number required. You will need good quality watercolour paper (from art shops) in the background colour of your choice – we have used cream – and acrylic paints in pastel shades of green, blue, pink, beige, grey, yellow, and black and white. You will also need fine-liner and fine-detail brushes, thin art cardboard to back the panels and 1/16in picture-frame moulding to frame them.

Trace the pattern or make a light photocopy on to watercolour paper.

Paint the larger areas of the pattern first, in delicate pastel shades – the grass in green, tree stumps in beige and grey-brown and the stems of bamboo in grey-green, shading from dark to light to give shape and definition. Add the stems of the flowering shrubs in beige and highlight the outlines with paler and darker shades. Paint the bamboo leaves in blue-green and the flowering shrub leaves in yellow-green with veins in a darker shade. Paint the stems and leaves of twining plants in dark green and add touches of lighter and darker colour to define and highlight. Paint the flowers in shades of pink, outlining the petals with darker pink and add dots of pink on the twining plants. Paint the birds in stronger colours in shades of blue, yellow and beige, and the butterflies and dragonflies in white with detail in black and grey.

Allow the paint to dry thoroughly, then cut out the panel within the line of the frame shown on the pattern. Glue the outside edge of the back of each panel and smooth it on to a piece of cardboard. Cut out the card around the panel and make a frame of 1/16in moulding, painted as required and cut with mitred corners. Glue the panel into the frame.

Fig 114 Pattern for the painted wall panels

— CHAPTER NINE —
The Tudor Room

The room in this chapter is made in the English vernacular style which was used throughout the sixteenth and seventeenth centuries when oak timber was still plentiful and the newly prosperous middle classes were building houses. Many of the houses built at this time are still inhabited today so the Tudor room could be decorated and furnished to suit any period you wish.

We have furnished our room as a kitchen and a parlour in a middle-class home of the early seventeenth century. In the kitchen the floor is beaten earth and the small window is unglazed – as glass was expensive it was only fitted in the windows of rooms used by the family and their guests. The parlour has a planked floor and the walls are covered with hangings of painted cloth which were made to imitate the expensive tapestries found in more affluent houses. All houses at this time were lit by candles or rushlights and cooking was done over an open fire. The women of all but the grandest households spun their own wool and most middle-class families played music and some could read.

Decorating ideas and furniture from this chapter can be used for other rooms in a Tudor dolls' house, which could include a still-room where the lady of the house distilled fruits and herbs to make preserves and medicines. For a Tudor bedroom, the pattern in Chapter 8 can be adapted to make a typical Tudor four-poster bed in oak-stained wood with fine wool hangings.

THE ROOM BOX
(Fig 115, photograph pages 158–9)

The pattern in Fig 115 will make a room box 16in wide, 10in deep and 8in high, which is a typical size for the rooms in a Tudor yeoman's house or small farmhouse. Our room has a large fireplace modelled in air-drying clay, painted to represent stone, with inglenook seats at either side of the hearth. The small, unglazed window and (non-opening) door in oak-stained wood, and the walls and ceiling, rough-plastered between the oak beams, are typical of small houses of this period. The floor in the kitchen is plastered and painted to represent beaten earth with areas of tiles made in air-drying clay. The parlour floor is self-adhesive wooden planking stained to represent oak. Measurements given on the patterns are for the room shown in the photograph but the methods can be adapted to any dolls-house room.

The room box is made in good quality ³⁄₈in plywood, and the base, back and sides are assembled in the same way as the room box described in Chapter 2 – except the window. For ease of access, do not pin and glue the top in place until the room is decorated.

THE CHIMNEY BREAST (Fig 116)

The chimney breast is made in 5mm (¹⁄₈in) Foamcore with a lintel of ⁷⁄₈in square wood and a mantelshelf and inglenook seat of ¹⁄₈in wood stained to represent oak. The stones are made in air-drying clay, shaped over blocks of 1¹⁄₁₆in wide scrap wood and glued on to the Foamcore backing with UHU or similar tacky craft glue.

Scale up the pattern on to Foamcore and use a steel ruler and craft knife to cut one front and four side pieces – two with the cut-out shown on the pattern to receive the lintel, and two without.

Glue and assemble the Foamcore pieces as shown in Fig 116b so that the inner side pieces form a slot to receive the lintel and mantelshelf. Cut small support struts (A) in Foamcore to fit, and glue the struts between the sides to strengthen the assembly.

Cut the mantelshelf in ¹⁄₈in wood and the lintel in ⁷⁄₈in square wood from the pattern. Use a Stanley knife and sandpaper to pare and shape the curved lower edge of the lintel. Hammer several ³⁄₄in pins into the back of the lintel to use for hanging cooking pots over the fire.

Glue the mantelshelf on to the lintel with back edges flush. Glue the assembly into the cut-out in the chimney breast.

Cut the seat-support blocks (B) 1 × 1³⁄₈in and ¹³⁄₁₆ × 1³⁄₈in, in balsa or scrap wood and glue the blocks to the inner sides of the hearth, behind the front, as shown by the dotted lines in Fig 116b.

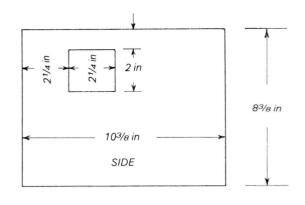

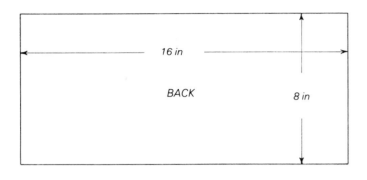

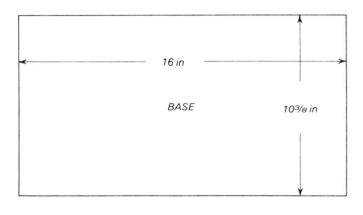

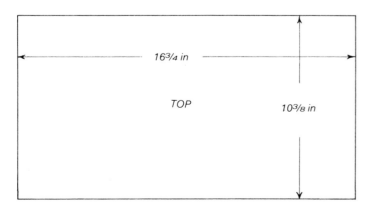

Fig 115 Plan for the Tudor room box

Glue the assembled chimney breast to the floor and to the back and side walls, so that the top edges are flush. (The chimney breast should not project above the walls of the room box.) The method for making the stones used to decorate the chimney breast is given on page 160.

DECORATING

The walls of the Tudor room are decorated with beams of $1/2 \times 5/32$in timber which are roughly cut and sanded to remove splinters, but not smooth. We used wood from a fruit crate from the local market, but any similar, slightly distressed wood would be suitable. We stained the beams with medium-oak woodstain before they were glued in place. The plaster between the beams is ready-mixed Tetrion (or similar filler) which is applied with a small flexible spatula (for example, the type used for cake icing). The door is made from $1/16$in wood planks, $11/16$in wide, stained to match the beams, with elaborate black-painted commercial metal hinges and a latch made from $1/8$in wood scrap. The unglazed window is framed with $3/8 \times 1/8$in woodstrip with mullions of $3/16$in square wood.

DOOR *(Fig 117)*

Cut four planks in $1/16 \times 11/16$in wood (the full height of the door) and glue and butt the planks together as shown.

Cut the door-head in $1/16$in wood and use a craft knife to incise and pare the carved decoration. Glue the door-head on to the door with the top and side edges flush.

Cut two planks $3/8 \times 1/4$in in $1/8$in wood scrap for the door-latch runners. Use a craft knife to shape the profile shown on the pattern.

Cut the door latch in $1/8$in wood scrap as shown. Stain or paint the pieces as required and glue the latch and runners on to the door. Glue the door hinges in place.

Mix a darker shade of oak woodstain (or burnt umber acrylic paint) and use a fine-detail brush to colour the cut-away areas in the carved decoration on the door-head. Paint a line at the lower edge of the door-head to indicate separation from the door. Paint areas of wear at the bottom edge of the door between the planks, and paint in knot-holes as required.

LEFT-HAND WALL *(Fig 118b)*

Cut a door-sill in $5/32 \times 3/16$in wood scrap, the same width as the door, and glue the sill to the floor, butted against the wall. Glue the door to the wall above the sill, leaving a slight gap between the bottom edge of the door and the sill. Cut two sill beams to fit the lower edge of the wall at either side of the door in $1/2 \times 5/32$in wood and glue in place.

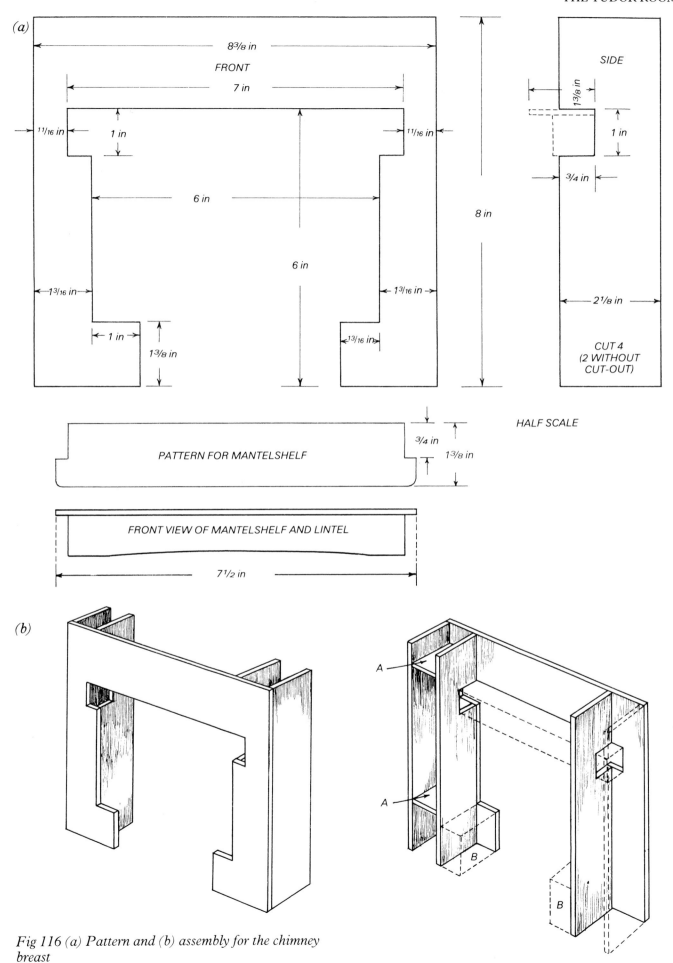

Fig 116 (a) Pattern and (b) assembly for the chimney breast

The Tudor Kitchen with its mellow stone and plaster
and oak furniture looks like a painting by one of
the Old Masters

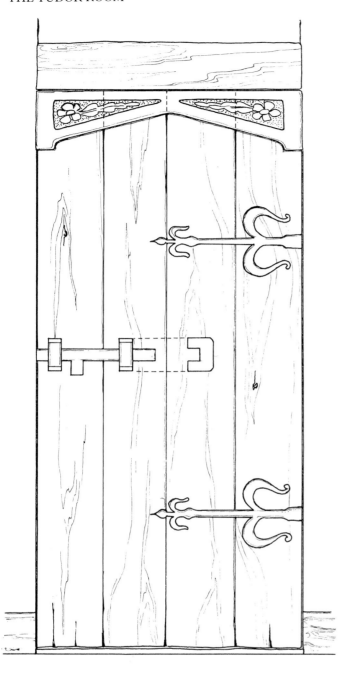

Fig 117 Pattern for the Tudor door

Cut two wall plates to fit the top edge of the wall as shown on the pattern and glue in place to leave a gap of ⅝in at the left side of the door to accommodate the end of the main ceiling-beam (A), and a gap of ½in at the right-hand (back) end of the wall to accommodate the back wall plate (B).

Cut four vertical posts in ½ × 5⁄32in wood. Note, that the left door post (beneath the main ceiling beam) is ⅛in shorter than the other posts. Glue the posts to each side of the door and to the ends of the walls as shown.

Cut the curved brace beam in 5⁄32in wood and glue to the wall as shown.

Cut the door-head beam in ½ × 5⁄32in wood and glue to the wall above the door, between the door posts.

RIGHT-HAND WALL (Fig 118c)

Face the window-opening edges with ⅜ × ⅛in woodstrip, glued in place. Cut three mullions in 3⁄16in square wood to fit tightly into the frame and glue in place to show a diamond profile as shown in Fig 119.

Cut a sill beam to fit the lower edge of the wall in ½ × 5⁄32in wood and glue in place.

Cut two wall plates to fit the top edge of the wall and glue in place to leave a gap of ⅝in above the window – to line up with the gap above the door and to accommodate the main ceiling beam (A).

Cut four vertical posts in ½ × 5⁄32in wood and glue to either side of the window, to the right (front) end of the wall and between the ends of the sill beam and wall plate.

Cut the curved brace beam in 5⁄32in wood and glue to the wall as shown.

Cut window-head and sill beams in ½ × 5⁄32in wood. Cut a ⅛in deep notch in the top edge of the window-head to correspond with the gap for the main ceiling beam. Glue the window-head and sill beams in place between the posts.

BACK WALL (Fig 118a)

Cut the sill beam in ½ × 5⁄32in wood to fit the lower edge of the wall and glue in place.

Cut the wall plate in ½in square wood to fit the top edge of the wall in one piece and glue in place.

Cut two vertical posts in ½ × 5⁄32in wood and glue between the sill beam and wall plate.

Cut the curved brace beam in 5⁄32in wood and glue to the wall as shown.

STONES (Fig 120)

This method for making and painting the stones which are used on the chimney breast in the Tudor room can also be used to make flagstone flooring. The stones are made in air-drying clay, eg grey Das, and painted with acrylic paints – we have used shades of burnt umber, yellow ochre, black and white, with touches of chrome green and red oxide to represent York stone.

Roll out the clay to approximately ⅛in thick and press the upper surface on to a piece of natural stone to impress the texture (see Chapter 1 page 19). When the clay is leather-hard, cut individual stones with a craft knife or scissors and leave to dry.

To shape the corner stones required for the fireplace, use blocks of 1³⁄16in wide scrap wood as moulds. Cut pieces of leather-hard clay, shape them on the mould as shown and leave to dry on the mould. Make a good selection of stones so that you can choose the best for the chimney breast.

When dry, glue the individual stones on to the Foamcore chimney breast, beginning at the bottom and building upwards, trimming stones as necessary

(a)

(b)

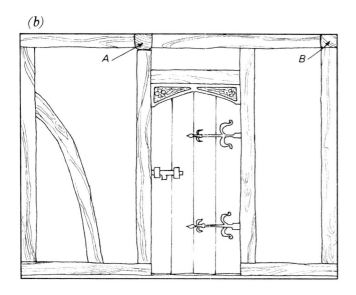

(c)

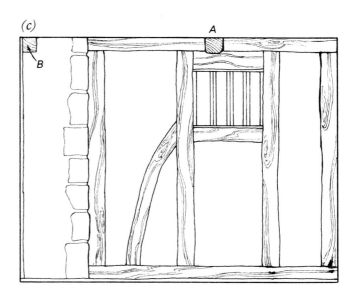

0   1   2   3   4   5   10   15 in

Fig 118 Plan of the decorating scheme for (a) the back wall, (b) the left-hand wall and (c) the right-hand wall of the Tudor room

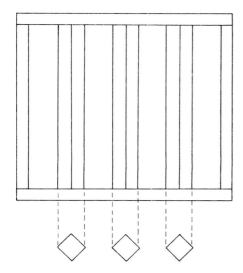

Fig 119 Pattern for the window

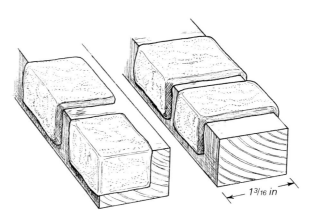

1³/₁₆ in

Fig 120 Method for shaping corner stones for the fireplace

161

A corner of the Tudor room showing the realistic planked door and the medieval floor tiles 'salvaged from the local abbey'

to improve the shape and fit. Glue corner stones on the left side to fit around the outside of the chimney breast (see Fig 118) and to both sides to fit around the insides of the hearth. Glue corner stones to the inglenook seats and flat stones above the hearth, and to fill the spaces between the corner stones. Leave a slight gap between the stones to fill with mortar later, but trim the edges so that they fit together well. (You may find it easier to glue the stones in place, paint them and apply the wall plaster with the room box lying on its back or side as you work.)

Mix shades of acrylic paint in burnt umber and yellow ochre with a little black and white, and paint the individual stones, varying the colour a little from one stone to the next. Apply touches of chrome green and red oxide with dry, old brushes to blend in with the painted colours. Leave the painted stones to dry, and apply a coat of matt spray-sealer if required.

For mortar, grout between the stones with Tetrion (or similar filler) applied with a craft knife, and clean away any excess filler with a damp cloth or cotton bud.

Cut an inglenook seat ($1\frac{1}{8} \times 2\frac{1}{2}$in) in $\frac{1}{8}$in wood, stain, and glue it on to the stone block on the left side of the hearth.

PLASTER

Apply Tetrion (or similar ready-mixed filler) to the

walls with a small flexible spatula, to fill the spaces between the beams to a depth of approximately $\frac{1}{16}$in to represent rough plastering. The finish should be smooth, but not too smooth. Allow the plaster to dry thoroughly.

The unpainted plaster finish resembles limewash, but if you wish the plaster may be painted with a colour wash, or a small stencilled pattern can be applied with a fine paint-brush. Authentic colours for a Tudor room include pale terracotta-pink, to represent powdered brick, or pale green to represent vegetable dyes mixed into the limewash.

FLOOR (Fig 121)

The floor of the Tudor Kitchen is plastered with Tetrion and painted with a wash of burnt umber acrylic paint to represent the beaten earth floor which was commonly used in small houses of this period. Areas of terracotta clay tiles, painted with designs in acrylic paint are set into the floor by the doorway and hearth. The hearth inside the large fireplace is floored with bricks, made from air-drying clay. Both the tiles and the brick hearth are made and glued to the floor before the plaster is applied.

MEDIEVAL FLOOR TILES

Medieval tiles of this type were salvaged from the abbeys and churches closed in the sixteenth century by Henry VIII, and re-used in many domestic interiors. The tenants of our house have found only a few but you may prefer to tile a larger area of your floor. The method can also be used to make tiles for other period houses, eg the hall or conservatory floor of a Victorian house.

Roll out the clay to a thickness of approximately $\frac{1}{16}$in as evenly as possible and leave to dry leather-hard. Cut the clay into individual tiles $\frac{3}{4}$in square with a craft knife and metal ruler and leave to dry.

Paint the patterns shown in Fig 121b and c on to the tiles, in yellow ochre acrylic paint with a fine-detail brush following the step-by-step guides. To make the floor shown in the photograph you will need twenty-four plain tiles, twelve tiles with pattern (b) and twenty tiles with pattern (c). When the painted tiles are dry, apply a coat of gloss acrylic sealer and allow to dry.

Glue the tiles to the floor as shown on the pattern, in an area by the door, an area by the hearth and a smaller area at the centre front of the room, butting the tiles closely together without mortar.

BRICK HEARTH

Roll out the clay to an even thickness of approximately $\frac{1}{8}$in and allow to dry leather-hard.

Score the individual bricks into the clay with a pointed tool and allow to dry thoroughly.

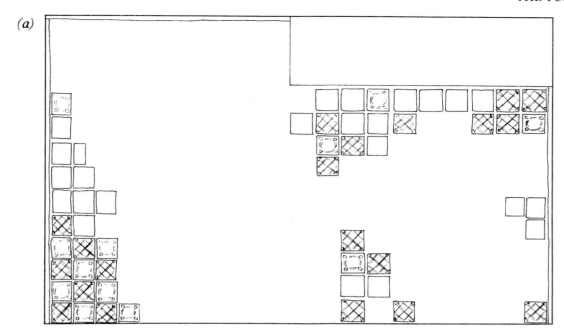

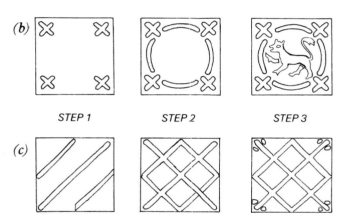

Fig 121 (a) Floor plan and (b and c) patterns for the medieval tiles

Paint the bricks with acrylic colours in dark red, ochre and burnt umber, varying the shades from brick to brick. Cut one piece to fit the area of the hearth and glue in place. If you wish to fit a flickering fire-light in the fireplace, drill a small hole through the back wall ½in above the hearth to feed the wires through.

BEATEN-EARTH FLOOR

Apply Tetrion (or similar ready-mixed filler) to the floor around the tiles and up to the edge of the brick hearth with a small flexible spatula, to a depth of 1/16in, and smooth the surface as evenly as possible. Clean any excess filler from the tiles or bricks immediately with a damp cloth or cotton bud and leave to dry. Paint the plaster with a wash of burnt umber acrylic paint, applying a second coat if necessary when the first is dry.

PLANKED WOOD FLOOR
(photograph pages 166–7)

Make a paper template of the floor area, to fit closely against the sill beams on each wall and to the front edge of the brick hearth. Trace the outline of the template on to a sheet of self-adhesive wooden flooring and cut out with sharp scissors. Paint the floor with medium-oak woodstain and a soft ½in-wide artists' paint-brush, working in one direction only. Leave to dry thoroughly. Apply a second coat of woodstain if necessary to intensify the colour and allow to dry. Peel off the backing paper and position the flooring, pressing it firmly in place on the plywood floor of the room.

CEILING *(Fig 122)*

The ceiling of the Tudor room has beams made from the same wood as the walls, stained to represent oak. The main beam is 5/8in square and the joists are 7/16in wide × ½in deep. The ceiling is plastered between the beams with ready-mixed Tetrion (or similar filler) and we have used cut-outs of embossed wallpaper to represent plaster mouldings. The ceiling of the room box is not fixed in place until it is decorated but if you are working on a fixed ceiling, turn the room upside-down if possible for ease of access.

Cut the main beam in 5/8in square wood to fit across the ceiling and locate the beam in the gaps left to accommodate it on the side walls.

Try the ceiling in place and (with the room upside-down) mark a line with a sharp pencil on the ceiling around the top edge of the walls – as shown by the dotted line on the pattern. Mark the position of both sides of the main beam. Glue the main beam to the ceiling on the marked lines, to meet the lines marked for the side walls. Cut and glue the joists to the ceiling to meet the main beam and the front edge, and to meet the main beam and the lines marked for the back wall and chimney breast.

Apply masking-tape to cover the outside edges of the ceiling to meet the marked lines – to prevent plaster covering these areas.

Apply Tetrion to the ceiling with a small flexible spatula, to a depth of approximately 1/16in between the joists, to meet the masked edge. Smooth the surface as evenly as possible, and while the plaster is still wet, carefully peel away the masking tape. Leave the plaster to dry thoroughly. Cut pieces of embossed paper to fit each plastered panel and glue on to the ceiling with wallpaper paste. When the paste is dry, apply a coat of off-white matt emulsion or acrylic paint over each plastered panel to blend the edges of the paper into the plaster and make a uniform texture on both.

Glue and pin the completed ceiling on to the room box. We framed the front edges of our Tudor room with 'beams' of the same wood used in the interior, glued in place with contact adhesive.

Finishing touches to the décor in the Tudor room include applying matt black paint to the back wall of the fireplace to represent soot, and small areas of very dilute burnt umber wash to the lower part of the walls to represent damp.

Fig 122 Pattern for the ceiling

FURNITURE

The furniture in the Tudor rooms is typical of the period – large, solid pieces made in plain wood and stained or painted to represent oak. We have used pine for the refectory tables, buffet and benches, but any 'real' wood with a suitable grain, planed to the appropriate thickness can be used – or you may prefer to make the Tudor furniture in commercial 'hobby' wood and woodstrip such as bass or jelutong.

LARGE REFECTORY TABLE
(Fig 123a, photograph pages 158–9)

Our refectory table is made in 5/32in wood for the top, and 7/32in wood for the legs and stretchers, stained to represent oak. (If you are using commercial wood, the patterns can be simply adjusted to standard 1/8in, 1/4in and 1/4in square thicknesses.)

Cut top (A), centre (B) and bottom (C) pieces for each leg in 7/32in wood, noting that (A) follows the dotted line on the pattern. Shape the curved edges on the pieces with a craft knife, then sandpaper and glue and butt the pieces together, applying pressure as the glue dries.

Cut the top centre panel 6in long, in 5/32in wood, and two top end panels in 7/32in wood. Glue and butt the ends to the centre panel so that the top surface is flush and the ends project 1/16in on the underside. Apply pressure as the glue dries.

Turn the table top upside-down and glue the legs in

(a)

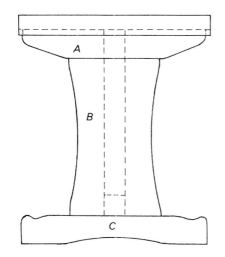

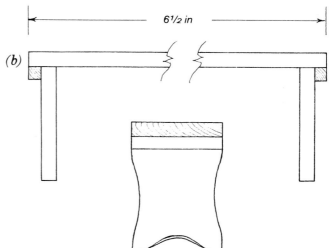

(b)

6½ in

Fig 123 Pattern for (a) the large refectory table and
(b) the bench

place, butted into the angles formed by the projection
of the top end panels.

Cut the stretcher and the stretcher post in 7/32in
wood to fit between the legs, and between the
stretcher and underside of the top. Glue the stretcher
and stretcher post in place as shown in Fig 124.

If required, apply a coat of wax polish and buff to a
soft sheen.

BENCH *(Fig 123b, photograph pages 158–9)*

The bench is made in 5/32in (or 1/8in) wood, with end
supports of 1/8in square woodstrip, stained with
medium-oak woodstain. The pattern may be used to
make a bench of any length required – ours are 4in
and 6½in long.

Cut two legs 1¼in long, in 5/32in wood and shape
the curved edges with a craft knife and sandpaper.

Cut a seat in 5/32in wood and two seat supports in
1/8in square woodstrip. Glue the seat supports to the
underside of the seat at each end so that the ends are
flush.

Fig 124 Assembly for the large refectory table

165

*The Tudor Parlour, where wall-hangings and a fine
collection of pewter display the owner's status*

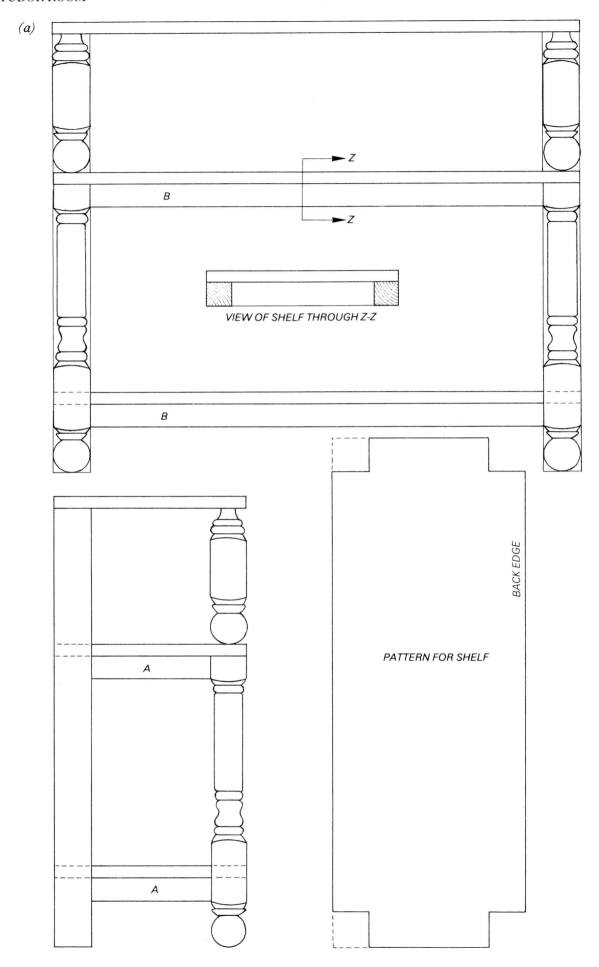

(a)

B

Z

Z

VIEW OF SHELF THROUGH Z-Z

B

A

A

BACK EDGE

PATTERN FOR SHELF

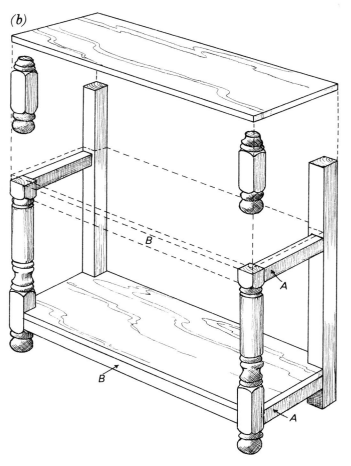

(b)

Fig 125 (a) Pattern and (b) assembly for the buffet

made in ⅛in wood, and ¼in and ⅜in square wood with four commercial turned newel posts which have a ⅜in square section. The pieces are stained before assembly.

Cut two back posts 4¾in long in ⅜in square wood. Cut two lower front posts 1⅛in long from commercial newel posts.

Cut four side shelf supports (A) 1¼in long in ¼in square wood. Glue the shelf supports between pairs of front and back posts and leave to dry.

Cut two shelves in ⅛in wood from the pattern. Cut notches in each corner of the lower shelf and the back corners of the upper shelf to accommodate the posts.

Cut four shelf supports (B) in ¼in square wood and glue the supports to the underside of each shelf so that the back and front edges are flush and allow to dry.

Glue the lower shelf on to the side shelf supports and to the back and front posts.

Glue the upper shelf on to the side shelf supports and lower front posts, and to the back posts.

Cut two upper front posts from the newel posts, ensuring that they are exactly the same length as the upper part of the back posts.

Cut the top in ⅛in wood. Glue the top on to the back posts. Glue each end of the upper front posts and fit them in place between the top and upper shelf to line up with the lower front posts, and leave to dry.

Apply wax polish and buff to a soft sheen.

Glue the legs into the angle formed on the underside of the seat by the seat supports. Allow the glue to dry and polish if required.

BUFFET (Fig 125, photograph pages 166–7)

The buffet is the earliest form of sideboard, and was used to display the family's collection of pewter or silver and other valuables in the parlour. Our buffet is

SMALL REFECTORY TABLE
(Fig 126, photograph pages 166–7)

Our table is made in ⁵⁄₃₂in and ⅛in wood, with stretchers of ³⁄₁₆ × ⁷⁄₃₂in and leg-ends of ⅛ × ⁵⁄₁₆in wood; stained with medium-oak woodstain. (If you are using commercial wood, the pattern can be simply adjusted to standard ⅛in wood and ³⁄₁₆in woodstrip.)

Cut two legs (A) in ⅛in wood, and top and bottom leg-end pieces (B and C) in ⅛ × ⁵⁄₁₆in wood. Shape the curved edges with a craft knife and sandpaper.

Using a piece of ¹⁄₁₆in scrap wood (or card) as a

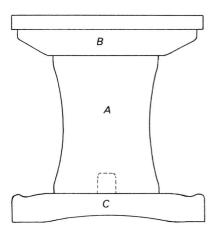

Fig 126 (a) Pattern for the small refectory table

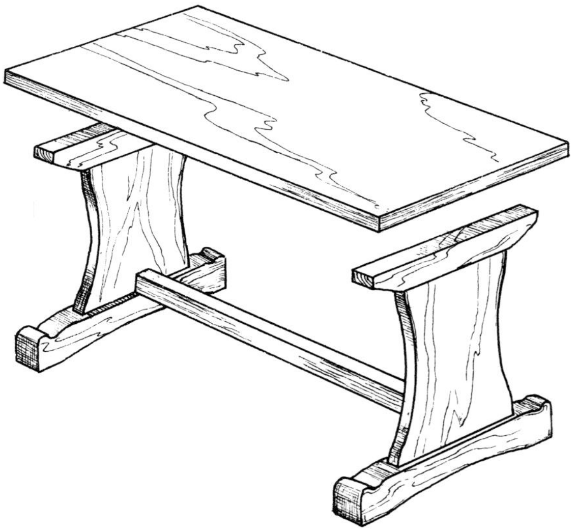

Fig 126 (b) Assembly for the small refectory table

spacer, glue and butt the leg-end pieces to the legs and apply pressure as the glue dries.

Cut the top in 5/32in wood. Glue the legs to the underside of the top, 1/4in from each end.

Cut a stretcher in 3/16 × 7/32in wood to fit between the legs, and sand the top edge to round off. Glue the stretcher between the legs to rest on the ledge formed by the top of the leg-ends.

If required, apply wax polish and buff to a soft sheen.

BOX-CHAIR (Fig 127, photograph page 162)

This early form of armchair would belong to the master of the house. Lesser beings would sit on stools or benches and children and servants were often not permitted to sit at all in the presence of the master and mistress. Our box-chair is made in 1/16in wood, and 1/4 × 1/16in, 1/18 × 1/16in, 1/8 × 1/4in, 1/2 × 3/32in and 1/4 × 3/32in woodstrip. The pieces should be stained before assembly, or the chair painted after assembly to represent oak.

Cut a back panel in 1/16in wood from the outline of the pattern in Fig 127a.

Cut two back-frame sides, a top, a bottom and two centre struts (A) and (B) in 1/16 × 1/4in woodstrip. Assemble and glue the back frame on the back panel as shown with top, bottom and side edges flush.

Cut strut (C) in 1/8 × 1/16in strip and glue on to the back. Cut the seat support (D) in 1/8 × 1/16in strip and glue centred on to strut (B) as shown.

Cut a front panel in 1/16in wood, following the outline of the pattern in Fig 127b.

Cut two front-frame sides, top and bottom in 1/4 × 1/16in strip. Use a craft knife to shape the curved top ends on the sides to match the front panel. Glue the front frame on to the front panel with edges flush.

Cut the centre strut (E) in 1/8 × 1/16in strip and glue on to the front panel as shown.

Cut the seat support (F) in 1/8 × 1/16in strip and glue to the back of the front panel 1/16in below the top edge.

Cut two side panels from the outline of the pattern Fig 127c in 1/16in wood. Cut the side-frame top and bottom in 1/4 × 1/16in strip and two struts in 1/8 × 1/16in strip for each side panel, and glue in place as shown.

Use a craft knife to chamfer the inner edges of the frames on the back, front and sides as shown.

Following the assembly guide Fig 127b, glue the sides behind the front so that the edges of the front and the frame of the sides are flush, and allow to dry thoroughly. Glue the back on to the sides.

Cut the seat in 1/16in wood to fit, and glue on to the back and front seat supports.

Cut a pair of arms, shaping the curves with a craft knife, and glue the arms on to the sides as shown in Fig 127a.

Cut the back crest-rail in 1/2 × 3/32in strip, shaping the curved top edges with a fretsaw or craft knife. Cut the carved decoration with the craft knife, paring away the shaded areas shown on the pattern.

Glue the crest-rail on to the back of the chair with the back edges flush.

Paint the (unstained) assembled chair to represent oak, and use a darker shade to emphasise the areas of carving on the back. Apply wax polish and buff to a soft sheen.

THREE-LEGGED STOOL
(Fig 128, photograph page 174)

The seat of the stool is made in 5/32in (or 1/8in) wood, with legs in 3/16in square wood, stained with dark-oak woodstain.

Cut the seat in 5/32in wood and drill three holes with a 1/8in bit, angled slightly outwards as shown.

Cut three legs in 3/16in square wood. Use a craft knife to pare the corners of each piece to round off, and taper the top end of each leg to fit snugly into the holes drilled in the seat.

Glue the legs into the seat. Trim the top of each leg flush with the top surface of the seat and the bottom end of each leg angled so that the stool stands square. Polish if required.

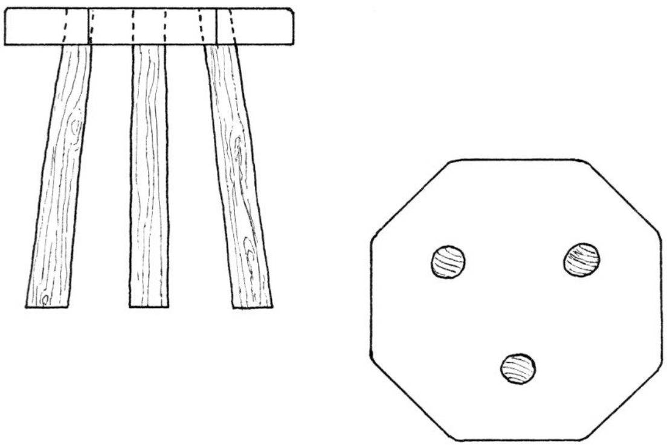

Fig 128 Pattern for the three-legged stool

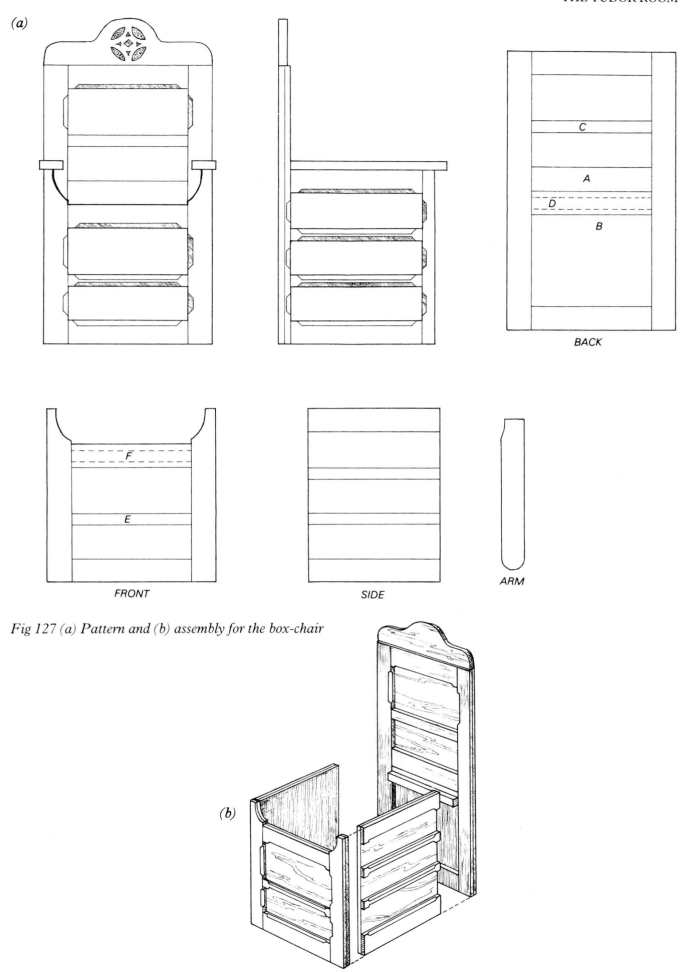

(a)

C

A

D

B

BACK

F

E

FRONT

SIDE

ARM

Fig 127 (a) Pattern and (b) assembly for the box-chair

(b)

ACCESSORIES

SMALL COFFER *(Fig 129, photograph page 174)*

The coffer is a box with a hinged lid and a lock which was used for storing small valuables or papers. It is made in $^1/_{16}$in wood with $^1/_8$in and $^3/_{16}$in moulding with two small metal strap hinges. We have made the coffer in wood, stained to represent oak before assembly.

Cut the base, back and front, $2 \times {}^7/_8$in, in $^1/_{16}$in wood. Pierce a keyhole in the front as shown. Cut two sides $^7/_8 \times {}^{13}/_{16}$in, in $^1/_{16}$in wood.

Glue the base behind the front. Glue the sides on to the base behind the front. Glue the back on to the base and sides.

Cut $^3/_{16}$in moulding with mitred corners and glue to the bottom of the front and sides as shown.

Cut the lid fractionally larger than the top of the box. Cut $^1/_8$in moulding with mitred corners and glue to the front and side edges of the lid, so that the moulding forms a lip around the box and is flush with the top surface of the lid.

Bend the flange of the hinge to form a right angle to fit over the lid, and glue the hinges to the lid and back of the box with superglue. Paint the hinges matt black.

Apply wax polish to the lid, front, sides and back of the coffer and buff to a soft sheen.

LARGE COFFER

To make a large box, for storage or seating, use the pattern Fig 64 and the instructions in Chapter 5 for the blanket box. Make the box in oak-stained wood and omit the curved lower edges on the plinth. Add a keyhole, carving or black-painted strap hinges as required. The sides and front of the box can be panelled, following the method used for the box-chair on page 170.

SPINNING WHEEL
(Fig 130, photograph pages 166–7)

The simple, early spinning wheel is made in $^1/_8$in wood, and $^3/_8$in and $^3/_{16}$in square woodstrip with $^1/_{16}$in dowelling spindles. The wheel is a $1^7/_8$in diameter commercial plastic wheel and the legs are turned wood scraps, though $^1/_8$in square woodstrip would be a suitable alternative. The parts are stained (or painted) to represent oak before assembly. The spinning wheel is dressed with natural sheeps' wool which may be taken from the hedgerow or purchased from chemist shops (drugstores).

Cut the base $3 \times 1^1/_2$in, in $^1/_8$in wood.

Cut the post $1^5/_8$in long, in $^3/_8$in square woodstrip and chamfer the top edges. Cut a $^1/_8$in deep step in the bottom end of the post so that it will fit on to the base, overhanging the side as shown.

Drill a $^1/_{16}$in hole in the centre of the wheel (if necessary). Cut a $1^1/_{16}$in long axle in dowelling to fit snugly into the hole in the wheel and drill a corresponding hole through the post as shown. Glue the post on to the base.

Cut two post supports in $^3/_{16}$in strip with ends angled to 45° as shown. Glue the supports to the post and base.

Cut two spindle-support sides (A) and a back (B) in $^1/_8$in wood. Drill $^1/_{16}$in holes in the sides to receive the spindle, and glue the support on to the base.

Cut four legs, $^5/_8$in long in turned wood (or $^1/_8$in square strip), and angle the top and bottom end of each leg as shown. Glue the legs to the underside of the base and allow to dry.

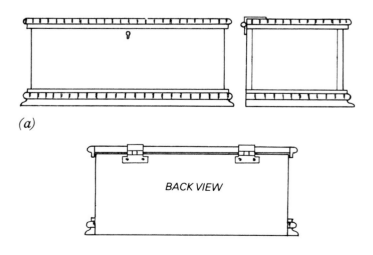

(a)

BACK VIEW

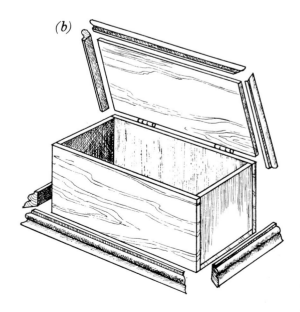

(b)

Fig 129 (a) Pattern and (b) assembly for the small coffer

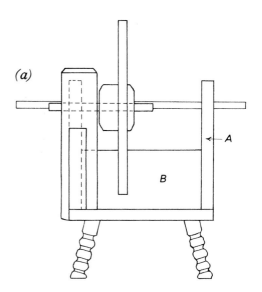

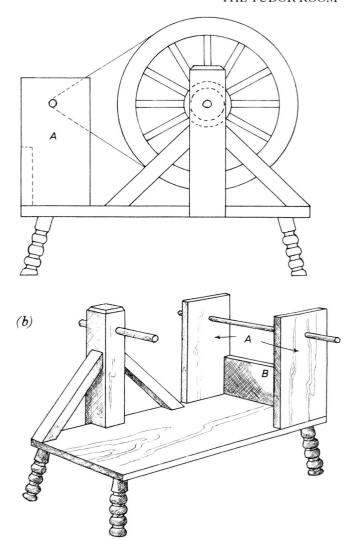

Fig 130 (a) Pattern and (b) assembly for the spinning wheel

Apply wax polish to the upper surface of the base, the post, supports and the wheel, and buff to a soft sheen.

Cut a spindle 2⅜in long, in dowelling and wind sheep's wool around the centre, securing with a little glue if necessary. Locate the ends of the spindle in the holes in the spindle-support sides.

Wind a thread of wool around the wheel, securing with a little glue and locate the axle through the wheel and the post. Secure the loose ends of wool thread from the wheel to the spindle.

Cut two pieces of fine dowelling, 1½in long, and wind wool around them, secured with a little glue, to make distaffs.

SALT BOX *(Fig 131, photograph pages 158–9)*

The salt box is made in ¹⁄₁₆in wood, stained to represent oak, with hinges of fine brown leather.

Cut the back and shape the curves with a fretsaw or craft knife and abrasive paper. Drill a hole as shown.

Cut the base and glue it to the back. Cut two sides and glue to the back and base.

Cut the front and chamfer the top edge to follow the angle of the sides. Glue the front on to the sides and base.

Cut the lid and chamfer the back edge to follow the angle of the sides. Cut two tiny pieces of thin leather, glue one end of each piece to the back of the lid and the other end of each piece to the back to hinge the lid on to the box as shown.

PAINTED WALL-HANGINGS
(photograph page 162)

The hangings (or tapestries) on the walls of the Tudor parlour are colour laser-copied on to white cotton fabric (or linen) from a catalogue or magazine illustra-

Fig 131 Pattern and assembly for the salt box

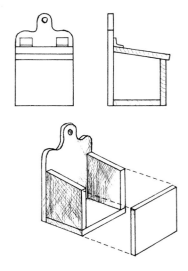

tion. Colour laser printing is the process used to print designs on T-shirts and reference to British Telecom Yellow Pages should produce a printer in your area.

Choose a picture of tapestry of the appropriate period – which can be enlarged (up to A4 size) or reduced if necessary in the printing process – and take

A small room in a Tudor dolls' house can be arranged with a few pieces of furniture and accessories to make a still-room

the picture with a piece of light-coloured natural fabric, such as cotton or linen, to the printer or copy shop. Try to ensure that the picture is printed squarely on the grain of the fabric.

Cut out the hanging and seal the edges with Fraycheck or similar – if necessary. Stick the top edge to the wall with double-sided tape – or hang the tapestry from narrow ribbon loops on a black-painted brass rod through eyelets screwed into the wall.

CANDLE HOLDERS (photograph pages 158–9)

The simple candle holders in our Tudor rooms are made from thick, strong wire and air-drying clay.

Cut a 1in piece of wire and push it into the bottom of a small wax candle. Mould Milliput around the lower end of the candle and part of the wire and pinch to shape it around the base of the candle, and to fit tightly around the wire.

Paint the candle holder with matt black paint and rub it with 'Treasure Gold' or a similar metallic wax to make a metallic finish. The wire end can be bent to a right angle with pliers and the candle holder glued into a small hole drilled in a beam, or the end can be glued into a small block of wood so that the candle will stand on the table.

LOG FIRE (photograph pages 158–9)

We have used a 'cast iron' fireback and a pair of fire-dogs from a specialist supplier (see Acknowledgements) to support a log fire, made from lengths of twig, sawn to size and charred by partly burning them. The logs are arranged and glued in place, covered with craft glue and sprinkled with ash and red and gold glitter.

If you prefer a light in the fireplace, dolls-house stockists can supply a 'flickering fire' unit which can be fitted beneath the logs and wired through a hole in the back wall of a room box, or into a lighting system in the dolls' house.

SHEEPSKIN RUG (photograph pages 166–7)

The rug is a piece of natural sheepskin with a short pile, simply cut to the shape of a full-size sheepskin.

— CHAPTER TEN —
The Garden

The project in this chapter is designed to represent the veranda of a house on a Caribbean island, surrounded by a small garden filled with exotic plants. We have painted the woodwork in sun-washed colours, paved the floor with tiles made in air-drying clay and roofed the veranda with cardboard to represent corrugated iron. Our veranda, fitted against a back wall with (non-opening) French windows and mock shutters, is furnished with commercial accessories and artists' equipment.

The methods can be adapted to make a veranda for any dolls' house by changing the measurements given on the patterns (and in brackets below). The roof could be tiled with slate, clay tiles or wooden shingles. If you do not have a garden, the plant-making methods can be used to make potted plants or hanging baskets, and the ideas in this chapter could be used to make a garden room or conservatory.

THE VERANDA
(Fig 132, pattern drawn ¹/₂ actual size, photograph pages 178–9)

To make the veranda you will need six turned spindles for the posts (we have used Houseworks porch-spindles), 5mm (¹/₈in) Foamcore, ¹/₈in wood and ³/₈in commercial handrail. You will also need ³/₈ × ³/₁₆in, ¹/₈ × ¹/₄in and ¹/₈in square woodstrip, ¹/₂in dentil-edge moulding, air-drying clay for the floor tiles and corrugated cardboard (or tiles) for the roof. We have used acrylic paints in cream, white and pale blue to decorate the veranda. You may find it easier to paint the various parts before assembly.

Note, that the veranda floor is constructed on a base of Foamcore supports as shown in Fig 133. Our base is 1³/₈in high to allow for a step, but the height may be adjusted to suit a dolls' house and the porch posts should be lengthened or trimmed accordingly.

To make the front of the veranda, trim four post spindles to length (10⁹/₁₆in) with the top ends cut at an angle of 21° as shown in Fig 132b. Cut three base-support fronts (A) (3¹/₂ × 1in) in Foamcore and glue them between the posts with the front edges flush.

Cut three friezes (B) (3¹/₂ × 1¹/₄in) in ¹/₈in wood and shape the curved edges with a craft knife and sandpaper. Using a spacer of ¹/₈in scrap wood, glue the friezes between the posts with the front edges recessed ¹/₈in and the top edges ³/₈in below the top of the posts. Allow to dry thoroughly.

Cut two base-support sides (C) (1 × 7in) in Foamcore and glue behind the posts at either side of the veranda front with the outer edges flush.

Cut a base-support back (D) in Foamcore to fit between the sides and glue in place with the back edges flush.

Cut the base-support struts (Ei and Eii) in Foamcore and glue (Ei) in place between the front and back, and (Eii) between (Ei) and (C) as shown in Fig 133. This completes the base support.

Cut two back posts (12³/₄in long) and glue them behind the base support with side edges flush.

Cut two side rails (F) to fit between the back and front posts in ³/₈ × ³/₁₆in woodstrip. Glue the side rails in place to fit flush with the outer edges of the posts and flush with the top of the front posts.

Cut the base floor (using a thin card template if required) in Foamcore as shown in Fig 133b, to fit on to the base support with front and side edges flush, and the back edge flush with the back edge of the posts. Glue the base floor on to the base support.

Cut two base sides in ¹/₈in wood to fit on to the base support and posts with all edges flush, and glue in place as shown in Fig 132b.

Cut a base front in ¹/₈in wood to fit on to the base support and posts with the ends flush with the base sides, and glue in place as shown.

If you are making the Caribbean garden shown in the photographs, make up the back wall and French windows described below before fitting and finishing the veranda. If you are making the veranda for a dolls' house, omit this section.

HALF ACTUAL SIZE

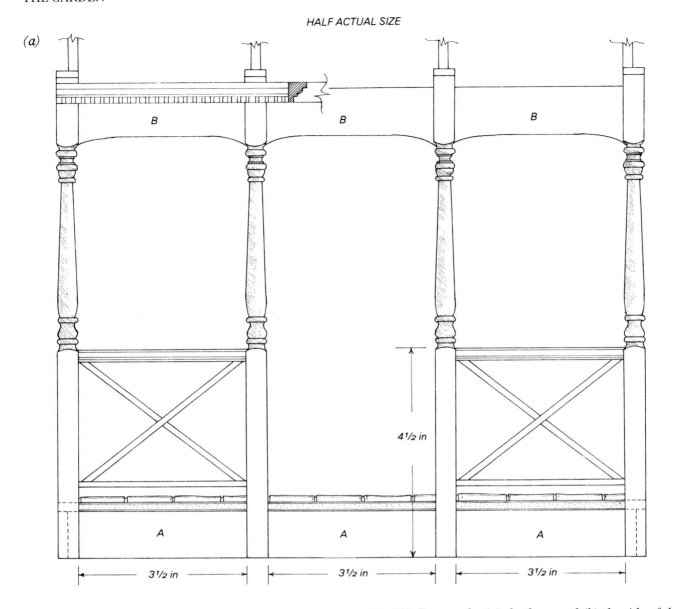

(a)

B   B   B

4½ in

A   A   A

3½ in   3½ in   3½ in

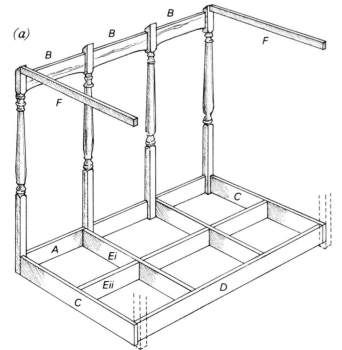

(a)

B
B
B
F
F
C
A   Ei
Eii
C   D

Fig 132 Pattern for (a) the front and (b) the side of the veranda

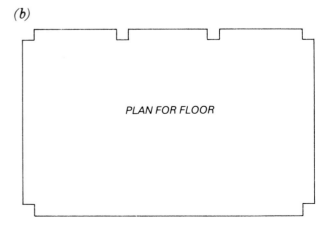

(b)

PLAN FOR FLOOR

Fig 133 Assembly of the base support of the veranda

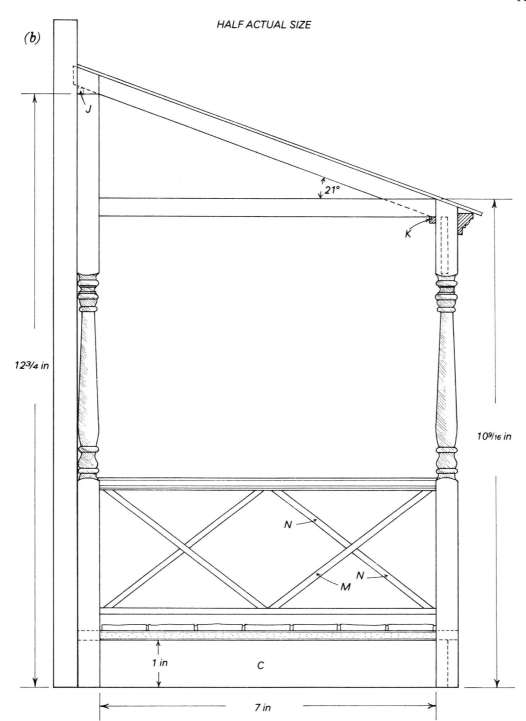

(b)

HALF ACTUAL SIZE

21°

J

K

12³/₄ in

10⁹/₁₆ in

N

M N

1 in   C

7 in

WALL WITH FRENCH WINDOWS *(Fig 134 pattern drawn ¹/₂ actual size, photograph pages 178–9)*

The wall behind the veranda is made in 9mm (¹/₄in) Foamcore framed with ¹/₂in L-shaped moulding in ¹/₈in thick wood, and planked with ¹/₂ × ¹/₁₆in woodstrip.

Cut a panel of Foamcore (12¹/₄in wide × 14¹/₄in high) to fit behind the veranda.

Cut L-shaped wood moulding with mitred corners to frame the top and sides of the Foamcore panel and glue in place.

Cut a base back (G) (1¹/₈ × ¹/₈in) to fit across the panel between the sides of the frame, and glue the base back to the panel with bottom edges flush.

Cut planks of ¹/₂ × ¹/₁₆in woodstrip to fit horizontally between the sides of the frame, and glue the planks on to the Foamcore panel, butted together to cover the area above the base back as shown in Fig 134. Paint the wall as required.

ASSEMBLY AND DECORATING *(Fig 136)*

Glue the veranda to the wall, and clamp and support

The Caribbean Garden where one can sit and watch the sun set over the sea

the assembly until the glue is dry. Glue the shutters to either side of the French windows to rest on the window-frames, splayed outwards. Cut mock-hinge barrels from a toothpick, paint and when dry, glue on to the shutters.

The veranda is most easily decorated before the roof is fitted. Paint any wooden parts not painted during assembly. We have plastered the sides of the base with Tetrion (or similar ready-mixed filler) and applied a wash of pale grey paint.

The floor tiles shown in the photograph are made in air-drying clay (Das or similar), rolled out to an even 1/8in thickness and cut into 1in squares (see page 19 for instructions for making clay floor tiles). Our tiles were painted with terracotta and grey acrylic paints. They were then glued on to the floor in a chequered pattern with a border of terracotta tiles cut to fit around the posts and overhang slightly at the front and side edges. We grouted the tiles with Tetrion.

To make the roof, cut a rafter (I) as shown in Fig 136 in 3/8 × 3/16in woodstrip, with the ends angled to fit tightly behind the front post and against the back wall resting on the back post. Cut three more rafters from this pattern. Glue a rafter to each end of the veranda as shown.

Cut two rafter supports (J and K) in 1/8in square strip and glue support (J) to the back wall and (K) to the back of the front posts to fit beneath the end rafters. Glue two centre rafters in place to rest on the supports behind the centre posts.

Cut two blocks (L) in 1/8in wood and glue on to the outer side of the posts and end rafters, to cover and strengthen the join.

Cut a roof support in 1/16in stiff art cardboard (posterboard) to fit on to the rafters butted against the back wall – overhanging the sides by 1/8in and the front by 1/2in. Cut notches in the back corners of the roof support (to accommodate the back frame) if

necessary so that it fits flush against the wall. Glue the roof support on to the rafters and posts.

Cut 1/2in dentil-edge moulding to fit across the front of the veranda, and glue on to the front posts and to the underside of the roof support.

Cut a corrugated cardboard roof to overhang the roof support by 1/8in at the sides and 3/4in at the front. Paint the roof – we have used grey and rust acrylic paints to represent rusty corrugated iron. Glue the roof on to the roof support, butted against the back wall. If you prefer to finish the roof with tiles, slates or shingles, glue tiles on to the roof support beginning at the front edge and overlapping each row of tiles as you work back to the wall.

To make the veranda railing, cut 3/8in handrail to fit tightly between the posts – at each side of the front, and from front to back on both sides (or on one side). Glue the handrail in place.

Cut bottom rails in 1/8 × 1/4in woodstrip to correspond with the handrails, and glue them between the posts, approximately 1/4in above the floor as shown in Fig 132. Allow to dry thoroughly.

Cut diagonal rails (M) in 1/8in square strip with ends angled to fit into the slot on the underside of the handrail and butted on to the bottom rail. Glue in place and allow to dry. Cut diagonal rails (N) in 1/8in square strip to fit either side of rails (M) and glue in place as shown.

Fig 136 Assembly for the veranda and back wall

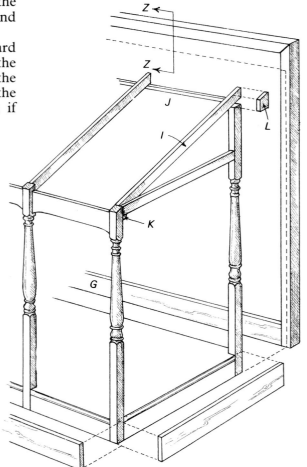

The veranda of a Caribbean house – or an English seaside cottage – makes the perfect place for artistic pursuits

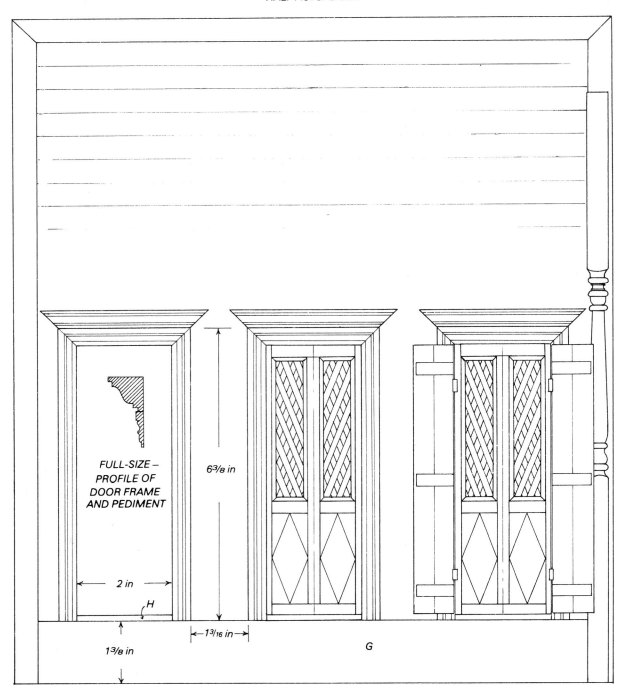

HALF ACTUAL SIZE

*FULL-SIZE –
PROFILE OF
DOOR FRAME
AND PEDIMENT*

6³⁄₈ in

2 in

H

1³⁄₈ in

1³⁄₁₆ in

G

Fig 134 Plan for the wall and French windows

FRENCH WINDOWS (Fig 135)

The window-frames are made from ³⁄₈in architrave moulding and have pediments of ³⁄₈in moulding. The windows are made in ¹⁄₁₆in wood, ¹⁄₈ × ¹⁄₁₆in, ¹⁄₄ × ¹⁄₁₆in and ¹⁄₈ × ¹⁄₃₂in woodstrip and ³⁄₃₂in moulding. The method can be used to make French windows for a dolls' house by adapting the measurements as required. You will find it easier to paint the various parts individually as they are assembled.

Cut two sides and one top with mitred corners for each window-frame in ³⁄₈in architrave moulding, and glue the frames on to the wall, above the base back as shown. Cut sills (H) (see Fig 134) for each window in ¹⁄₈in square strip and glue into the bottom of the window-frame between the sides.

Cut pediment moulding with ends mitred at 45° for each window (see Fig 134) and glue on to the wall above the window-frame.

To make *each* window: cut two frame sides in ¹⁄₈ × ¹⁄₁₆in strip. Cut frame top, bottom and vertical and horizontal dividers in ¹⁄₄ × ¹⁄₁₆in strip. Assemble the frame to fit into the window-frames as shown in Fig 134 – but do not glue the frames into the window-frames at this stage.

Cut a back panel in ¹/₁₆in wood to fit the lower part of the window as shown in Fig 135b and glue behind the frame. Cut diamond-panels in ¹/₁₆in wood and glue on to the front of the panels as shown.

Cut ³/₃₂in moulding with mitred corners to frame the inner edges of the open upper parts of each window and glue in place as shown, with the back edges flush.

Cut ¹/₈ × ¹/₃₂in woodstrip and glue diagonally across the back of each window opening, to form a lattice. To ensure that the lattice follows the profile of the diamond-panels, mark points (A) and (B) shown on the pattern Fig 135b in pencil on the back of each window, and glue the first lattice-strip on these points. The strips are then glued ¹/₈in apart in one direction (reversed for the other window of each pair) to fill the opening. Glue the cross strips diagonally behind the strips to complete the lattice.

We have painted a fine black line down the centre of the vertical divider on each window to indicate division into a pair of French windows, and painted the wall black inside the window-frames to create the impression of a shaded interior.

Glue the windows on to the wall to fit into the window-frames and sills.

Cut two shutters (5⁷/₈ × ⁷/₈in) for each window in ¹/₁₆in wood, and paint or score to indicate planking if required. Cut three battens for each shutter in ¹/₁₆in wood and glue the battens on to the shutters. Paint the shutters as required, but do not glue them in place until the veranda is fitted to the wall.

(a)

Fig 135 (a) Pattern and (b) assembly for the French windows and shutters

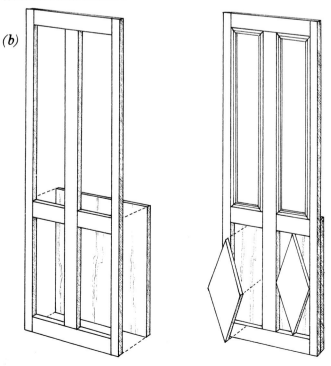

(b)

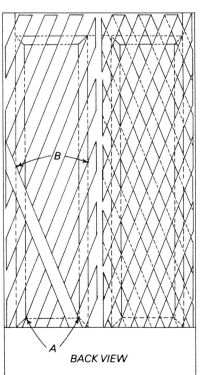

BACK VIEW

183

GARDEN BASE

(photograph pages 178–9)

Our garden base is made in ³⁄₈in plywood, and is 13 × 19in. We glued the veranda and wall assembly on to the base in the right-hand back corner with side and back edges flush. The step is made in ½in balsa wood (6½ × 1½in) with the sides faced with ⅛in wood and plastered with Tetrion (or similar), and painted to match the veranda base. The step is tiled to match the veranda floor.

We painted the surface of the base with earth-coloured acrylic paint mixed with a little white glue, and sprinkled landscaping powder (from hobby shops) and fine sand on to the wet paint. We used pieces of natural cork (from hobby shops) glued on to the base to form landscaping and provide support for the plants. Finally, green and brown lichen was glued into the nooks and crannies in the bark.

PLANTS

(Fig 137, photograph pages 178–9)

The methods described here can be used to make plants for the garden or potted plants for the house or conservatory. In the garden the plants can be glued into holes pierced in the cork landscaping for support. Planters, tubs and flower pots are available from most dolls-house shops in a wide variety of styles suitable for any period dolls' house. Fill the bottom of planters and pots with Blu-tac or plasticine for weight, with a layer of Oasis or similar flower arranging material above. Spread craft glue over the top of the Oasis and sprinkle with a little garden compost or peat to represent earth. The wire stems of the plants can be glued and pushed into a hole pierced with a darning needle in the filling.

The plants in the Caribbean garden include an artificial 'banana tree' from a gift shop, which was removed from its pot and glued on to the base; and live air-plants from the garden centre which were supplied with their own glue and need an occasional spray with water. We have also used commercial metal ivy and other leaves, painted with a cellulose metal primer and acrylic paints, and twined around the post and rail of the veranda, with sprays of dried flowers glued in place.

PALMS

The large palm tree was made from etched brass leaves and a sectional white-metal trunk supplied as a kit which was assembled and painted with metal primer and acrylic paints. We modelled small coconuts in air-drying clay, glued them on to the assembled palm tree with superglue and painted them green.

The small palms were assembled from commercial brass leaves painted with shades of glossy green enamel paint, on stems carved from balsa wood with sprays of painted dried flowers. The monstera or Swiss-cheese plant is made up from metal leaves superglued on to florists' wire stems, bound together with green plastic florists' tape to make a trunk.

HANGING BASKET OF ORCHIDS

The hanging basket on the veranda is made from a sphere of Oasis (or similar flower-arranging material) with a length of wire twisted around it to make the hanger. Cover the ball of Oasis with craft glue and press moss (or lichen) tightly around it. To make the orchids, glue florets of dried sea-lavender on to wire stems and paint the florets yellow. Glue artificial flower stamens into the florets and cut leaves in green plastic florists' tape to wrap around the stems. Vary the orchids by painting the stems with white rings to represent dried-off leaves and add pieces of white-painted stem to represent aerial roots. Glue the stems and push the orchids into the moss-covered Oasis ball.

FERN *(Fig 137a, photograph page 186)*

The fern is made from green crêpe-paper florists' tape and green wire artificial flower stems. Cut a stem and fold crêpe-paper tape, doubled over the wire. Cut the leaf shape as shown. Paint the leaf with green and yellow acrylic paints and add touches of burnt umber at the edges. Use small sharp scissors to snip fringed edges around the leaf. Make approximately twelve leaves for each plant, varying the sizes and colours a little. Bunch the leaves together, with the smallest at the centre, glue the stems to secure and push into the pot. Arrange the leaves to curl outwards naturally.

GERANIUMS *(photograph page 186)*

The geranium leaves are green-painted commercial metal leaves on stems. The flowers are florets of dried sea-lavender glued on to the stems with superglue through the hole in the base of the floret, and painted with red and pink acrylic paint.

The yucca leaves shown with the geraniums are made from sticky-backed paper ('Post-it' notes or similar) folded over wire stems as shown in Fig 137b. Cut long narrow leaf shapes and paint them dark green. Paint fine stripes in pink and purple on the leaves and arrange them with the geraniums in the pot.

LILIES *(Fig 137, photograph pages 178–9)*

The lily leaves are made from sticky-backed paper with stems of green florists' wire, and the flowers are cut from large pearlised white plastic sequins with green-painted artificial flower stamens.

Fold the paper over the wire stem and cut the leaf shape as shown. Paint the leaves medium green, add veins in dark green and paint gloss varnish on the upper surface of the leaf. Cut lily shapes from the sequins to include the sewing hole at the lower end of each flower. Push the end of the stamen through the hole to form a stalk and secure with a touch of superglue if necessary. Bunch the flowers and leaves together, secure with glue and push the stems into the pot. Pinch the leaves to shape and arrange the plants naturally.

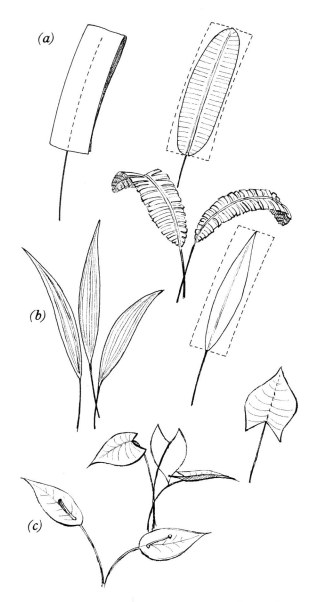

Fig 137 Patterns and assembly for (a) ferns, (b) yucca leaves and (c) lilies

*If you don't have a garden, you could furnish a small
room in the dolls' house as a garden room*

Stockists, Magazines and Books

The dolls-house hobby has grown so popular in Britain and America, and more recently in Australia, that there are now shops everywhere and it would be impossible to list them all. If you are new to the hobby, we advise that you subscribe to one of the dolls-house magazines or directories listed here where you will find information about shops in your area. Please include a SAE or IRC (International Reply Coupons) with all enquiries.

BRITISH SUPPLIERS AND MAGAZINES

For a comprehensive list of British craftspeople and suppliers we recommend that you contact:
The Dollshouse Information Service,
Ash Grove,
Cross in Hand,
Heathfield,
Sussex TN21 0QG

or
The Dollshouse Hobby Directory,
Nexus Special Interests Ltd.
Nexus House,
Boundary Way,
Hemel Hempstead,
Hertfordshire HP2 7ST

The following magazines are specialist dolls-house publications which contain a wealth of information, including articles, how-to projects, advertising and listings of dolls-house fairs around the country. They are available on subscription from the addresses given below.

The International Dolls House News,
Nexus Special Interests Ltd.
Nexus House,
Boundary Way,
Hemel Hempstead,
Hertfordshire HP2 7ST

Dolls House World including
The Home Miniaturist
Ashdown Publishing Ltd.
Avalon Court,
Star Road,
Partridge Green,
West Sussex RH13 8RY

Dolls House and Miniature Scene,
5 Cissbury Road,
Ferring,
West Sussex BN12 6QJ
(Tel: 01903 506626)
(available from WH Smith)

US SUPPLIERS AND MAGAZINES

In the US, the dolls-house hobby is so large that there are literally thousands of suppliers. The beginner is advised to look for a local miniatures shop which will probably stock most things you will need for the projects in this book. For more information, there is an annual mail order suppliers directory called *The Miniatures Catalogue* which can be ordered from Hobby Book

Distributors, 3150 State Line Road, North Bend, Ohio 45052. This address is also the American office of *Dolls House World* magazine.

There are a number of American magazines, but the best known is *The Nutshell News*, available from Kalmbach Miniatures Inc., 21027 Crossroads Circle, PO Box 1612, Waukesha, Wisconsin 53187.

British magazines such as *The International Dolls House News* (see above) can also be sent to subscribers in America, and contain much information which is relevant to them. Most British suppliers will send catalogues and goods to America, but please enclose an IRC with all enquiries.

STOCKISTS, MAGAZINES AND BOOKS

AUSTRALIAN SUPPLIERS AND MAGAZINES

In Australia the dolls-house Hobby is fairly new, but growing rapidly and there are a number of specialist shops, mail order suppliers and craftspeople. However, as the country is so large, we suggest that you contact *The Australian Miniaturist*

Magazine as a starting point. The address is
PO Box 467,
Carlingford,
New South Wales 2118,
Australia.

British magazines such as *The*

International Dolls House News (see above) can also be sent to subscribers in Australia, and contain much information which is relevant to them. Most British suppliers will send catalogues and goods to Australia, but please enclose an IRC with all enquiries.

BOOKS

For a very wide-ranging catalogue of books on dolls' houses, miniatures, architecture, furnishings and crafts, contact
The Mulberry Bush,
9 George Street,
Brighton,
Sussex BN2 1RH
(Tel: 0273 493781/600471)

If you are building, decorating and furnishing a dolls' house, you may find the following books useful.

Atkinson, Sue,
Making and Dressing Dolls' House Dolls,
David & Charles, 1992

Calloway, Stephen,
The Elements of Style,
Mitchell Beazley, 1991

Dodge, Venus and Martin,
Making Miniatures,
David & Charles, 1989

Dodge, Venus and Martin,

The New Dolls' House DIY Book,
David & Charles, 1993

Hardyment, Christina,
Home Comfort,
Viking/National Trust, 1992

Nickolls, Brian,
Making Dolls' Houses,
David & Charles, 1991

Yarwood, Doreen,
The English Home,
Batsford, 1979

Acknowledgements

Carol and Nigel would like to thank the following people for supplying the items used in the book.

CHAPTER 1
The whitewood dolls' house, Anglesey Dolls' Houses; brick and slate cladding materials, Reuben Barrows; stained-glass window, Black Country Miniatures; dolls-house lighting, Wood 'n Wool Miniatures. Wood, woodstrip, mouldings and turnings used throughout the book, Borcraft Miniatures; furniture hinges, Jennifers of Walsall; miniatures jig, Sussex Crafts.

CHAPTER 2
Ceiling beams and tongue and groove boards, Borcraft; oil lamp, Wood 'n Wool; brass scales and tins, Country Treasures; Devon pottery, Bryntor; white-metal kitchen-range kit, lockbox, mincer and ornaments, Phoenix; porcelain, Stokesay Ware; spongeware, Carol Lodder.

CHAPTER 3
Brick cladding, Reuben Barrows; lighting, Wood 'n Wool; white-metal lockbox, coat hooks, pump and mangle kit, Phoenix; clothes airer and metal brackets, Black Country; taps and pipes, Sussex Crafts; fish and vegetables, Rohanna Bryan; copper and tins, Country Treasures; stoneware, Carol Lodder; doll (undressed), Isabel Wood.

CHAPTER 4
White-metal fireplace kits and ornaments, Phoenix; wooden flooring, Hobby's; gas lights, Wood 'n Wool; art nouveau fireplace, Sussex Crafts; soft-furnishing trimmings, Miniature Supplies; porcelain, Carol Lodder; desk accessories, Terence Stringer; dressed doll, Sunday Dolls.

CHAPTER 5
Wooden flooring, Hobbys; oil lamp, Wood 'n Wool; pottery and spongeware, Carol Lodder; recorder, Johnny Blenkinsop; shaving accessories, Terence Stringer; doll (undressed), Isabel Wood.

CHAPTER 6
Microwood veneer and lights, Hobby's; reeded moulding, Borcraft; white-metal record player and electric fire, Phoenix; books, Blackwells; plant, Rohanna Bryan.

CHAPTER 7
Lights, Wood 'n Wool; Aga kit, Gable End Designs; turned legs, Borcraft; white-metal kitchen-range kit and crockery, Phoenix; paper plates, Country Treasures; porcelain, Pat Venning; bone china, Stokesay Ware; fruit and vegetables, Rohanna Bryan; dressed doll, Sunday Dolls.

CHAPTER 8
Door and fireplace kits, broken pediment, cornice mouldings and bed posts, Borcraft; moulded resin frieze and mirror, Sussex Crafts; wooden flooring, Hobby's; lighting, Wood 'n Wool; furniture kits, Blackwells; carved wall brackets and silver cup and cover, Terence Stringer; silver tray, Gordon Blacklock; porcelain, Carol Lodder; dressed dolls, Sunday Dolls.

CHAPTER 9
Wooden flooring and plastic wheel, Hobby's; fireback, and irons and barrels on stands, Sussex Crafts; flickering fire unit, Wood 'n Wool; pail-yoke, Dolphin Miniatures; lute and recorder, Johnny Blenkinsop; pottery, Carol Lodder.

CHAPTER 10
Porch spindles, Blackwells; metal leaves, monstera, palm and terracotta pots, Scale Link; metal leaves, Phoenix; artists' equipment, Jays Crafts; metal brackets, Black Country.

Listed below are the addresses of the craftspeople and suppliers of the items used in the book. We hope this will also be of interest to readers in America and Australia as most British suppliers are willing to export their goods and some have American and Australian distributors. Many of the craftspeople listed here attend miniatures fairs, so overseas readers who are planning a trip to Britain should have the opportunity to see them. Please note that all enquiries to the addresses listed here should be accompanied by a SAE or an IRC (International Reply Coupon) or you cannot reasonably expect a reply. This list includes shops, craftsmen and mail-order suppliers, and, as all make a charge for their catalogues, we suggest that you make an initial enquiry (or telephone) for the current catalogue price and details of opening hours etc.

Anglesey Dolls Houses, 5a Penrhos Industrial Estate, Holyhead, Anglesey LL65 2UQ (Tel/Fax: 01407 763511)

Black Country Miniatures, 63 Church Street, Halesowen, West Midlands B62 9LQ (Tel: 0121 561 5052)

Reuben Barrows, 30 Wolsey Gardens, Hainault, Ilford, Essex IG6 2SN (Tel: 01992 719593)

Borcraft Miniatures, Unit W25, Robin Mills Business Centre, Leeds Road, Greengates, Bradford, West Yorkshire BD10 9TE (Tel/Fax: 01274 622577) (American Distributor) Karens Mini Mouldings, PO Box 1287 Santa Theresa, New Mexico 880088, USA

Phoenix Model Developments, The Square, Earls Barton, Northampton NN6 0NA (Tel: 01604 810612)

W. Hobby Limited, Knights Hill Square, London SE27 0HH (Tel: 0181 761 4244) (Annual catalogue available from WH Smith)

Wood 'n Wool Miniatures, Unit 1, Old Co-op Yard, Kellet Road, Carnforth, Lancashire LA5 9LR (Tel: 01524 720277)

Blackwells of Hawkwell, 733-5 London Road, Westcliffe on Sea, Essex SS0 9ST (Tel: 01702 72248)

Jennifers of Walsall, 51 George Street, Walsall, West Midlands WS1 1RS (Tel: 01922 23382)

Country Treasures, Rose Cottage, Dapple Heath, Admaston, Rugeley, Staffs WS15 3PG (Tel: 01889 500 652)

Stokesay Ware, 37 Sandbrook Road, Stoke Newington, London N16 0SH (Tel: 0171 254 5254)

Gable End Designs, 190 Station Road, Knowle, Solihull, West Midlands B93 0ER (Tel: 01564 777607)

Bryntor Miniatures, 60 Shirburn Road, Torquay, Devon TQ1 4HR (Tel: 01803 323393)

Dolphin Miniatures, The Gallery, The Square, Whimple, Exeter EX5 2FL (Tel: 01404 822607)

Carol Lodder, Brooks Cottage, Belchalwell, Blandford, Dorset DT11 0EG (Tel: 01258 860222)

Johnny Blenkinsop, Amberwood, Hackthorne, Durrington, Salisbury, Wiltshire SP4 8AS (Tel: 01980 52397)

Terence Stringer, Spindles, Lexham Road, Litcham, Norfolk PE32 2QQ (Tel: 01328 701891)

Pat Venning Porcelain, Pineways, Faircross Avenue, Weymouth, Dorset DT4 0DD (Tel: 01305 773325)

Sussex Crafts, Hassocks House, Compton Brow Lane, Horsham, West Sussex BH13 6BX (Tel: 01403 254355) (Mail order only)

Sunday Dolls, 7 Park Drive, East Sheen, London SW14 8RB (Tel: 0181 876 5634)

Scale Link Ltd, Rear, Talbot Hotel, Blandford Road, Iwerne Minster, Blandford, Dorset DT11 8EF (Tel: 01747 811 817)

Jay Crafts, 12 Sutherland Drive, Birch Hill Park, Birchington, Kent CT7 9UE

Index

Numbers in *italics* refer to illustrations